GIANTS, GODS & DRAGONS

EXPOSING THE
FALLEN REALM AND THE PLOT TO IGNITE
THE FINAL WAR OF THE AGES

SHARON K. GILBERT
DEREK P. GILBERT

From the authors of *VENERATION*

DEFENDER

CRANE, MO

Giants, Gods, and Dragons: Exposing the Fallen Realm and the Plot to Ignite the Final War of the Ages
by Sharon K. Gilbert and Derek P. Gilbert

© Copyright 2020 Defender Publishing.
All rights reserved.
Printed in the United States of America.

All Scripture is taken from the English Standard Version (ESV) unless otherwise noted.

Cover design by Jeffrey Mardis.

ISBN: 9781948014397

With thanks to our Savior and King,
to Whom we dedicate this book.

If we err, then the fault is ours.
If anything we write has merit for His kingdom,
then it is He who inspired it.

CONTENTS

PART III
UNVEILING THE FUTURE AND THE END OF TIME

FOREWORD

ALL EYES ARE ON PROPHECY

The mood on the Monday following Palm Sunday of 2020 was somber and reflective—not only because of the historic implications of Christ's prophetic entry into Jerusalem or because Passover this year coincided with Resurrection Week. The quiescent mood precipitated from palpable fear. Fear of disease. Fear of economic insecurity. Fear of death.

But there was also a very real concern that our freedoms are now eroding. In recent years, Christians have endured constant pressure to compromise our convictions. And now, thanks to COVID-19, churches across the United States and the UK remained closed or are forced to submit to government oversight. While bars and gambling institutions are considered vital, churches—places where solace and comfort might be found during times of great stress—have been deemed non-essential to society.

COVID-19 has changed everything. But disease isn't the only "rider" now roaming the globe. Unrest and insurrection dominate headlines as protestors destroy the foundations of liberty. Suddenly, almost overnight, the world has changed completely, as if someone flipped a switch. Families, workplaces, churches, grocery stores, and public transport are forced into the "new normal." Businesses, large and small alike, are torched, as if to satisfy the hunger of an increasingly angry mob—or possibly an angry "god." The world teeters on the brink of utter and endless chaos.

Black is the trending color, but it has nothing to do with skin—and everything to do with anarchy. As we write this opening, black flag protests are gathering momentum in Israel in a troubling echo of a similar campaigns more than a century ago: the 1885 Black Flag Revolt in South Africa; 1883's Black Flag Army of brigands who fought against French occupation in Vietnam; even an 1880s newspaper, *Le Drapeau Noir* ("the Black Flag"), that advocated for anarchy and the return of the Paris Commune. Regarding this last item, it's believed that a London organization calling itself "Black International" may have sponsored French Bread Riots of 1883—which, by the way, were led by Louise Michel, a woman who'd played a major role in the 1871 Paris Commune insurrection.

Why is "black" used again and again by rebels and insurrectionists? It is claimed to represent "the people," but a better explanation is that a black flag lacks any symbol to identify those behind it. Black equals an absence of light. Nothing. A void, with no country, no nation, and no formal government.

However, the truth is far more deceptive: Black represents darkness. Defiance. It represents Chaos, the original rebel.

Because of the "new normal," our economy has taken a nosedive, grocery prices have skyrocketed, and woe to those who want to buy a pound of beef! Meatpacking houses in the US operate beneath the corporate umbrellas of only a few companies (China owns at least one of these), leading to supply-chain issues due to outbreaks in the factories. Supply chains have taken a further hit as states assert protectionist tactics regarding incoming traffic. Some states have overcome such restrictions by implementing a fleet of inhuman, autonomous semi-trucks. Self-driving vehicles have been in the news as prototype and futuristic ideas for over a decade, but now they're a reality.

In addition, to reduce human-to-human interactions, our "new normal" includes AI algorithms that take orders online or via the phone, warehouse robots that select products and place them into boxes, other robotic helpers that seal the boxes and add the labels, and still others that load them onto self-driving trucks. With humans confined to their homes, the computerized world of Skynet's Terminator is emerging. The Internet of Things, the IOT, serves as the inorganic replacement for a biologically based, human workforce, while at the same time providing us with constant entertainment and all the goodies our government checks can pay for—bread and circuses aplenty.

As a result, humans are becoming both product and producer. We fill the Internet with requests, web pages, blogs, videos, likes, and emojis while consuming each and every byte with the relish of a hungry child. Think of that the next time you spend half the day on social media. For years, these companies have trained us to make social-media platforms our virtual gathering place, news portals, and entertainment hubs. We consume and regurgitate like trained puppies.

But even as we learn our new roles, a few begin to awaken. The tragedy of COVID-19 has served as the crucible to awaken our senses. Bibles and books on prophecy are flying off virtual shelves as those who once laughed at any mention of "end times" and the return of Christ now eagerly learn all they can about the Savior. Signs in the heavens add to this phenomenon and shout warnings to all.

Comets ATLAS and SWAN, along with numerous other NEOs (near-earth objects), are streaking towards us. On April 29th of this year, 1998 OR2, which is 2.5 miles wide, hurtled past us. The trajectory showed that the space rock would skootch by with plenty of room to spare, but Yarkovsky effects (basically, heat, cold, collisions with seen and/or unseen forces) could easily have altered its path. The earth escaped a major collision once again.

And, yes, both ATLAS and SWAN are green. The idea that a green comet could become visible to the naked eye or with garden telescopes evokes the *chloros* horse and its deadly rider of Revelation 6, Thanatos, who wields the curved blade, the *rhomphaia*, as he spreads contagion. Atlas was the Greek Titan who served as a living link between heaven and earth as he bore the weight of the former on his shoulders as a punishment from Zeus for his role in the Titanomachy. Atlas was also the grandfather of Hermes (AKA Mercury), the messenger God, and perhaps a cognate for Thanatos, for both were liminal figures who ushered souls to Hades. Oh, yes—Hermes had a son named Pan. Sound familiar? The more you know about mythology, the better you'll understand the context of our Bible.

And if all that isn't enough, Anak Krakatau, the volcano that killed more than four hundred people in the deadly tsunami it triggered sixteen months ago, has once again erupted. On April 10, 2020, Good Friday, the mountain spewed ash and lava fifteen kilometers high.[1] Anak Krakatau is the "son" of the infamous Krakatau volcano that erupted, sending the sound of its thunderous boom around the world in 1883 and causing a period of global cooling from the ash.

Another recent article published at *Esquire* noted the convergence of apocalyptic events with this headline: "An Extremely Normal Weekend of Pestilence, Locusts, a Fire in Chernobyl, and a Volcano."[2] The Chernobyl fire released plumes of radiation into the region, leading many to reach for their Bibles. In case you don't recall it, *Chernobyl* is the Ukrainian word for "Wormwood." Yes, that's right. Wormwood.

Boy, the prophetic alarm bells can't get much louder. It's as though the riders of Revelation have formed up and are galloping past, isn't it? Conquest, War, Famine, and Death have taken over the world.

That's the purpose of this book. We're going to unmask the spirits behind the chaos: the giants, the small-*g* gods, and the ancient dragons. We'll dive into why the spiritual war exists at all as we examine the historic impact and timelines of prophecy: where we've been, how we got here, and where we're heading.

And because dragons really do exist and play a major role in the beginning and ending of time, we'll open with a short bit of fiction. We've both explored the role of dragons in ancient cosmology, and Sharon has applied some of this to her novels in *The Redwing Saga* series. Here, we present the prologue to Book 5, *Realms of Fire*, and follow the steps of the saga's main character, Charles Sinclair, as he remembers a pivotal event in his childhood.

And if you're unfamiliar with the series, it's written using nineteenth-century British spelling.

Eyes of the Dragon

Prologue from Realms of Fire, Book 5 in *The Redwing Saga*

10th June, 1860 – Rose House

The boy's azure eyes popped open, wide as saucers. Something had awoken him—something scratchy and tempting. Something ethereal with a raspy voice that spoke in whispers.

His bedchamber was shrouded in velvety darkness, the only sound the somnolent ticking of a gold and black marble clock that sat upon the mantelpiece opposite the curtained bed. The curious clock featured a magnificent figure of King Arthur astride a pure white steed. The figure's position altered with the hands; the delicate changes provided by interlocking brass wheels and fine-toothed gears. On the quarter hour, the heroic king's mighty horse would advance along a concealed track towards a terrifying, fire-breathing dragon. As the rider moved ever closer, the armoured arm would slowly lift the sword higher; until, at the chiming of the hour, it pointed straight into the serpent's mouth, slaying the worm and ending his fiery reign.

The clock should have inspired a sense of history and pride in the child, but the bellicose ballet of cold marble and crimson fire ground into the sensitive boy's bones with a terrifying sense of dread. He'd hidden the clock numerous times, but the nursemaid always discovered its hiding place and returned it to the mantel. The child had learnt to shut out the persistent ticking—which often took on a grating, growling sound. Born of rare privilege and high position, the boy nearly always felt completely alone.

Charles Robert Arthur Sinclair III, known in peerage circles by the courtesy title Lord Loudain, stood tall and straight as he emerged from the warm feather bed that morning. He had measured four-foot-one-inch precisely the previous day, when his ageing nanny, Mrs. Millicent Caswell, had placed her charge against the door frame of the nursery's play area.

"You'll be tall as a cedar one day, young lord!" she'd declared happily. "You might even outgrow your good father, and all the young ladies o' the county'll think you a grand catch."

The bashful boy had smiled patiently, as he generally did when trying to understand the strange amusements of adults. Most found humour in the oddest of moments, and very few appreciated the beautiful complications of the remarkable world all around them; for they seemed caught up in life's trivialities—or worse, in matters so deep and troublesome that no amount of study could unravel them.

Take his parents' recent arguments, for instance.

Ordinarily, Robby and Angela Sinclair had nothing but gentle endearments for one another, but beginning in late April of that year— following a masked ball at Haimsbury House—everything changed. Charles had gone with them to London, but he'd come down with a fever, leaving him with very little memory of that strange week. Once he recovered, the family abruptly left London and returned to their Cumbria estate, and his gentle parents commenced a distressing series of shouting matches—all of them centred on a foreigner named Prince Aleksandr Koshmar and a mysterious black mirror.

As Charles secured the buttons on his shoes, the determined five-year-old decided to search out this troublesome looking glass and discover just why his father hated it so very much.

Mrs. Caswell slept in a small bedchamber just beyond the main play area, but the fifty-two-year-old nanny snored like a bear, making it a simple matter to slip past her room without causing the woman to stir. Once through the apartment's exterior door, the youth hastened to the nearest staircase. The main wall of the broad landing held an arched window seat that overlooked the eastern park. Charles tiptoed to the cushioned seat and climbed up, peering through the leaded panes. Dawn's first rays were just beginning to paint the green hills of Eden Valley in a shimmering, watercolour pink; a stark contrast to the sapphire blue shadows cast by the statues and trees within the estate's formal gardens. The landscape looked foreboding and eerily foreign to the child's eyes that morning; as though he'd awakened to an entirely different realm.

Leaving the window, he passed by the east-wing servants' staircase. Charles could hear the rattle of copper pans and kettles rising up through the open stairwell, accompanied by the aroma of baking rye bread, cinnamon buns, and French butter sponge cakes. The hall's head baker, Mrs. Celia Carson, and her two assistants rose at four each morning to prepare large wooden bowls of dough and kindle the oven fires. Usually, Charles would visit Carson for a cup of tea and a plate of warm biscuits, but not this morning. His destination stood high above, inside the centuries-old home. Upward, all the way to the attics.

Built four hundred years ago, the original limestone castle overlooked the western bank of Eden River. The main drive followed an old Roman road, leading modern visitors towards the west elevation of the expanded home. Consequently, the fortified castle at its heart remained concealed behind the magnificently amended wings and Palladian façade of the 18th century additions. Despite its antiquity, Charles found the original castle fascinating, and often came here to play; picturing himself as the son of a warrior marquess, learning to wield a sword whilst on horseback, or fire arrows from the defensive towers. He would wander through the armoury and run his small hands along a great blade that some claimed was nearly a thousand years old. It was called *Lann Lasair*, the "fire sword," and it rested upon a bed of claret velvet, securely locked within a protective glass case. Despite its age, the ancient sword gleamed as though newly forged, and Charles sometimes imagined that it spoke to him, whispering of blood and destiny.

That morning, however, the sword and the towers held no charm for the boy. He walked briskly past the armoury and pulled open a thick oak door that led to the south tower. A black rat scuttled past his feet as the iron-banded portal creaked open. A blast of stale air swept across the boy's smooth face like wispy fingers of some ghostly knight.

The boy froze, wondering if he shouldn't return to bed and await his nanny's call to breakfast.

No, he told himself. *This is important. I have to see that mirror for myself.*

With fierce determination for so young a heart, the lad forged ahead, slowly climbing the narrow stone steps. The well-worn, winding stairs led to a crenulated turret where archers and musketeers once took shelter as they fought invaders from other lands and other kingdoms. Charles held his lamp high as he ascended the hand-hewn risers. His sensitive nose discerned the musty odour of centuries-old mildew as he proceeded up the anti-clockwise curve. Along the case, arrow slits provided modest hints of dawn's maturing light. At three feet high and one foot wide, the windows had seen many battles, their casement stones marked by blood stains; the last bits of life from long-forgotten men.

Charles gazed upon the shadowed ground below, picturing the hills covered in the warm blood of horses and warriors and kings; the river's clear water choked with the bloated bodies of the dead and dying. The vision sent a cold sense of dread through his bones, but the valiant child pressed onward, up the claustrophobic staircase, until he arrived at the final door. It required all his strength to push the heavy structure, but once through, he emerged into a dark chamber used now as storage. The flickering yellow flame of his lantern struggled to cut through the deep shadow. Rather than provide comfort, the dancing tongue of fire made the forest of books, sea cans, and wooden crates appear to undulate like angry trees in fields of endless night. The tall boy whispered a prayer and advanced into the unwelcoming landscape.

A series of persistent scratching sounds caught his ear, soon turning into whispers in a thousand languages all at once; seductive words without translation that simultaneously terrified and tantalised the intelligent child. In one corner stood a suit of armour, the helmet's empty eye holes greedily watching his passage. Along the north wall, a row of sturdy bookcases guarded family histories and ledgers. Elsewhere, painted cupboards, wooden toys, musical instruments, bird cages, and scrolled iron bedsteads, patiently waited to be summoned; forlorn and abandoned, as if they'd come here to die.

The child's remarkable blue eyes accommodated to the low light as he continued through the haunted maze. Though bathed in shadow, the attics felt familiar, for Charles had wandered through these aisles of Haimsbury's *disjecta membra* many times. What imaginative five-year-old wouldn't find such a collection fascinating?

But where is the mirror? he wondered.

With only the candle's light as guide, he threaded a path through the crowded field of debris and dust. Charles passed through a series of connecting doorways, moving from the original castle to the newer sections, where modern reliquaries guarded the unused treasures of the grandest home in all Cumbria.

This newer loft included a series of round windows that ran parallel to the eaves, allowing dawn's light to enter. The scratching sound seemed to grow louder here, and he noticed several slender tree branches tapping against the leaded panes. An adult would assume this to be the source of the scratching, but Charles doubted the delicate willow limbs could have awoken him this far from his bedroom. No, the persistent sounds *must* have another cause.

He felt certain the mirror was to blame.

As he passed through the tightly packed goods, the boy puzzled through the events of the previous night. The eve of his birthday had commenced with the arrival of his father's good friend, Martin Kepelheim, just after breakfast. Then, shortly after luncheon, Prince Aleksandr Koshmar had unexpectedly appeared on their doorstep, offering armloads of gifts for Charles and far too many kisses for his mother.

Usually a generous host, Robby Sinclair showed little warmth for the intruding foreigner, and the two men had nearly come to blows following a seemingly innocent chess match after supper. By half past nine, his mother retired, blaming a sudden headache, and Koshmar followed soon after. Charles's father had whispered something to the departing prince, who'd clicked his heels and bowed before climbing to the upper storey. Robby Sinclair then ordered a decanter of his strongest whisky and drew Martin Kepelheim into the Pendragon room for a hushed discussion. Suspecting something amiss, Charles stood at the door, eavesdropping on the troubling discourse.

His father and Kepelheim argued over the mirror, mentioning a curse upon the Haimsbury family that reached far into the past—something to do with the Sinclair blood. Charles had overheard talk like this before, when he'd hidden in his father's library and listened to the inner circle members as they debated the possible identity of a future child; apparently desired by some villainous group called Redwing. Since that day, the boy had tried to discover anything he could regarding this mysterious Redwing group, but thus far, he'd found very little. His father seemed to connect Redwing to the black mirror—and to the Russian prince, Aleksandr Koshmar. *Who was he? And why did his mother so enjoy the interfering man's company? Moreover, how did it connect to the mirror?*

Though young, Charles had a uniquely designed logic to his mind, with the ability to perceive patterns amongst a tangle of disparate threads. *Was the Russian more than he appeared? Might Koshmar be evil? And why did these persistent scratching noises bring forth images of gloomy places and stones of fire?* He gazed out the windows, wondering if the noise was meant to lure him into the attics. If so, then he'd meet the challenge head-on; just as his father would.

As Charles progressed deeper into the dusty attic, his lantern fell upon a series of surfaces: wood, metal, cloth, even the odd jewel. Then, to his surprise, the buttery beam produced what looked like a companion beacon. A second, brighter light that shimmered seductively from the northeast corner.

It's a reflection! the boy realised.

A velvet drape covered most of the tall mirror, but a tiny hole, the size of a penny, allowed the light to shine forth like a radiant eye. A deep chill ran along his long arms, and Charles paused, suddenly overwhelmed with dread.

There's something in there.

Swallowing his fear, the child reached for the velvet cloth that shrouded the mirror. His fingers went numb, and a seductive voice whispered into his thoughts.

Hello, boy. The answers to all your questions lie within. Unveil me and behold the Face of Destiny!

Charles paused, praying the voice was his imagination.

Come find me, boy.

Warning bells clanged inside his mind, and Charles longed for the safety of his father's arms. He started to leave, but as he turned to go, the thick velvet draping slid away, as though a ghostly hand removed it. The cloth pooled on the wooden planks near his feet.

The mirror was unlike any the boy had ever seen. Rather than silver, the black surface was formed of polished obsidian, and its beveled edges etched with shapes that had the regularity of language. Charles reached out to touch the forbidding glass, intending to trace the unfamiliar words, but to his utter shock, his hand passed into it, as through an open window—or doorway.

The glass rippled, and the boy's reflection disappeared, replaced by crimson eyes set into a dazzling face.

"*Hello, boy,*" an enormous Dragon whispered out of swirling grey mists. "*Let's play.*"

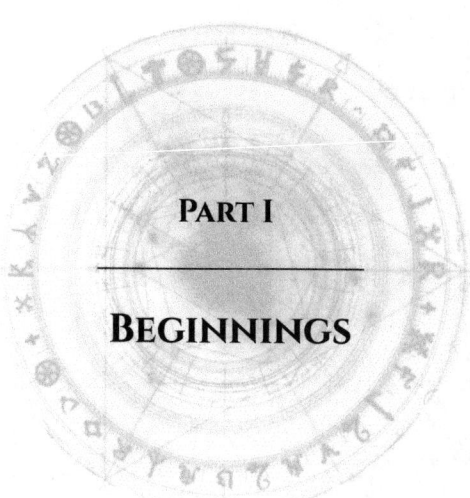

PART I

BEGINNINGS

Remember this and stand firm, recall it to mind, you transgressors,
    remember the former things of old; for I am God,
    and there is no other; I am God, and there is none like me,
declaring the end from the beginning and **from ancient times
things not yet done**, saying,
    "My counsel shall stand, and I will accomplish all my purpose,"
    calling a bird of prey from the east, the man of my counsel
from a far country. **I have spoken, and I will bring it to pass;**
    I have purposed, and I will do it.

        —ISAIAH 46:8–11, EMPHASIS ADDED

For a brief second, Charles saw a vision of things to come: poisonous
air, a darkened sun, eternal night, nocturnal creatures consuming
the flesh of all those who refused to take the mark.

    Hell on earth.

    When the Dragon ruled.

        —SHARON K. GILBERT, *REALMS OF FIRE*, CHAPTER 19

ORDO AB CHAO:
THAT OLD DRAGON—THE TWISTING SERPENT

In that day the LORD with his hard and great and strong sword
will punish Leviathan the fleeing serpent, Leviathan the twisting
serpent, and he will slay the dragon that is in the sea.

—ISAIAH 27:1

Everything has a start. A plant, a person, an idea. Even the universe had a
beginning. In Genesis, chapter 1, we're told that God created the heavens
and the earth. Then, only two verses in, we read something that may not
make sense when we first read it, because something happened to the
earth. Rather than being described as "good" and perfect, as we see in later
verses regarding creation, our world is described as "void" and "without
form." Now, why would God create something that's basically unfinished?

Simple answer: He didn't.

It's our belief that the LORD created everything in perfect condition,
but that something catastrophic occurred between verses 1 and 2 that so

scarred the original creation it rendered the earth "void" and "without form." We believe that "something" was a cataclysmic rebellion, led by a primordial being we refer to as "Prisoner Zero." Scholars have named this conflict the *Chaoskampf*: an ancient war that formed the pattern for what's to come in our future. To understand the end times and the book of Revelation, we must understand the Chaoskampf, for it is the history of a long, spiritual war that will one day end with a new heaven and a new earth: A return to a pristine, former glory. The end from the beginning— the beginning from the end.

As God promises in Isaiah 46:11, "*I have spoken,*" says Yahweh. "*I will bring it to pass. I have purposed it, and I will do it*" (emphasis added). What does He mean by this? What is God vowing to accomplish? What ancient prophecy awaits final fulfillment? That question requires some time to unpack, for it's one of those frequently "missed" prophecies that, as with Poe's *Purloined Letter*, has been staring us in the face the entire time. But its form and shape emerge once we take the Bible as a whole and realize that Revelation cannot be understood without first discerning the implications of Genesis.

The end from the beginning. A series of rebels and rebellions.

Prisoner Zero. The Chaos Dragon. The Nachash. The Watchers. The Nephilim. Babel. Satan. The Antichrist.

Most of you are familiar with the prophecy of Ezekiel 38, where we read that Gog leads a confederation against Israel. His objective will be Zion, the *har mô'ēd*, God's mount of assembly. Gog comes from the north, but "north" in this case is not so much a geographic direction as it is *spiritual north*, consistent with the Jewish tradition of evil always descending upon Israel from "the north." Historically, the most fearsome enemies always attacked from that direction. Assyria and Babylon were the big two, and these would enter Israel from either Lebanon or Syria, because crossing the Syrian desert to the east was foolish.

Likewise, *supernatural* threats to Israel also came from the north: Bashan, the entrance to the Canaanite underworld; Mount Hermon, El's mount of assembly and the site of the Watchers' rebellion; and Mount

Zaphon, the home of Baal's palace, were all located to the north of Israel. This is the proper context for viewing the war of Gog and Magog depicted in Ezekiel 38 and 39:

> Son of man, set your face toward Gog, of the land of Magog, the chief prince of Meshech and Tubal, and prophesy against him and say, Thus says the Lord GOD: Behold, I am against you, O Gog, chief prince of Meshech and Tubal. And I will turn you about and put hooks into your jaws, and I will bring you out, and all your army, horses and horsemen, all of them clothed in full armor, a great host, all of them with buckler and shield, wielding swords. Persia, Cush, and Put are with them, all of them with shield and helmet; omer and all his hordes; Beth-togarmah from the uttermost parts of the north with all his hordes—many peoples are with you.
>
> Be ready and keep ready, you and all your hosts that are assembled about you, and be a guard for them. After many days you will be mustered. In the latter years you will go against the land that is restored from war, the land whose people were gathered from many peoples upon the mountains of Israel, which had been a continual waste. Its people were brought out from the peoples and now dwell securely, all of them. You will advance, coming on like a storm. You will be like a cloud covering the land, you and all your hordes, and many peoples with you. (Ezekiel 38:2–9)

Gog is the personal name of a Reubenite,[3] but it's also the name of a spirit entity, that which animates Antichrist, the great supernatural end-times enemy of God and Israel. Speculation linking the identity of Gog to any Russian leader is misguided. First, while there may be Russians in the coalition that comes to Jerusalem for the Battle of Armageddon, Russia *as a nation* is not part of Ezekiel's prophecy. With all due respect to Bible teachers who hold the "Russia is Magog" view, identifying *Rosh* as Russia and *Meshech* as Moscow is folk etymology, making connections simply because the words sound the same. Language doesn't always work like that. For example, "dear" and "deer" sound the same, but you aren't going to mistake your spouse for Bambi.

More importantly, the grisly sacrificial feasts of Ezekiel 39:17–20 and Revelation 19:17–21 confirm that the war of Gog ends at Armageddon. It's the same conflict. So, unless we create a plausible scenario that includes a Russian Antichrist, we have to let that theory go.

We can agree, however, that the Beast that emerges from the sea in Revelation 13:1 is the Antichrist figure, but did you know this relates back to Prisoner Zero? The sea (*Yam* in Hebrew) is most properly understood as an entity. *Yam* is a proper name and represents Chaos, the very rebel that God subdued in the first two verses of the Bible.

> In the beginning, God created the heavens and the earth. The earth was without form and void, and darkness was over the face of the deep. And the Spirit of God was hovering over the face of the waters. (Genesis 1:1–2)

The Hebrew word translated as "deep" is *tehom*, which is a cognate—that is, the same word in a different language—to the Akkadian *Têmtum*, which, in turn, is a variant of *Tiamat*, the Sumerian chaos monster who was defeated by the warrior god, Marduk, to bring order to creation. Similar myths were common in the ancient Near East (ANE): Baal vs. Yamm, Teshub vs. Illuyanka, Zeus vs. Typhon.

But the original version is Yahweh vs. Leviathan.

Now, the most obvious difference between the biblical account and the others is that the fight between God and Chaos, if there *was* a fight, was over by the end of the second verse in the Bible. We see references to it in later chapters—for example, Psalm 74:12–17—but there is no hint that God had any trouble bringing Chaos to heel. He merely placed His Spirit over the deep and it obeyed. "Down! Stay!" No weapons needed. Just His Word.

Not so with pagan versions of this epic moment in history. In every case, the warrior god required outside help, weapons, and multiple battles to subdue the sea monster representing Chaos. But Chaos, being a supernatural creature, is (for the present) only restrained, not dead.

Now, here's where Typhon comes in.

According to the Greek poet Hesiod, Zeus threw the serpentine chaos-monster Typhon into Tartarus to share a cellblock with the infamous Titans.[4] We can be reasonably sure the Titans/Watchers are presently in Tartarus; Hesiod and Homer agreed on that point, and Peter confirmed it (see 2 Peter 2:4, and note that the Greek word translated "hell" is *tartaroo*—Tartarus).

The Greeks believed the battle between Zeus and Typhon took place at Mount Kasios, which was their name for Baal's holy mountain, *Zaphon*, and scholars have long noted that Typhon's name resembles Zaphon so closely they are most likely etymologically linked.[5] This gives us a clear connection between Zaphon, the mountain where the Antichrist/Gog will marshal his forces, and the chaos-god Typhon. And while this entity is called a dragon (with a hundred heads no less!) by Hesiod,[6] Typhon is described elsewhere as "a hybrid between man and beast,"[7] with many wings, coils of vipers for legs, and a human head. That is, the Greek god of chaos was a human-animal chimera, similar to the way ancient Mesopotamians described the *apkallu*, who were—yep, you guessed it—the Watchers/Titans.

In other words, the Greeks remembered that a monstrous deity connected to Satan/Baal's mount of assembly was buried in Tartarus—the abyss, which is represented in the Bible by the sea. In Revelation, the Beast, which is described as a chimeric entity like the chaos-monster Typhon, *emerges* from the sea (*Yam*)—the abyss—to become the Antichrist (Gog) and lead the war against God's holy mountain, Zion:

> Then the dragon became furious with the woman and went off
> to make war on the rest of her offspring, on those who keep the
> commandments of God and hold to the testimony of Jesus. And
> he stood on the sand of the sea.

And I saw a beast rising out of the sea, with ten horns and seven heads, with ten diadems on its horns and blasphemous names on its heads. (Revelation 12:17–13:1)

The verses above suggest that it is *the dragon* who stands on the shore when the Beast, the Antichrist/Gog, rises from the abyss. Please note that Satan/Baal's mount of assembly, Zaphon, today called Jebel al-Aqra, sits on the shore of the Mediterranean Sea.

All that leads to the $64,000 question: Could the Antichrist actually *be* the spirit of Chaos, known also as Leviathan, Tiamat, Têmtu, and the Dragon?

In his book, *The Day the Earth Stands Still,* Derek and his coauthor, Josh Peck, explored the idea of the "return of chaos." While the book deals primarily with the occult origins of beliefs common to the UFO community, the research revealed a strange attraction to the god of chaos within UFO circles.

Occultists Kenneth Grant and Austin Osman Spare (who learned his craft directly from Aleister Crowley—the man who called himself the "Great Beast 666"), developed Crowley's occult system into what Grant called the "Typhonian Tradition." That's been further developed into something practitioners today call "chaos magick." But chaos magick isn't anything new; Job 3:8 makes a reference to those "who are ready to rouse up Leviathan."

The key detail is this: Around 1955, Grant claimed he detected a "Sirius-Set current" in Crowley's teachings. Set, brother of Osiris, was the Egyptian god of storms, war, and chaos. This so-called "current" convinced Grant and others that the chaos-god's home could be found near the star Sirius, and that Set (Typhon/Chaos) was in contact with "chosen ones" on earth, and was planning a big comeback.

If you know your Bible, then you also know that Chaos is coming back, but not in the way the practitioners of chaos magick believe.

Now, while the chaos-god Typhon wasn't one of the original Titans, he was believed to be their half-brother and is sometimes referred to as a Titan. Interestingly, at least one of the early church fathers thought a Titan would return at the end of days. Irenaeus, a Christian theologian of the second century, offered these thoughts on John's prophecy of the Antichrist:

> Although certain as to the number of the name of Antichrist, yet we should come to no rash conclusions as to the name itself, because this number [666] is capable of being fitted to many names.... *Teitan* too, (TEITAN, the first syllable being written with the two Greek vowels ε and ι), among all the names which are found among us, is rather worthy of credit. For it has in itself the predicted number, and is composed of six letters, each syllable containing three letters; and [the word itself] is ancient, and removed from ordinary use; for among our kings we find none bearing this name Titan, nor have any of the idols which are worshipped in public among the Greeks and barbarians this appellation. Among many persons, too, this name is accounted divine, so that even the sun is termed "Titan" by those who do now possess [the rule]. This word, too, contains a certain outward appearance of vengeance, and of one inflicting merited punishment because he (Antichrist) pretends that he vindicates the oppressed. And besides this, it is an ancient name, one worthy of credit, of royal dignity, and still further, a name belonging to a tyrant. **Inasmuch, then, as this name "Titan" has so much to recommend it, there is a strong degree of probability, that from among the many [names suggested], we infer, that perchance he who is to come shall be called "Titan."**[8] (Emphasis added)

To his credit, Irenaeus declined to say *absolutely* that the Antichrist would be named Titan. He reasoned that if the precise name had been important, John would have revealed it instead of a number. Still, it's intriguing, isn't it? And consider this: Jesus demonstrated His mastery over Chaos to the disciples one night on the Sea of Galilee:

On that day, when evening had come, he said to them, "Let us go across to the other side." And leaving the crowd, they took him with them in the boat, just as he was. And other boats were with him. And a great windstorm arose, and the waves were breaking into the boat, so that the boat was already filling. But he was in the stern, asleep on the cushion. And they woke him and said to him, "Teacher, do you not care that we are perishing?" **And he awoke and rebuked the wind and said to the sea, "Peace! Be still!" And the wind ceased, and there was a great calm.** He said to them, "Why are you so afraid? Have you still no faith?" And they were filled with great fear and said to one another, **"Who then is this, that even the wind and the sea obey him?"** (Mark 4:35–41; emphasis added)

So, is it truly possible that an entity such as Typhon/Set/Leviathan could *be* the Antichrist?

The answer is yes.

In Revelation 12:3, Satan is described as "a great red dragon, with seven heads and ten horns," and he entered Judas Iscariot,[9] the betrayer of Jesus. Since Satan was able to possess or control Judas, then it's logical that the Beast, whatever spirit it is, can and will do the same with another human host. Remember: What we perceive with our natural eyes is not the full picture, for "even Satan disguises himself as an angel of light."[10]

Let's look at Revelation 9. When the fifth of the trumpet-blowing angels sounds his horn, a star falls from heaven to earth with a key to the abyss. We believe that this moment marks the return of the old gods:

He opened the shaft of the bottomless pit, and from the shaft rose smoke like the smoke of a great furnace, and the sun and the air were darkened with the smoke from the shaft. Then from the smoke came locusts on the earth, and they were given power like the power of scorpions of the earth. They were told not to harm the grass of the earth or any green plant or any tree, but only those people who do not have the seal of God on their foreheads. They were allowed to torment them for five months, but not to kill them, and their torment was like the torment of a scorpion when it stings someone. And in those days people will seek death and will not find it. They will long to die, but death will flee from them.

In appearance the locusts were like horses prepared for battle: on their heads were what looked like crowns of gold; their faces were like human faces, their hair like women's hair, and their teeth like lions' teeth; they had breastplates like breastplates of iron, and the noise of their wings was like the noise of many chariots with horses rushing into battle. They have tails and stings like scorpions, and their power to hurt people for five months is in their tails. They have as king over them the angel of the bottomless pit. His name in Hebrew is Abaddon, and in Greek he is called Apollyon. (Revelation 9:2–11; emphasis added)

In the preceding verses, we see the entities that the world thousands of years ago called Titans, Watchers, Anunnaki, and even *Apkallu* angrily roar out of the abyss. That's where they are now—the abyss—but they'll soon be given a short time to torment humanity. Five months. One hundred and fifty days. The same it took for their children, the Nephilim, to die in the Flood:

And the waters prevailed upon the earth 150 days. (Genesis 7:24)

Thus, the Watchers will take revenge on God's most prized creation—man—in return for the punishment of watching their own children, the Nephilim/Rephaim, destroyed in the Flood of Noah. Granted, the description of the things from the pit doesn't exactly match the Mesopotamian images of *apkallu* or Greek sculptures of the Titans. Remember, though, that those entities were sent to the bottomless pit around the time of the Great Flood. Hundreds of years, and maybe a thousand or more, had passed by the time the Sumerians began to create images of *apkallu* on cylinder seals and clay tablets. Those descriptions captured handed-down, oral traditions of supernatural human-animal hybrids, however, which is basically what John describes for us in Revelation.

The Titans, the Watchers of the Bible, return when Apollyon opens the pit. And for humans without the protective seal of God on their foreheads, it will literally be hell on earth.

THE INFLUENCE OF EVIL:
IN THE GARDEN OF THE LORD

Now the serpent was more crafty than any other beast of the field
that the LORD God had made.

—GENESIS 3:1

We've learned a bit about the original rebel: the entity called Chaos. And
we've considered how this might also be connected to the Titans of old. Now,
let's dig a bit deeper into Prisoner Zero's ultimate end. The Chaoskampf
left the original earth in a state of imperfection, the consequence of the
real original sin. But even then, the LORD had determined the direction of
His thoughts. Regardless of the Dragon's plans, He had always known the
Rebel would rouse once more to defy Him. Remember, nothing surprises
the Lord. Nothing at all. We can take comfort in that. We can rest upon
Him in the same way a child might rest upon his father's shoulder. We
allow Him to make the decisions, for He knows best.

The Chaoskampf must have galled, confused, and amazed the first
created beings, those elder brothers who sang together as morning stars
in the days of creation! And God's response to Prisoner Zero, for the
swift and destructive actions of the LORD of Hosts (meaning "Yahweh
of Armies") to Chaos/Typhon/Leviathan, demonstrated to all the Divine
Assembly members just what the dire consequences of rebellion would
be—the wages of sin. But it also revealed the LORD's endless mercy; for
Yahweh could have destroyed Chaos right away—with nothing more
than a word. Instead, He chose to humble and constrain the ancient rebel
dragon beneath the power of His Spirit until the time of the end. Then, all
the elder brothers and all the humans from Adam forward will witness the
final judgment of the first rebel, when Leviathan is finally punished for his
rebellious deeds. And all who have practiced evil and rebelled against the
LORD will earn their just reward in the Lake of Fire, after which:

> Then I saw a new heaven and a new earth, for the first heaven
> and the first earth had passed away, and **the sea was no more.**
> (Revelation 21:1; emphasis added)

How comforting are these last words! The sea was no more! Oh,
but for now, even as a prisoner, Chaos exerts an evil influence upon all
creatures, both in our physical world and in the spirit realm. Prisoner
Zero's evil may have inspired the second rebellion, which occurred in a
very special garden.

Did you know that Eden was the original holy mountain of God? Yes,
Eden was a garden, but it was a garden set upon a mountain. We learn
this from Ezekiel 28:

> Son of man, say to the prince of Tyre,
> Thus says the Lord GOD:
> "Because your heart is proud,
> and you have said, 'I am a god,
> I sit in the seat of the gods,

in the heart of the seas,'...
You were the signet of perfection,
full of wisdom and perfect in beauty.
You were in Eden, the garden of God;
every precious stone was your covering,
sardius, topaz, and diamond,
beryl, onyx, and jasper,
sapphire, emerald, and carbuncle;
and crafted in gold were your settings
and your engravings.
On the day that you were created
they were prepared.
You were an anointed guardian cherub.
I placed you; **you were on the holy**
mountain of God;
in the midst of the stones of fire you walked.
You were blameless in your ways
from the day you were created,
till unrighteousness was found in you.
In the abundance of your trade
you were filled with violence in your midst,
and you sinned;
so I cast you as a profane thing from
the mountain of God,
and I destroyed you, O guardian cherub,
from the midst of the stones of fire."
(Ezekiel 28:2, 12–16; emphasis added)

Eden was more than just a garden. More than a paradise. It was the where the divine council met, the "seat of the gods" on "the mountain of God." Adam and Eve were there, and they served alongside the "elder brothers"—or *elohim*—as members of the LORD's divine council.

Although Ezekiel 28:1–19 is addressed to the King of Tyre (probably

Ithobaal III, who reigned between 591 and 573 BC), most commentators agree that these passages are really aimed at the divine rebel in Eden. Some try to de-supernaturalize the section and apply the verses to Adam, but verses 17 through 19 describe punishments that cannot refer to Adam's post-Garden life ("I exposed you before kings, to feast their eyes on you"— *what* kings does the writer mean?).

You might say that the Garden of Eden was the earth's first temple, God's dwelling place amongst humanity. Ezekiel 28 makes the point in its condemnation of the rebel in the Garden:

> By the multitude of your iniquities,
> in the unrighteousness of your trade
> you profaned your sanctuaries. (Ezekiel 28:18a; emphasis added)

Now here, the word translated as "sanctuaries," *miqdash*, is the same word used to describe the tabernacle built by Moses per God's instructions. This verse, then, identifies Eden on God's holy mountain as a sacred space, unique and set apart from all other places on earth; the place where Yahweh walked and talked with man. From the moment Adam and Eve disobeyed God's command to refrain from eating the fruit of the tree of the knowledge of good and evil, human history has been the chronicle of His plan to redeem us—to bring humanity back to His mountain—and of the Enemy's attempts to thwart that plan.

It was also in Eden that the Enemy first employed a PSYOP (psychological operation). And these PSYOPs have formed a major component in the enemy's arsenal ever since. In this case: "You will be as gods."

Many false religions (and false teachings within the Body of Christ) can be boiled down to that one insidious lie. And the Enemy keeps using it, because *it keeps working*. The apostles contended with this lie in the first century, and this PSYOP is still alive and well in the twenty-first. Doctrines from belief systems as diverse as speculative Freemasonry and the New Age movement are built around the idea that we are all divine and could return to that transhuman, *übermensch* state, if we'd just recognize and develop the spark within us.

Of course, that's a bald-faced lie. Instead of achieving godhood, Adam and Eve lost their immortality, died spiritually, got kicked out of their home (the garden), were expelled from the divine council, and were evicted from the holy mountain.

All because they listened and believed a serpent's lie.

We've already discussed the first rebel, Chaos; but who is this second enemy? Who is the serpent in the garden?

The name "Satan" means "accuser," and it's written *ha-shaitan* in the Old Testament. It is not a personal name, but a job title—"*the* satan." *Ha-shaitan* means "the accuser" or "the adversary." Think of it as performing the office of prosecuting attorney—the one who accuses the defendant of a crime.

> Now the serpent was more crafty than any other beast of the field that the LORD God had made. (Genesis 3:1)

The word translated as "serpent" in this verse is *nachash*. It's based on an adjective that means "bright" or "brazen," like shiny brass. The noun *nachash* can mean "snake," but it can also mean "one who practices divination." In Hebrew, it's not uncommon for an adjective to be converted into a noun—the term is "substantivized." If that's the case here, *nachash* could mean "shining one," which is consistent with other descriptions of the Satan figure in the Old Testament.

For example, in Isaiah 14, the character is called "Lucifer" in the King James translation, based on the Latin words chosen by Jerome (*lux* + *ferous*, meaning "light bringer"). But the original Hebrew text actually names him—not "Light Bringer"—but *Helel ben Shachar*, which means "shining one, son of the dawn." Interestingly, *Šahar* (i.e., *Shachar*) was the name of a Canaanite deity: *Shachar* ("Dawn"), twin brother of *Shalim* ("Dusk").

Now, consider this in Daniel 10:

I lifted up my eyes and looked, and behold, a man clothed in linen, with a belt of fine gold from Uphaz around his waist. His body was like beryl, **his face like the appearance of lightning, his eyes like flaming torches, his arms and legs like the gleam of burnished bronze**, and the sound of his words like the sound of a multitude. (Daniel 10:5–6; emphasis added)

Obviously, "shining one" is an apt description of the angel who had to battle the prince of Persia (a supernatural being) to bring his message to Daniel.

Another example occurred about nine hundred years before Daniel, when the Israelites began to complain (and complain and complain) on their way out of Egypt. In response, God sent *saraph nachash* ("fiery serpents") to torment them.[11] *Saraph* is the root word of *seraphim*, which roughly means "burning ones." The Hebrew words *saraph* and *nachash* are used interchangeably, so rather than "fiery serpents," the actual translation should read "*saraph* serpents."

Deuteronomy 8:15 praises Yahweh for bringing Israel through "the great and terrifying wilderness, with its fiery serpents," reinforcing the interchangeability of *saraph* and *nachash*.

Now, if the mental image of flaming snakes isn't weird enough, the prophet Isaiah twice referred to *flying* serpents (*saraph `uwph*, in Isaiah 14:29 and 30:6). And in his famous throne-room vision, Isaiah saw:

…the LORD sitting upon a throne, high and lifted up; and the train of his robe filled the temple. Above him stood the seraphim. Each had six wings: with two he covered his face, and with two he covered his feet, and with two he flew. (Isaiah 6:1–2)

Again, the root word of "seraphim" is *saraph*, the same word translated "serpent" in Numbers and Deuteronomy. In fact, aside from the Isaiah 6 passage above, every single mention of "seraphim" in the Old Testament refers to serpentine beings!

Throughout the ancient Near East, the flying serpent was a well-known symbol, especially in Egypt. Therefore, it would have been very familiar to the Israelites. The *uraeus*, a cobra standing on its coiled body with its hood extended, was a royal symbol of protection used by pharaohs and Nubian kings. Tutankhamun's death mask is an excellent example; and interestingly, the *uraeus'* hood is depicted with six distinct sections that look a lot like six wings.

The bottom line is this: What Adam and Eve saw in the garden wasn't a talking snake, but a *nachash*—a radiant, divine entity, very likely of serpentine appearance.

But consider also that a good, one-word English term to describe a flying, fiery serpent is "dragon."

Now, since you're paying attention, you'll remember that the divine rebel in Eden, the *nachash* of Genesis 3, is called a "guardian cherub" in Ezekiel 28. As we just showed you, *nachash* and *saraph*, the singular form of seraphim, are interchangeable terms. But if the rebel in Eden was one of the seraphim, how could he also be one of the cherubim?

Good question.

Did you know that cherubim are mentioned more frequently than the seraphim in the Old Testament? They are usually referenced in descriptions of the mercy seat on top of the Ark of the Testimony (Ark of the Covenant) and in reference to carved decorations in Solomon's Temple. Two exceptions are the cherubim who guard the entrance to Eden and the four cherubim Ezekiel saw in his famous "wheel within a wheel" vision by the Chebar canal.

Most of us today have a mental image of cherubim that was shaped by artists in the Middle Ages—cute, chubby little boys with dinky wings who filled up the empty space in religious paintings. Nothing could be farther from the biblical and archaeological truth. Cherubim are scary, dangerous creatures we do not want to mess with.

The cherubim of the mercy seat are usually shown as a matched pair of plainly recognizable angels perched on top of the Ark of the Covenant with their outstretched wings touching in the middle. The Bible doesn't describe this pair of cherubim, telling us only that they have wings and faces. Why? Because everybody in the fifteenth century BC knew what a cherub looked like, and they knew it was right and proper for them to serve as Yahweh's throne-bearers. You see, God appeared to men above the mercy seat "enthroned on the cherubim." (See Numbers 7:89; 1 Samuel 4:4; 2 Samuel 6:2; Psalms 80:1 and 99:1; and Isaiah 37:16.)

But the cherubim Ezekiel saw looked like something from a nightmare:

> ...this was their appearance: they had a human likeness, but each had four faces, and each of them had four wings. Their legs were straight, and the soles of their feet were like the sole of a calf's foot. And **they sparkled like burnished bronze**.
>
> Under their wings on their four sides they had human hands. And the four had their faces and their wings thus: their wings touched one another. Each one of them went straight forward, without turning as they went.
>
> As for the likeness of their faces, each had a human face. The four had the face of a lion on the right side, the four had the face of an ox on the left side, and the four had the face of an eagle.
>
> Such were their faces. And their wings were spread out above. Each creature had two wings, each of which touched the wing of another, while two covered their bodies. And each went straight forward. Wherever the spirit would go, they went, without turning as they went.
>
> As for the likeness of the living creatures, their appearance was like burning coals of fire, like the appearance of torches moving to and fro among the living creatures. And the fire was bright, and out of the fire went forth lightning.
>
> And the living creatures darted to and fro, **like the appearance of a flash of lightning**. (Ezekiel 1:5–14; emphasis added)

While these living creatures aren't identified as cherubim in these verses, they are specifically called cherubim in Ezekiel 10—and we'll see them again in the throne room of God when we get to the book of Revelation.

> And every one had four faces: the first face was the face of the cherub, and the second face was a human face, and the third the face of a lion, and the fourth the face of an eagle. (Ezekiel 10:14)

Wait—why a cherub instead of an ox for the fourth face? Is there some connection between the cherub and the ox?

Actually, yes.

The word "cherub" probably comes from the Akkadian *karibu* (the "ch" should be a hard "k" sound). It means "intercessor" or "one who prays." The *karibu* were usually portrayed as winged bulls with human faces, and huge statues of the *karibu* were set up as divine guardians at the entrances of palaces and temples. This is the role of the cherubim "at the east of the garden of Eden...to guard the way to the tree of life."[12]

Cherubim were the gold standard for guarding royalty in the ancient Near East. In Assyria they were called *lamassu*, and the Akkadians called them *shedu*. They were sometimes depicted as winged lions rather than bulls, and they were often incorporated into the thrones of kings. So, the function of the biblical cherubim, guarding the tree of life and carrying the throne of God, was entirely consistent with what the neighbors of the Israelites knew about these beings. Based on what archaeologists have found in the Levant (modern-day Syria, Lebanon, Jordan, and Israel), the cherub was more like a winged sphinx than a humanoid with wings.

The presence of cherubim in the Bible isn't an accident or an invention of the Hebrew prophets. The cherubim were known by different names by the other cultures of the ancient Near East, but they served a similar role in all of them. The cherubim were supernatural bodyguards for the throne of Yahweh, and their imagery was appropriated by earthly kings.

So, we've identified, as best we can, the *nachash*, one of the entities—gods, if you will—who was a member of the assembly on God's holy mountain. But what about the other gods? Who else was in Eden with God, Adam, Eve, and the *nachash*? What do we know about them?

Actually, we know more than you'd think. Unfortunately for us, English doesn't convey the full sense of the Hebrew words that describe the supernatural beings in the Bible. For example, our English word "angel" covers a range of entities—*cherubim, seraphim, ophanim, malakim, bene elohim*, and others in Hebrew, as well as archangels and Watchers. That's made it easier for scholars and theologians to get around the idea that multiple gods are clearly described in the Bible.

We know those gods were in the Garden, or Yahweh would not have inspired Ezekiel to call Eden "the seat of the gods." And it's possible they're mentioned in Ezekiel 28, just not in the way we expect.

Scholars generally agree that Ezekiel 28 is linked to Isaiah 14, another account of the divine rebel being tossed out of Eden:

> How you are fallen from heaven,
> O Day Star, son of Dawn!
> How you are cut down to the ground,
> you who laid the nations low!
> You said in your heart,
> "I will ascend to heaven;
> above the stars of God
> I will set my throne on high;
> I will sit on the mount of assembly
> in the far reaches of the north." (Isaiah 14:12–13)

Ezekiel 28 and Isaiah 14 describe the same event, so we have confirmation of other divine beings in Eden. In the Ezekiel account, God describes how the "anointed guardian cherub" was cast out of Eden, where he'd once walked "in the midst of the stones of fire." Compare that with what we discussed above about the brazen, glowing, or burning appearance of the beings encountered by Moses, Daniel, and Isaiah. And in Psalm 104:4, we read that God "makes his messengers winds, His ministers a flaming fire."

In the Isaiah 14 passage above, we also see a reference to the "stars of God." Scholars agree that "stars" in the Old Testament often refer to the *bene ha'elohim* ("sons of God"). For example, when Yahweh rebuked Job for his lack of faith:

Where were you when I laid the foundation of the earth?
Tell me, if you have understanding.
Who determined its measurements—surely you know!
Or who stretched the line upon it?
On what were its bases sunk,
or who laid its cornerstone,
when the morning stars sang together
and all the sons of God shouted for joy?
(Job 38:4–7; emphasis added)

The divine rebel in Eden was cast out of the Garden and the divine council for his pride and his desire to set his throne "above the stars of God"—sons of God who appear as beings of fire and light. If we read the passages in Ezekiel 28 and Isaiah 14 as consistent with one another, then the "stones of fire" in Eden *were* the sons of God that the *nachash* wanted to rule from his own "mount of assembly in the far reaches of the north."

Apologists for the Bible often try to de-supernaturalize the puzzling references to fiery, flying serpents by offering naturalistic explanations. Some suggest that the fiery serpents of Numbers 21 were saw-scaled vipers, dangerous venomous snakes native to the Sinai Peninsula. Others claim that the verses are proof that dragons or pterodactyls were alive during the Exodus. Both suggestions miss the point. We need to keep our eyes on the supernatural.

By the way, if you had to come up with a single word to describe a "flying, fiery serpent," what would you choose? If we had to guess, we'd bet on "dragon."

Well, the consequences of the rebellion in Eden were immediate and harsh:

The LORD God said to the serpent, "Because you have done this, cursed are you above all livestock and above all beasts of the field; on your belly you shall go, and dust you shall eat all the days of your life.

I will put enmity between you and the woman, and between your offspring and her offspring; he shall bruise your head, and you shall bruise his heel."...

Then the LORD God said, "Behold, the man has become like one of us in knowing good and evil. Now, lest he reach out his hand and take also of the tree of life and eat, and live forever—"

Therefore the LORD God sent him out from the garden of Eden to work the ground from which he was taken. He drove out the man, and at the east of the garden of Eden he placed the cherubim and a flaming sword that turned every way to guard the way to the tree of life. (Genesis 3:14–15, 22–24)

Well-meaning Christians for generations have pointed to Genesis 3:14 as the moment in history when snakes lost their legs. Again, that misses the point. God didn't remove the legs of snakes; He described the punishment of the *nachash* in figurative language. Even casual observers of the animal kingdom know that snakes don't eat dust.

What happened was this: The *nachash* was cast down from the peak of the supernatural realm, "full of wisdom and perfect in beauty," to be the lord of the dead. What a comedown! Isaiah 14 makes a lot more sense when you keep a supernatural worldview in mind:

Sheol beneath is stirred up
to meet you when you come;
it rouses the shades to greet you,
all who were leaders of the earth;
it raises from their thrones
all who were kings of the nations.

All of them will answer
and say to you:
"You too have become as weak as we!
You have become like us!" (Isaiah 14:9–10)

Refer to our previous book, *Veneration,* for a deep dive into the significance of those verses. The "shades" Isaiah mentioned were the Rephaim (root word *rapha*), divinized royal ancestors of the pagan Amorites who surrounded ancient Israel. Moses did not invent the Rephaim when he wrote the Pentateuch. They were well known to their neighbors, and their worship was a central part of the lives of the pagans of the ancient Near East.

For Adam and Eve, the banishment affected the two of them and all their descendants through the present day. Instead of living with God as members of His council, we humans have struggled for millennia to make sense of a world that often seems to make no sense. The memory of our brief time in the Garden of God has echoed down through the long and many centuries since, and it may be the source of our belief that mountains are somehow special: reserved for the gods.

Eden was a lush, well-watered area "on the holy mountain of God," where Yahweh presided over His divine council. The council included the first humans along with the loyal *elohim* (those who had not sided with Chaos during that *first rebellion*). Adam and Eve walked and talked with the supernatural "sons of God" who (based on clues scattered throughout the Bible) were beautiful, radiant beings.

And, at least some of them were serpentine in appearance.

The long war between Yahweh and the sons of God who rebelled is not just about control of the spirit realm, it's also about whether humanity will be restored to its rightful place "in the seat of the gods"—among the divine council on the holy mountain of God. We see God's battle plans and references to previous skirmishes in the Bible, but a day is coming when He will destroy all enemies.

3

EAST OF EDEN

He drove out the man, and at the east of the garden of Eden he placed the cherubim and a flaming sword that turned every way to guard the way to the tree of life.

—GENESIS 3:24

Then Cain went away from the presence of the LORD and settled in the land of Nod, east of Eden.

—GENESIS 4:16

Ejection from the Garden must have been a crushing disappointment for humanity's first couple. Forget about the burden of living under the curse; toiling to coax enough food from the ground to survive; the pain of bringing new life into the world; and all the rest. The realization that they had disappointed their Creator and condemned their children and their children's children—all their descendants until the end of time—to live separate from Him must have been nearly unbearable.

The Bible gives us very little about the rest of their lives. We only know the names of three of their children: Cain, Abel, and Seth. There must

35

have been others, and at least two of them were girls, because Cain and Seth both married and had children of their own. If you find this concept produces cognitive dissonance, you're not alone; but remember that no law had yet been decreed regarding familial relations and marriage. And humanity's genetic diversity at this point was far greater than at present. After all, Adam married a woman whose entire genome was based on his rib. Suffice to say that God, who created the DNA in the first place, had it all under His perfect control, so we'll just trust in Him and move on, eh?

Secular archaeologists and historians won't agree with much of what we believe about human history. That's okay. We Bible-believing Christians don't reject science when we interpret data through a biblical lens—in fact, some of us have science degrees! The discipline known as "science" (meaning "knowledge") is the process by which we collect and record information to test theories about the way things are. It is the result of how we're made. A reflection of our God-breathed design. Scientific analysis is what we do with that information after it's collected. As Christians, it's not the science we question, it's the analysis. Whether you hold to "young earth" or "old," belief in an omnipotent Creator is at the heart of Christian doctrine.

Despite any prejudicial slants regarding God, most scholars agree that human civilization emerged in the Fertile Crescent (the land between the Tigris and Euphrates rivers) around 10,000 BC. (Note: We're using dates that are generally accepted by a consensus of scholars so we don't get bogged down arguing about the timeline. That's outside the scope of what we're trying to do here.) Agriculture, cities, writing, trade, science, and organized religion all developed in a broad arc that stretched from Egypt through the Levant and down into Mesopotamia.

Curiously, the evidence uncovered thus far supports the idea that Adam and Eve, and later Cain, traveled east of Eden to begin their lives (Note: We place the Garden of Eden in the vicinity of Jerusalem). As such, the first evidence of civilization appears at Sumer, today's southeastern Iraq, where it emerged fully formed with no preliminary steps.

A few scholars speculate that earlier attempts at organizing what we call "civilization" lies at the bottom of the Persian Gulf. The theory goes that Eden, from which all humans came, stood in the "Gulf Oasis," a lush valley watered by the Tigris and Euphrates rivers, as well as the Karun River from Iran and the Wadi Batin from Saudi Arabia. The Persian Gulf rose rapidly between 6000 and 5000 BC, during the Neolithic Wet Phase, and as the Gulf moved northward, people moved ahead of it, leaving the evidence of their earlier settlements hidden beneath the gulf's waves.

Scholars refer to as this civilization as the Ubaid culture. Of course, that's not what the people who lived in it called themselves; we don't know their proper name, because they never invented writing. The Ubaid civilization gets its name from Tell al-`Ubaid, a small settlement mound in southeast Iraq where two well-known archaeologists, Henry Hall and Sir Leonard Woolley, first dug up bits of Ubaid pottery between 1919 and 1924.

Archaeologists who study the Ubaid culture agree that its influence spread from Eridu in southeast Iraq, eventually going as far as what is today northwest Iran, northern Syria, southern Turkey, and the Levant (Syria, Lebanon, Jordan, and Israel).

The Ubaid civilization was typified by large, unwalled villages, rectangular multi-room mud-brick houses, high-quality pottery, and the first public temples. Crop irrigation developed by about 5000 BC, so cereals and grains could grow in the dry climate that again dominated the region. The first city in Mesopotamia, and therefore the oldest city in the world, appeared around 5400 BC. Although agricultural settlements like Jericho (c. 9000 BC) and Jarmo, east of modern-day Kirkuk in Iraq (c. 7100 BC) are older, Eridu was remembered by later Sumerians as the first city, with a degree of specialization among its citizens not seen before in other settlements.

The Sumerian King List, dated to about 2100 BC, records it this way:

After the kingship descended from heaven, the kingship was in Eridu. In Eridu, Alulim became king; he ruled for 28,800 years.[13]

Interestingly, the Bible may actually support this account.

Cain went away from the presence of the LORD and settled in the land of Nod, east of Eden. Cain knew his wife, and she conceived and bore Enoch. **When he built a city, he called the name of the city after the name of his son, Enoch. To Enoch was born Irad,** and Irad fathered Mehujael, and Mehujael fathered Methushael, and Methushael fathered Lamech. (Genesis 4:16–18; emphasis added)

Some scholars, such as Egyptologist David Rohl, believe it's possible that the "he" in the second sentence refers to Enoch, not to Cain; thus, the final word "Enoch" might be a later addition—in which case the builder of the city *was* Enoch, and it was named for *his* son, Irad—hence the name Eridu.

To speculate a little further, we can apply a rudimentary translation to the name "Alulim" and come up with "fourth man" (*A* = prefix + *lu* = "man" + *lim*, a contraction of *limmu* = "four"). Again, this is speculative and it may be way off base, so don't take it as gospel. But if it's correct, then Alulim might have been Irad, the "fourth man," or fourth generation, after creation—Adam, Cain, Enoch, Irad—and the first king of the first city on earth, Eridu, the city that bore his name.

Regardless of its origins, what is most interesting about Eridu is that, besides being the oldest city in Sumer, it was the home of the oldest and largest ziggurat (a step pyramid) in Mesopotamia. This was the temple of one of the most important gods of the ancient Near East. He was known as Enki to the Sumerians and Ea to the later Akkadians and Babylonians. Enki was the god of the *sweet* waters, those needed for life. To illustrate this, he was depicted with two streams of water flowing from his shoulders to represent the Tigris and Euphrates rivers, the main sources of fresh water in Mesopotamia. Consider the hubris of the fallen "gods" who dared to lay claim to Christ's imagery—the source of Living Water. Once again, these rebels twist truth.

Along with An (or Anu), the sky-god, and Enlil, the king of the pantheon, Enki was one of the three most important gods in Sumer. He arrived very early in Sumer from a place called Dilmun, probably the island of Bahrain in the Persian Gulf. In fact, the Sumerians believed Enki personally created Eridu, elevating it from the marshy ground on what was then the shore of the gulf.

Enki was the god of magic, craftsmanship, and wisdom. Although Enlil was king of the gods, Enki was the keeper of the *mes* (sounds like "mezz"), decrees of the gods that formed the fundamental concepts and gifts of civilization—everything from religious practices to social interaction to music.

The Babylonian creation myth, the *Enuma Elish*, describes how everything on earth came into being after Marduk defeated the chaos-goddess Tiamat. (Yes, this is another lie from the Fallen Realm.) Marduk was the son of Enki, the chief god of Babylon. However, the older Sumerian story credits Enki with giving life to all things, including mankind, and names Enlil the slayer of Tiamat.

Apparently, the fallen realm squabbles over who gets credit for stealing God's ideas. And this explains how worship of these entities passed from one region to another—one might call it the ebb and flow of power over the centuries. Each city in Mesopotamia had a patron god or goddess. The importance of a deity was, as you'd guess, tied to the fortunes of its city. Just as Eridu was the home of Enki, Enlil was chief deity at Nippur; Inanna (Ishtar) was supreme at Uruk; the sun-god Utu was the patron deity of Sippar; and so on. To give you an idea of the incredible amount of time we're dealing with, Enki ruled in Eridu for about 3,500 years before Marduk entered the picture and replaced Enlil at the head of the Mesopotamian pantheon—an event linked to Babylon's emergence as the region's dominant power in the eighteenth century BC.

For context, that's about the same amount of time that's passed between Moses leading the Israelites out of Egypt and our current day.

Oh, and there's one more aspect of life in the ancient Near East we'd like to call to your attention. It's something we only hear about from fringe pseudo-scholars who blame the phenomenon on extraterrestrials. (Think big hair.) Scholars, that is archaeologists and sociologists, have known at least since the late 1940s that before the people of Mesopotamia had even learned how to write, they'd already begun turning their children into coneheads.

Based on human remains dated to between about 10,000 BC and 3500 BC, it appears that cranial deformation was widespread in the Ubaid culture and at Eridu, the world's first city. If Cain or his son established Eridu, then we can place them at ground zero for head-shaping. An archaeological dig at Eridu just after World War II revealed about a thousand bodies that had been buried during the Ubaid period. Of the 206 sets of remains the archaeologists exhumed, "all of the crania had been deformed in one fashion or another."[14]

Got that? That's 206 out of 206. Not a few, and not just the elites, but every person from every stratum of the Eridu culture had a deformed skull.

However, instead of asking why the Ubaid peoples engaged in this strange practice, the lead archaeologist decided "earth pressure" following burial must be the cause, even though none of the skulls was cracked or broken, which we would expect if the deformations had been placed under enough pressure to turn them into coneheads.

Evidence of head-shaping has been found at sites all over Iraq, southwestern Iran, eastern Turkey, the valleys of the Zagros mountains, and the western shores of the Persian Gulf, dated from 7500 BC to about 4000 BC. After that, the practice seems to disappear.[15]

Now, it's worth asking: Who wakes up one morning in 7000 BC and decides to wrap something around a baby's skull to see if it makes his head pointy? What inspires that? And why was Eridu (the city built by Cain or his son) the starting point for this unusual practice?

A 1992 study concluded that the practice of head-shaping, which is found in cultures the world over, must have originated in the Near East because it was so widespread there. However, the researchers believed the deformation may have been unintentional, but was probably "incidental to patterns of head-gear."[16]

Yeah, right.

And here's another bit of data to chew on (assuming you're not full yet). At Eridu and nearby sites in ancient pre-Flood southern Sumer, and *only* there, archaeologists have found about 120 terracotta figurines that scholars call *ophidian*, meaning "snake-like." These figurines are slender bipeds, adorned with button-like protuberances, more often female than male, and often in poses that are exclusively mammalian—for example, a female lizard-like figure suckling an infant.

Pop quiz: Who can name a reptile that suckles its young? None that we can identify. At least, none within the material world.

Now, ancient astronaut evangelists on cable TV shows claim to have an answer for this phenomenon. These reptilian mothers were our space ancestors, the Anunnaki who came from the stars to create humanity by tinkering with ape DNA.

Now let's give them a bit of credit. They are thinking along the right lines, but by ignoring the supernatural, they miss the most likely answer.

The aforementioned scholars point out in their paper that (as of 1992), there had been no serious study of these figurines regarding their meaning to the ancients, just as there is no scholarly literature on the origins of human cranial deformation.

While there hasn't been much academic attention paid to the ophidian idols (let's just admit their probable usage), there have been several papers published within the last ten years on head-shaping in the ancient Near East. Still no conclusions as to why or how the practice began, but it is clear that the people who lived in the region—descendants of the refugees from Eden—made a habit of this odd practice. Cain has a lot to explain.

We'll never know for certain why all this happened, but we can speculate. Perhaps, the people who formed the earliest human civilizations copied a look that someone, somewhere, had seen and decided was the physical ideal. We still do this. Modern-day teens copy hairstyles and fashion from magazines and television, and men emulate the latest Marvel hunk, right? Except that the ophidian style head-shaping fashion statement didn't change with the seasons; it appears to have been worn by nearly everybody for more than six thousand years!

For it to last that long, it must have conveyed some advantage to those who practiced it. Think back to what we discussed about the serpentine *nachash* and seraphim, and remember that at least one of them rebelled against Yahweh. Is it possible that the citizens of the prehistoric Near East were trying to curry favor with a god?

As mentioned earlier, Eridu is considered to be the center of the Ubaid culture. The Ubaid period is defined as the civilization in the ancient Near East just before the time of Nimrod and the Tower of Babel, roughly between 6500 BC and 3800 BC. It would have begun not long after Adam and Eve got kicked out of the Garden.

Now, remember that God wanted humanity to "have dominion over the fish of the sea and over the birds of the heavens and over every living thing that moves on the earth" (Genesis 1:28)? He did not direct mankind to form into stratified groups, with one person atop the social pyramid. We weren't to take dominion over each other. As Jesus told His disciples thousands of years later, "You know that the rulers of the Gentiles lord it over them, and their great ones exercise authority over them. It shall not be so among you" (Matthew 20:25–26a).

Adam and Eve were created to work the land. God designed humans to be self-sufficient—growing our own food, tending our own flocks, and helping each other whenever and however we're needed. When you live that kind of life, you're too busy to dominate your neighbors. And since you don't depend on handouts for your family's daily bread, government cannot dictate to you. It makes sense that Israel was led by judges in times of trouble during its early years, but a king wasn't part of the original plan—even though God, who knows the end from the beginning, surely saw what was coming and let the Hebrews make Saul king anyway.

Now, archaeologists and sociologists have noticed two other aspects of civilization that commenced during the Ubaid period: first, the transition from a rural to an urban society, and second, their society becoming increasingly stratified. The evidence (primarily grave goods) indicates that, as people moved from the country to the city, the rich got richer and the poor got poorer. Just like today.

The Ubaid period also saw the construction of the first temples in Mesopotamia. Each of their cities worshiped a "city god" for whom the locals built a temple. And each of these temples had a granary for collecting the offerings of the commoners. Of course, this required somebody to oversee offerings and storage of the commodities, but also the recording of who provided the offering and how much was given—a ledger of sorts, requiring a new skill: writing. Archaeologists and sociologists believe this led to an elite class of hereditary leaders and priests who determined which folks deserved to receive grain from these granaries during times of famine. Substitute "income tax and social security income" for grain offerings, and it's clear that things haven't changed all that much in the last eight thousand years.

We can only speculate how such a system emerged. Logically, it's a pretty good guess that the rebel entities who'd rose up against Yahweh at this early stage had set themselves up as these city gods. It's also conceivable, based on what we know about angels from the Bible, that one or more of them appeared to the pre-Sumerians (possibly even Cain) and explained that, as gods, 1) they each needed a house or temple, and 2) each temple required a priest-king to oversee the offerings and ensure that all the city gods were pleased. The result? The upper class (kings, priests, and scribes) increasingly lived in luxury, while the peasants worked the land to support them. There was no middle class.

From the point of view of the Fallen Realm, destroying the world was much easier when you only had to manipulate a handful of useful idiots who then convinced the rest of the people to do things your way. As evidence, archaeologists have concluded that the Ubaid period was a time of increasing disparity between the classes,[17] but they miss the hidden truth because they fail to examine the evidence through a spiritual lens. Instead, they dissect more tangible data, such as climate, technology, and artistic expression (i.e., those ophidian figurines). They blindly miss the possibility that the unseen realm may have guided these cultural changes—

one might say they gave mankind secret knowledge. And it was done to corrupt humanity and render it unfit for God's purposes. The long war lies at the heart of all history. But if Christians remain blind and don't admit to these truths, then we can bet secular historians, archaeologists, and anthropologists won't bother to put on those "spiritual eyeglasses."

Now, we've mentioned how the fallen, small-*g* gods tricked humans into building temples in their honor. What about a ziggurat? What about Babel?

For generations, well-meaning Bible teachers have presented the story of the Tower of Babel as an object lesson on the dangers of pride. The flannel-board version presents them as foolish people who were so arrogant, they thought they could build a tower high enough to reach heaven.

With respect to all our Sunday school teachers, that's not quite the entire story. In fact, it's an insult to the intelligence of our ancestors and it's a disservice to people in church who want to know the real reason Yahweh was so offended by this construction project. No, He wasn't threatened by it. The builders and their overseers weren't just people who'd gotten too big for their britches. They'd fallen hook, line, and sinker for lies, and the clue to the sin of Babel is in the name.

The Hebrew prophets loved to play with language, and we often find words in the Bible that sound like the original but make a statement—for example, Beelzebub ("lord of the flies") instead of Beelzebul ("Baal the prince"), or Ish-bosheth ("man of a shameful thing") instead of Ishbaal ("man of Baal"). Likewise, the original Akkadian words *bāb ilu*, which mean "gate of god" or "gate of the gods," is replaced in the Bible with *Babel*, based on the Hebrew word meaning "confusion."

And, contrary to what you've been taught, Babel was not in Babylon. It's an easy mistake to make. The names sound alike. Babylon is one of the most famous cities of the ancient world, and it had a bad reputation, especially to Jews and Christians. Under the aegis of the megalomaniacal King Nebuchadnezzar, the army of Babylon sacked Jerusalem and carried off the hardware for service in the Temple. So, it makes sense that some believe a building project that so offended God that He personally intervened *must* have been built at Babylon, right? But there's a problem with linking Babylon to the Tower of Babel: Babylon didn't exist when the structure was built. In fact, it didn't even become a city until about a thousand years *after* the Tower of Babel incident, and even then, it remained an unimportant village for about another five hundred years. A lot can happen in five hundred years. For instance, what was London like in 1520? Or the Americas? What inventions have arisen since then? Oxcarts have been replaced with autonomous cars, flying machines take people from one continent to the other in just a few hours, and even children can communicate at the speed of light by tapping a screen.

Five hundred years is a long time!

Who commissioned the construction of the tower? Traditions and sources outside the Bible identify the builder as a shadowy figure named Nimrod, who lived sometime between 3500 and 3100 BC, a period of history called the Uruk Expansion. This tracks with what little the Bible tells us about Nimrod. In Genesis 10:10, we read "the beginning of his kingdom was Babel, Erech, Accad, and Calneh, in the land of Shinar." To clarify, the land of Shinar is Sumer and Erech is Uruk. Consider this: Uruk was so important to human history that Nimrod's homeland is *still* called Uruk, five thousand years later. We just spell it differently—Iraq.

Accad, mentioned above, was the capital city of the Akkadians, which thus far remains undiscovered, but its influence covered the land between Babylon and ancient Assyria. Babylon itself was northwest of Uruk, roughly three hundred miles from the Persian Gulf in what is today central Iraq. But it wasn't founded until around 2300 BC, at least seven hundred years after Nimrod, and it wasn't really Babylon as we think about it until the old Babylonian Empire emerged in the early part of the second millennium BC.

Where, then, should we look for the infamous Tower of Babel? Remember, the oldest and largest ziggurat in Mesopotamia was at Eridu, the first city of the Sumerians. In recent years, scholars have learned that the name "Babylon" was interchangeable with other city names, including

"Eridu."[18] So when we read about Babylon, it doesn't always mean *the* Babylon of ancient texts.

Eridu, the city of Enki, never dominated the political situation in Sumer after its first two kings, Alulim and Alalgar, unlike Ur, Uruk, Nippur, and other prominent worship centers. But Eridu was so important to Mesopotamian culture that more than three thousand years later, Hammurabi, the greatest king of the Old Babylonian Empire, was crowned not in Babylon, *but in Eridu*—even though Eridu had ceased to be a city about 1,300 years earlier![19]

Even as late as the time of Nebuchadnezzar, 1,100 years after Hammurabi, the kings of Babylon still sometimes called themselves LUGAL.NUN[ki]—King of Eridu.

Why? What was the deal with Eridu? It was the first city, the place where "kingship descended from heaven," a city possibly built by Cain or his son, and it may have named for Cain's grandson, Irad.

Think about that for a moment. Eridu, its name interchangeable with Babylon, may have been established by the first murderer on earth— meaning it may have been Cain, not Nimrod, who founded the *original* Babylon!

Archaeologists have uncovered eighteen levels of the temple to Enki at Eridu. The oldest levels of the *E-abzu*, a small structure less than ten feet square, date to the founding of the city around 5400 BC. Fish bones were scattered around the building. Enki seems to have been a fan of Euphrates River carp.

Now, stop and take that in: The first small shrine to Enki may have been built by Cain or one of his immediate descendants. And consider that the spot remained sacred to Enki long after the city was deserted, around 3100 BC.[20] The temple remained in use until the fifth century BC, nearly five thousand years after the first crude altar was built to accept offerings of fish to the god of the subterranean aquifer, the *abzu*.

Now, at this point we should tell you that *abzu* (*ab* = water + *zu* = deep) is very likely where we get our English word "abyss."

And the fog begins to lift.

Another clue: The name "Enki" is a compound word. *En* is Sumerian for "lord," and *ki* is the word for "earth." Thus, Enki, god of the *abzu*, was "lord of the earth."

Do you remember Jesus calling someone "the ruler of this world"? Or Paul referring to "the god of this world"? Who were they talking about?

Yeah. Satan.

And here's another piece to our puzzle: Nimrod was of the second generation after the Flood. His father was Cush, son of Ham, son of Noah. In Sumerian history, the second king of Uruk after the Flood was named Enmerkar, son of Mesh-ki-ang-gasher.

The Hebrew writers of the Old Testament, doing what they loved to do with language, transformed the name "Enmer"—the consonants *N-M-R* (remember, there were no vowels in ancient Hebrew)—into Nimrod, which makes it sound like *marad*, the Hebrew word for "rebel." Clever, huh?

Now, get this: An epic poem from about 2,000 BC called "Enmerkar and the Lord of Aratta" preserves the basic details of the Tower of Babel story.

We don't know exactly where Aratta was, but informed guesses range from northern Iran to Armenia, which would be interesting. Not only is Armenia located near the center of an ancient kingdom called Urartu, which may be a cognate for Aratta, but it's also where Noah landed his boat—the mountains of Ararat. So, it's possible that Nimrod/Enmerkar was trying to intimidate the people—his cousins, basically—who settled near where his great-grandfather landed the ark. But we just don't know. Wherever it was, Enmerkar muscled this neighboring kingdom to compel them to send building materials for a couple of projects near and dear to his heart.

Some background: The poem refers to Enmerkar's capital city Uruk as the "great mountain." This is intriguing, since Uruk, like most of Sumer, sits in an alluvial plain where there are no mountains whatsoever. Uruk was home to two of the chief gods of the Sumerian pantheon: Anu, the sky-god, and Inanna, his granddaughter, the goddess of war and sex (and by sex, we mean the carnal, extramarital kind).

While Anu was pretty much retired, having handed over his duties as head of the pantheon to Enlil, Inanna played a very active role in Sumerian society. For example, scholars have translated ritual texts for innkeepers to pray to Inanna, asking her to guarantee that their bordellos turn a profit.

Apparently, part of the problem between Enmerkar and the king of Aratta, whose name, we learn from a separate epic, was Ensuhkeshdanna, was a dispute over who was Inanna's favorite. One of the building projects Enmerkar wanted to tackle was a magnificent temple to Inanna, the *E-ana* ("House of Heaven"). He wanted Aratta to supply the raw materials. This wasn't only because there isn't much in the way of timber, jewels, or precious metal in the plains of Sumer, but because Enmerkar wanted the lord of Aratta to submit and acknowledge that he was Inanna's chosen one. So Enmerkar prayed to Inanna:

> My sister, let Aratta fashion gold and silver skillfully on my behalf for Unug [Uruk]. Let them cut the flawless lapis lazuli from the blocks, let them … the translucence of the flawless lapis lazuli … build a holy mountain in Unug. Let Aratta build a temple brought down from heaven—your place of worship, the Shrine *E-ana*; let Aratta skillfully fashion the interior of the holy jipar, your abode; may I, the radiant youth, may I be embraced there by you. Let Aratta submit beneath the yoke for Unug on my behalf.[21]

Notice that Inanna's temple was, like Uruk, compared to a holy mountain. And given the type of goddess Inanna was, the embrace Enmerkar wanted was more than just—ahem—a figure of speech.

To be honest, some of the messages between Enmerkar and Ensuhkeshdanna about Inanna were the kind of locker room talk that got Donald Trump into trouble during the 2016 presidential campaign. But we digress.

Well…no. Let's continue the digression for a minute. We should stop for a brief look at Inanna's role in human history. The goddess has been known by many names through the ages: Inanna in Sumer, Ishtar in

Babylon, Astarte in Canaan, Aphrodite in Greece, and Venus across the Roman world. Let's just say the image we were taught of Aphrodite/Venus in high school mythology class was way off.

Since we'd like to keep this a family-friendly book, we won't dig *too* deeply into the history and characteristics of Inanna. Scholars don't completely agree on the details, anyway. But it's safe to say Inanna wasn't a girl you'd bring home to meet your mother.

In fact, she wasn't always a girl, period. You see, while Inanna was definitely the goddess with the mostest when it came to sex appeal, she was also androgynous. She was sometimes shown with masculine features like a beard. On one tablet (although from much later, in the first millennium BC, almost three thousand years after Nimrod), Inanna says, "When I sit in the alehouse, I am a woman, and I am an exuberant young man."[22] Her cult followers included eunuchs and transvestites, and she was apparently the first in history to make a practice of sex reassignment:

> She [changes] the right side (male) into the left side (female),
> She [changes] the left side into the right side,
> She [turns] a man into a woman,
> She [turns] a woman into a man
> She ador[ns] a man as a woman,
> She ador[ns] a woman as a man.[23]

This poem is wonderfully ironic, given our twenty-first century progressive ideal of gender fluidity. Even though the passage was written five thousand years ago, we see a personified Sumerian goddess, the Lady Inanna, portrayed as a woman who craved sex and fighting just as much, if not more, than men. Inanna took on all comers in love and war, and did so with greater skill and more delight than men or other gods. Today, Inanna's personality is celebrated by modern scholars as complex and courageous, transcending traditional gender roles, turning this ancient goddess into an icon of independent man/woman/other-hood.

There is an ongoing debate among scholars as to whether the

priesthood of Inanna was involved in ritual sex. The concept of divine marriage was common in ancient Mesopotamia, but generally the participants were a god and his consort. It appears that the rituals were intended to please the god so he'd be receptive to the requests from a city or kingdom under his protection.

However, as a *harimtu*, which might mean "temple prostitute" or may simply refer to a single woman, Inanna herself participated in the rite with a king. And since she was the dominant partner in the ritual coupling, gender roles might not have been as clearly defined as we would assume.

From a Christian perspective, however, Inanna isn't complex at all. She's a bad Hollywood screenwriter's idea of a fifteen-year-old boy's fantasy woman. Inanna is selfish, ruled by her passions, and destructive when she doesn't get her way. The Sumerian hero Gilgamesh, who ruled Uruk two generations after Enmerkar, is remembered partly for rejecting Inanna. As he pointed out in the story, every one of the men in her life suffered horrible consequences—for example, Dumuzi the Shepherd, who ruled as a king in Bad-Tibara, the second city in Sumer to exercise kingship after Eridu.

In the myth, even though Inanna married Dumuzi, she was happy to throw him under the bus when demons tried to drag her younger son, Lulal (patron god of a city named Bad-Tibara), down to the netherworld. At Inanna's urging, the demons spared Lulal and took Dumuzi instead. Dumuzi's sister pleaded for him, so Inanna agreed to allow her to take his place for half the year, thus making Dumuzi the first of many "dying and rising gods" in the ancient Near East.

More than two thousand years later, one of the abominations God showed the prophet Ezekiel was women at the entrance of the north gate of the Temple weeping for Dumuzi, called Tammuz in the Bible.

Well, for his impudence at daring to remind Inanna about the fate of Dumuzi and the other poor shlubs who'd succumbed to the charms of the wild goddess, she flew up to heaven in a rage and demanded that her father, the sky-god Anu, unleash the Bull of Heaven on Gilgamesh. That didn't go well for the Bull of Heaven, but sadly for Gilgamesh, his best friend Enkidu was killed by the gods as punishment for spoiling Inanna's revenge.

We shared all of that with you to make a point: *This* is the deity Enmerkar/Nimrod wanted to make the patron goddess of his city, Uruk (replacing her father Anu, ironically)! Could it be that veneration of the violent, sex-crazed, gender-bending Inanna was responsible for Yahweh's decision to stop Nimrod's artificial holy mountain?

Probably not. Inanna has enjoyed a very long run as one of the most popular pagan deities in history. And why not? Selling humans on the concept of sex as worship is easy.

Looking at the values of our modern society, it's no stretch to say that Inanna is the spirit of the age. Gender fluidity is the flavor of the month among progressives in the West. The values of Inanna—immediate gratification and sex with whomever, whenever—are considered more open-minded, tolerant, and loving than the virtues of chastity, fidelity, and faithfulness introduced by Yahweh long after Inanna was first worshiped as the Queen of Heaven.

Ironically, this means that so-called progressive ideas about gender and sexual morality are actually *regressive*! The enlightened think they're cutting-edge, breaking new ground and smashing old paradigms when in fact they're just setting the calendar back to more than a thousand years before Abraham.

If Yahweh had genuinely intervened to put a stop to the cult of Inanna, she would be long forgotten, like Enki.

No, the transgression of Nimrod was much more serious. Besides building a fabulous temple for the goddess of prostitutes, he also wanted to expand and upgrade the *abzu*—the abyss.

Let the people of Aratta bring down for me the mountain stones from their mountain, **build the great shrine for me, erect the great abode for me, make the great abode, the abode of the gods,** famous for me, make my me prosper in Kulaba, make the *abzu* grow for me like a holy mountain, **make Eridug [Eridu] gleam**

for me like the mountain range, cause the *abzu* shrine to shine forth for me like the silver in the lode. When in the *abzu* I utter praise, when I bring the me from Eridug, when, in lordship, I am adorned with the crown like a purified shrine, when I place on my head the holy crown in Unug Kulaba, then may the … of the great shrine bring me into the *jipar*, and may the … of the *jipar* bring me into the great shrine. May the people marvel admiringly, and may Utu (the sun god) witness it in joy.[24] (Emphasis added)

That's the issue Yahweh had with it right there. This Tower project wasn't about hubris or pride; it was to build the abode of the gods, an artificial mount of assembly, right on top of the *abzu*.

Could Nimrod have succeeded? Ask yourself: Why did Yahweh find it necessary to personally put a stop to it? A lot of magnificent pagan temples were built in the ancient world, from Mesopotamia to Mesoamerica. Why did God stop this one?

We can only speculate, of course, but there's a reason or we wouldn't have a record of it. The simple fact that it's in the Bible at all means it's an important enough lesson that God wanted to preserve it for us. Calling Babel a story about the sin of pride is easy, but it drains the narrative of its spiritual and supernatural context. And frankly, it makes God seem a bit insecure. Doesn't He want us to work hard to reach our goals?

Well, Inanna gave Enmerkar the answer he wanted (said Enmerkar, anyway; history is always written by the winner), so the king chose a messenger to carry this message to the lord of Aratta:

Lest I make the people fly off from that city like a wild dove from its tree, lest I make them fly around like a bird over its well-founded nest, lest I requite (?) them as if at a current market rate, lest I make it gather dust like an utterly destroyed city, lest like a settlement cursed by Enki and utterly destroyed, I too utterly destroy Aratta; lest like the devastation which swept destructively, and in whose wake Inanna arose, shrieked and yelled aloud, I too wreak a sweeping devastation there—let Aratta pack nuggets of gold in leather sacks, placing alongside it the *kugmea* ore; package up precious metals, and load the packs on the donkeys of the mountains.[25]

Enmerkar justified his demand and his threat by claiming that Inanna had chosen him and Uruk as her favorites and sent his messenger off across "seven mountains" to reach Aratta. That's possibly coincidental, but an interesting reference nonetheless, considering end-times prophecies about the seven mountains of Babylon the Great (see Revelation 17:1–14, especially verse 9). Unintimidated, the lord of Aratta, Ensuhkeshdanna, refused to submit. Instead, he proposed a series of challenges that he believed were impossible to fulfill, but Enmerkar, with the help of Enki, succeeded anyway.

There's more to this story, which was apparently so popular in Mesopotamia, even as late as the Old Babylonian era (early third millennium BC, more than 1,500 years later), that several other surviving Sumerian epics read like sequels to a hit movie. Without getting bogged down in details, we can draw a few broad conclusions from the tale: The king of Uruk, whom we believe was Nimrod, wanted to build a fabulous temple to the goddess of sex and war as a centerpiece of his capital city. More important, Enmerkar/Nimrod wanted to rebuild and expand the ancient, pre-Flood temple of Enki, the god Sumerians thanked for the gifts of civilization (the *mes*) and for creating the *apkallu* (the Watchers)—even though their intervention in human affairs, according to later Babylonian myth, was responsible for the deluge.

But there's another fascinating detail recorded in "Enmerkar and the Lord of Aratta": In the story, Enki confused the speech of humans, who had formerly spoken the same language.

Once upon a time there was no snake,
there was no scorpion,
There was no hyena, there was no lion,
There was no wild dog, no wolf,

There was no fear, no terror,
Man had no rival.
In those days, the lands of Subur (and) Hamazi,
Harmony-tongued Sumer,
the great land of the decrees of princeship,
Uri, the land having all that is appropriate,
The land Martu, resting in security,
The whole universe, the people in unison
To Enlil in one tongue [spoke].
(Then) Enki, the lord of
abundance (whose) commands are trustworthy,
The lord of wisdom, who understands the land,
The leader of the gods,
Endowed with wisdom, **the lord of Eridu**
Changed the speech in their mouths,
[brought] contention into it,
Into the speech of man that (until then)
had been one.[26] (Emphasis added)

The elements of the Babel account are all there in "Enmerkar and the Lord of Aratta": the pride that drove Nimrod to dominate the known world, construction of a Tower/ziggurat that Yahweh found offensive enough to bring to a halt (building the abode of the gods over the abyss!), and the supernatural confusion of languages that gave the Tower its Hebrew name, Babel.

In our view, the evidence is compelling. It's time to correct the history we've been taught since Sunday school: Babel was not at Babylon; it was at Eridu. The Tower was the temple of the god Enki, "lord of the earth," the god of the abyss. Its purpose was to create an artificial mount of assembly, the abode of the gods, to which humans had access.

That was something that Yahweh could not allow.

The end of "Enmerkar and the Lord of Aratta" is mostly missing, but it appears that Enmerkar ultimately triumphed over his rival. Other stories suggest that Enmerkar later marched the army of Uruk to Aratta and conquered it.

This is consistent with archaeological evidence of the Uruk Expansion, which covers the period from about 3500 BC to about 3100 BC. Although scholars usually downplay the violence that created the world's first empire, Uruk spread its influence as far away as northwest Iran and southeastern Turkey. Pottery from Uruk has been found are more than five hundred miles away from the city. To put it into context, Uruk at its peak controlled more territory than Saddam Hussein's Iraq.

This was not a peaceful endeavor. An ancient city called Hamoukar in northeast Syria was destroyed and burned by an army from Uruk sometime around 3500 BC.[27] Scholars have identified the origin of the army by the pottery they left behind. Hamoukar was overwhelmed and then burned by attackers who used clay bullets fired from slings to defeat the city's defenders. Strangely, what appears to have been a trading post from Uruk outside the city was destroyed, too, suggesting that maybe the men sent by Uruk to keep the locals in line had gone native.

That was how the kingdom of Nimrod obtained materials like jewels, copper, silver, lead, gold, timber, wine, and other things that were scarce in the plains of Sumer.

Of course, there is no way we'll ever know for certain that Nimrod was Enmerkar and that he was responsible for the Uruk Expansion—which is a polite way of describing the process of conquering everybody within a two-month march of home. Artifacts from Uruk are found everywhere in the Near East, especially a type of pottery called the beveled-rim bowl. This is significant because it offers a glimpse into the way the society of Uruk was organized.

More on that later in the book. For now, we'll just observe that the unprecedented growth of the Uruk empire between about 3500 BC and 3100 BC suggests that the mass-produced, beveled-rim bowls are evidence of the stratification of Urukian society. As in the Ubaid culture, citizens of Uruk found themselves working for hereditary leaders—kings, who justified their rule as ordained by the gods.

As an example, the Sumerian myth *Enki and Inanna* tells the story of how the divine gifts of civilization, the *mes*, were stolen from Enki by Inanna and transferred from Eridu to Uruk. Enki, always ready for a romp with a goddess, tried to ply Inanna with beer. She maintained her virtue while Enki got drunk, offering her gift after gift as his heart grew merry and his mind grew dim. When he awoke the next day with a hangover, Inanna and the *mes* were no longer in the *abzu*. The enraged god sent out his horrible *gallu* demons (sometimes translated "sea monsters") to retrieve them, but Inanna escaped and arrived safely back at Uruk, where she dispensed the hundred or so *mes* to the cheers of a grateful city. Enki realized he'd been duped and accepted a treaty of everlasting peace with Uruk. This tale may be a bit of religious propaganda to justify the transfer of political authority to Uruk, or it may represent a dim memory of a power struggle in the spirit realm thousands of years ago.

One more thing: We mentioned earlier that archaeologists at Eridu have found eighteen construction layers at the site of Enki's temple. Some of those layers are below an eight-foot deposit of silt from a massive flood. The most impressive layer of construction, called Temple 1, was huge, a temple on a massive platform with evidence of an even larger foundation that would have risen up to almost the height of the structure itself.

Here's the thing: Temple 1 was never finished. At the peak of the builders' architectural achievement, *Eridu was suddenly and completely abandoned.*

> …the Uruk Period…appears to have been brought to a conclusion by no less an event than **the total abandonment of the site**…. In what appears to have been an almost incredibly short time, drifting sand had filled the deserted buildings of the temple-complex and obliterated all traces of the once prosperous little community."[28] (Emphasis added)

Why? What would possibly cause people who'd committed to building the largest ziggurat in Mesopotamia at the most ancient and important religious site in the known world to just stop work and leave Eridu with the *E-abzu* unfinished? Could it be…

> "Come, let us go down and there confuse their language, so that they may not understand one another's speech." So the LORD dispersed them from there over the face of all the earth, **and they left off building the city.** (Genesis 11:8–9; emphasis added)

Just as the rebellious sins of the *nachash* and the chaos-dragon forced their Creator to act, the sin at Babel would not be permitted to continue. The Lord of Armies personally intervened. Yahweh mixed the speech of the Sumerians "that (until then) had been one."

The consequences of the sins at Babel were immediate and severe. Not only did Yahweh scatter the people, He told mankind that we'd have to deal with the lesser *elohim*—the small-*g* gods—from then on.

It's not immediately obvious in the Genesis account, but Moses reminded the Israelites of what went down in the aftermath of Yahweh's divine intervention at Babel:

> When the Most High gave to
> the nations their inheritance,
> when he divided mankind,
> **he fixed the borders of the peoples**
> **according to the number of the sons of God.**
> **But the LORD's portion is his people,**
> **Jacob his allotted heritage.** (Deuteronomy 32:8; emphasis added)

Most English translations render the last words of verse 8 "sons of Israel." The English Standard Version translators follow most of the existing copies of the Septuagint and the texts of Deuteronomy found among the Dead Sea Scrolls. But even just on a logical basis, "sons of God" makes more sense. Israel (Jacob) wasn't around when God divided mankind after Babel. He wouldn't be born for another 1,200 to 1,500 years.

This is important. Getting this verse right makes a lot of things in the Bible easier to understand. Making the case linguistically requires going back to a couple of earlier passages in Deuteronomy.

> And beware lest you raise your eyes to heaven, and when you see the sun and the moon and the stars, all the host of heaven, you be drawn away and bow down to them and serve them, **things that the LORD your God has allotted to all the peoples under the whole heaven.** (Deuteronomy 4:19; emphasis added)

> All the nations will say, "Why has the LORD done thus to this land? What caused the heat of this great anger?" Then people will say, "It is because they abandoned the covenant of the LORD, the God of their fathers, which he made with them when he brought them out of the land of Egypt, and went and served other gods and worshiped them, **gods whom they had not known and whom he had not allotted to them.**" (Deuteronomy 29:24–26; emphasis added)

The word rendered "inheritance" and "heritage" in Deuteronomy 32:8–9 is the Hebrew *nakhal,* and the word translated "portion" is the Hebrew *kheleq.* In the Deuteronomy 4 and 29 passages, "allotted" is based on the Hebrew *khalaq,* the same root used to describe Israel's status in chapter 32. Israel is the allotted heritage of Yahweh, and the other gods were allotted to "all the peoples under the whole heaven." So after Babel, the nations of the world were divided, geographically and spiritually, according to the number of the sons of God.

The concept of territorial spirits is biblical, although it's not often mentioned in Sunday morning services. The most obvious example is in a previously cited passage from the book of Daniel:

> I lifted up my eyes and looked, and behold, a man clothed in linen, with a belt of fine gold from Uphaz around his waist....

Then he said to me, "Fear not, Daniel, for from the first day that you set your heart to understand and humbled yourself before your God, your words have been heard, and I have come because of your words. **The prince of the kingdom of Persia withstood me twenty-one days, but Michael, one of the chief princes, came to help me, for I was left there with the kings of Persia**, and came to make you understand what is to happen to your people in the latter days. For the vision is for days yet to come."…

But now I will return to fight against the prince of Persia; and when I go out, behold, the prince of Greece will come. But I will tell you what is inscribed in the book of truth: there is none who contends by my side against these except Michael, your prince. (Daniel 10:5, 12–13, 20–21; emphasis added)

There are a couple of intriguing questions here: Who was the man Daniel saw? And who is the prince of Persia?

Some scholars think Daniel saw an angel of high rank, while others note similarities between the description of the angel and John's description of Jesus in the book of Revelation. However, Jesus wouldn't need help dealing with another spirit being, so Daniel's visitor must have been an angel. It may have been Gabriel, whom Daniel saw in the two previous chapters, but then why didn't he just identify the man since he'd seen him at least twice before? The bottom line: It was an angel, possibly one not named in Scripture.

The prince of Persia was certainly a spirit being, because a human opponent wouldn't have been able to hold him at all, much less for three weeks! But identifying that entity is an impossible task. We can speculate, though, that it was one of the seventy *bene elohim* who were allotted to the nations.

How do we know there were seventy? Good question. The nations are named in Genesis chapter 10, in the section called the "Table of Nations." Quick quiz: How many nations are listed in Genesis chapter 10? Right, seventy.

Now, go back to our earlier chapter on Mount Hermon if you need to look this up: How many sons of El gathered in the assembly on Mount Hermon?

Seventy.

Is this a coincidence? *No!*

These seventy *bene elohim* apparently presented themselves to the ancient world as their gods. The aftermath of Babel is where the concepts of holy ground and national gods began. It was Dagon for the Philistines, Chemosh for Moab, Molech for Ammon, Marduk for Babylon, Hadad (Baal) for the Canaanites, and so on. "But the LORD's portion is his people, Jacob his allotted heritage" (Deuteronomy 32:9).

The Mesopotamians were already heading down that path when God made the arrangement formal. Every city in Sumer had a temple that was home to the city's patron god. This sometimes led to war as local kings went out to conquer on orders of their god. (To be fair, that claim has been made by alleged Christians from time to time.) The political situation in Sumer and the greater ancient Near East often reflected the relative position of various gods within the pantheon.

So how did the rebellion work out for those seventy sons of God? About as well as it did for the Watchers on Mount Hermon. Because the *bene elohim* rebelled and began accepting worship, Yahweh passed judgment on them, too. Refer back to Psalm 82. The gods are under a death sentence, and a day is coming when God inherits all the nations!

4

THE WATCHERS:
THE GENESIS 6 INCURSION

Concerning the elect I said, and took up my parable concerning
them:
>   The Holy Great One will come forth from His dwelling,
>   And the eternal God will tread upon the earth,
>   (even) on Mount Sinai,
>   And appear from His camp,
>   And appear in the strength of His might
>   from the heaven of heavens.
>   And all shall be smitten with fear
>   And the Watchers shall quake,
>   And great fear and trembling shall seize them
>   Unto the ends of the earth.
>   —I Enoch 1:3–5 (H. R. Charles, trans.)

Mount Hermon is the highest, most majestic peak in the Levant. At
9,200 feet above sea level, it dominates the Golan Heights on the border
between Israel and Syria, anchoring the southern end of the Anti-Lebanon
Mountains. It has been considered sacred for most of human history.

Mount Hermon was a holy site as far back as the Old Babylonian period, nearly two millennia before Christ, and maybe even earlier. In the Old Babylonian version of the Gilgamesh epic, which dates to the eighteenth century BC (roughly the time of Jacob and Joseph), "Hermon and Lebanon" were called "the secret dwelling of the Anunnaki." The Ninevite version of the poem, written about six hundred years later, describes the monster slain by Gilgamesh, Humbaba (or Huwawa), as the guardian of "the abode of the gods."[29]

The Anunnaki were the seven chief gods of the Sumerian pantheon: Anu, the sky-god; Enlil, king of the gods; Enki, god of the earth; Ninhursag, mother goddess of the mountains; Inanna (Babylonian Ishtar), goddess of sex and war; Nanna (Sîn in Babylon), the moon-god; and Utu (Shamash), the sun-god. They are mentioned in texts found in what is today southeastern Iraq that date back to the twenty-seventh century BC. So, it's possible that the more recent versions of the Gilgamesh story from Babylon and Nineveh remember more ancient traditions. We'll discuss later why those ancient traditions may have been brought to Babylon from Syria, far to the west.

The name "Hermon" appears to be based on a root word that means "taboo," similar to the Hebrew word *kherem*, or "devoted to destruction." The word is often translated into English as "under the ban."

The first appearance of the word in the Bible is in Exodus 22:20:

Whoever sacrifices to any god, other than the LORD alone, shall be **devoted to destruction** [*kherem*]. (Emphasis added)

But this condemnation, or "the ban," wasn't just invoked against disobedient Israelites. Some of the inhabitants of Canaan were also declared *kherem* by Yahweh—specifically those that were known to be giants, or at least descended from giants.

That begs the question: Where did the giants come from? A curious episode is recorded in the first four verses of Genesis chapter 6:

When man began to multiply on the face of the land and daughters were born to them, the sons of God saw that the daughters of man were attractive. And they took as their wives any they chose. Then the LORD said, "My Spirit shall not abide in man forever, for he is flesh: his days shall be 120 years."

The Nephilim were on the earth in those days, and also afterward, when the sons of God came in to the daughters of man and they bore children to them. These were the mighty men who were of old, the men of renown. (Genesis 6:1–4)

Scholars have debated the meaning of the term "Nephilim" for millennia. Most believe it comes from a Hebrew root, *naphal,* meaning "to fall" or "cast down"—literally, "fallen ones."

However, Bible and ancient language scholar Dr. Michael S. Heiser (author of the excellent book *The Unseen Realm,* which is highly recommended), at his website www.SitchinIsWrong.com (a reference to the late Zecharia Sitchin, who popularized the idea that the Sumerian gods, the Anunnaki, were extraterrestrial astronauts who created humanity from ape DNA), contends that this cannot be the case:

The form *nephilim* cannot mean "fallen ones" (the spelling would then be *nephulim*). Likewise *nephilim* does not mean "those who fall" or "those who fall away" (that would be *nophelim*). The only way in Hebrew to get *nephilim* from *naphal* by the rules of Hebrew morphology (word formation) would be to presume a noun spelled *naphil* and then pluralize it. I say "presume" since this noun does not exist in biblical Hebrew—unless one counts Genesis 6:4 and Numbers 13:33, the two occurrences of *nephilim*—but that would then be assuming what one is trying to prove! However, in Aramaic the noun *naphil(a)* does exist. It means "giant," making it easy to see why the Septuagint (the ancient Greek translation of the Hebrew Bible) translated *nephilim* as *gigantes* ("giant").[30]

In short, the Jewish scholars who translated the Old Testament into Greek about two hundred years before the birth of Jesus clearly understood that the Nephilim were giants, not just men who "fell away" from God.

Likewise, the Hebrew words translated "sons of God" in the passage, *bene elohim*, refer to divine beings, not mortal men. Now, that hasn't been the consensus among Christian scholars since about the fifth century, thanks to the great theologian Augustine. He popularized the "sons of Seth" theory to explain away the weird supernatural element of the passages above. In short, the Sethite view is that the sons of God were men from the godly, righteous line of Seth who began intermarrying with women from the corrupt, wicked line of Cain.

Frankly, this defies logic on several points:

1. How likely is it that all the Sethite men were good while all the Cainite women were bad?
2. Cainite men never married Sethite women?
3. Why would these unions produce Nephilim, understood to be giants by Jewish rabbis and early Christians alike?
4. Why would these unions lead to wickedness so great that God had to wipe out everything that walked the earth except Noah, his family, and the creatures in the ark?
5. Every other use of *bene elohim* in the Hebrew Scriptures refers to divine beings.

Problems with the supernatural understanding of the text usually focus on whether angels and humans could successfully produce children. Proponents of the Sethite view often point to Jesus' teaching on the resurrection of the dead:

For **in the resurrection** they [people] neither marry nor are given in marriage, but are **like angels in heaven.** (Matthew 22:30; emphasis added)

The key words here are "in the resurrection" and "in heaven." Noah's neighbors were mortal, flesh-and-blood humans—not yet resurrected—and the angels who "came in to the daughters of man" were most definitely *not in heaven*.

There are several examples in the Bible of divine beings interacting with humans in physical ways—eating, drinking, and even engaging in a dustup in front of the house of Lot (Genesis 19:5–11). Why couldn't they procreate as well?

The final nails in the coffin of the Sethite view are the references to this event in the New Testament. Both Peter and Jude refer to the only example in Scripture where angels transgressed:

> For if **God did not spare angels when they sinned**, but cast them into hell and committed them to chains of gloomy darkness to be kept until the judgment; if he did not spare the ancient world, but preserved Noah, a herald of righteousness, with seven others, when he brought a flood upon the world of the ungodly; **if by turning the cities of Sodom and Gomorrah to ashes he condemned them to extinction**, making them an example of what is going to happen to the ungodly... (2 Peter 2:4; emphasis added)

> **And the angels who did not stay within their own position of authority, but left their proper dwelling**, he has kept in eternal chains under gloomy darkness until the judgment of the great day—**just as Sodom and Gomorrah and the surrounding cities, which likewise indulged in sexual immorality and pursued unnatural desire**, serve as an example by undergoing a punishment of eternal fire. (Jude 6–7; emphasis added)

If there was any doubt about what the angels did after they descended—what sin they committed that such deserved punishment—then Peter and Jude clarified things by specifically identifying the sin of the angels as *sexual* by linking it to the sins of Sodom and Gomorrah. Crossing the species barrier between angel and human is just as taboo as transgressing the one between human and animal.

It is significant that the phrase translated "cast them into hell" in 2 Peter 2:4 is the Greek word *tartaroo*, a verb meaning "thrust down to Tartarus." This is the only time in the New Testament that the word is used, meaning it requires special attention. Our Western concept of "hell" is vague and one-dimensional; we think of it as little more than an underworld domain with lots of fire and demons. But this is far different from the concept known to the Greeks. To them, Tartarus was an entirely separate domain from Hades, a place of torture and torment much lower than Hades in Greek cosmology. In fact, it was believed to be *as far below Hades as earth is below heaven.*

Let that sink in for a minute. Tartarus might be called the very center of the earth!

And Peter, under the inspiration of the Holy Spirit, chose that specific word, *tartaroo*, to describe the punishment reserved for angels who engaged in illicit sexual relations with human women.

The extrabiblical books of I Enoch and Jubilees expand on this story, adding extra detail and context not found in the Bible. Mount Hermon is where two hundred Watchers, a class of angelic being mentioned in chapter 4 of the book of Daniel, descended and began cavorting with human women. From these unions came the Nephilim, the giants of Genesis 6.

The Watchers, according to I Enoch, were led by Semjâzâ, whose name is thought to be a combination of *shem* (meaning "name") and *azaz* (possibly meaning "rebellion"). Some list Semjâzâ as one of the *archon* class of *elohim*, a ruler. But whatever his name meant in heaven, his choice to descend to Mount Hermon certainly made him infamous.

Apparently, this former ruler in heaven worried that his companions might soon regret their rebellious choices and allow their leader to take the fall for what they'd all proposed to do. After all, each of them knew how the Lord of Armies had dealt with Chaos, and they'd probably heard God pronounce judgment upon the *nachash* in the garden, vowing to one day crush his head, just like the heads of Leviathan will be crushed.

Here is the excerpt from the Book of Enoch:

> And Semjâzâ, who was their leader, said unto them: "I fear ye will not indeed agree to do this deed, and I alone shall have to pay the penalty of a great sin." And they all answered him and said: "Let us all swear an oath, and all bind ourselves by mutual imprecations not to abandon this plan but to do this thing." Then sware they all together and bound themselves by mutual imprecations upon it. And they were in all two hundred; who descended [in the days] of Jared on the summit of Mount Hermon. (Book of Enoch 6:3–6a; R. H. Charles, trans.)

The gift these Watchers offered to human women (and possibly to their families/husbands) in exchange for sexual favors was forbidden knowledge, the same deal the *nachash* offered Adam and Eve in Eden. As payment for the pleasures of the flesh, Semjâzâ and his rebellious companions offered charms, enchantments, astrology, metallurgy (read that as weaponry for warfare), cosmetics, and writing, among other things—presumably arts that humans would have developed or discovered on their own, given time.

However, the products of these illicit unions were giants, the Nephilim, whose stature and abilities far surpassed their human relatives. Believing themselves gods, these "men of renown" pillaged the earth and endangered all of humanity. The Nephilim consumed everything that men possessed; when that wasn't enough, they began to eat people, and they finally turned on one another. Enoch describes these cannibalistic colossi as creatures of insatiable desire who threatened to pollute and even terminate the bloodline of the future Messiah by violence—but also by corrupting the human genome. It was a military move by the fallen realm, who thought to remove any possibility of defeat by polluting human DNA, while at the same time, creating their own army of superhumans.

They probably thought themselves pretty clever—but the Lord of Armies had seen their ploy long before, for He knows all and sees all, even from the foundation of the world.

But wait, as they say on television, there's more! Not only did the Watchers corrupt human DNA, but the Book of Jasher suggests they transgressed against all creation by "the mixture of animals of one species with the other" (Jasher 4:18).

Was this the source for the "legends" of centaurs, griffins, and satyrs? Are they just legends? We know that Yahweh sent a Flood to rid the earth of all flesh that breathed air, with the exception of eight people: Noah, his wife, three sons, and their wives, along with the animals God Himself directed to board the ark. The worldwide Flood that followed killed all that remained, including the Nephilim (for they, too, breathed the air). And as punishment for their sins, the fathers of these Nephilim, the Watchers, were thrust down to Tartarus, and are now chained there, where they'll stay until "the judgment of the great day."

But did you know that these giants didn't completely perish—that they are still with us today? The physical forms of the Nephilim certainly died, but their illicitly begotten spirits became what we now call demons:

And now, the giants, who are produced from the spirits and flesh, shall be called evil spirits upon the earth, and on the earth shall be their dwelling. Evil spirits have proceeded from their bodies; because they are born from men and from the holy Watchers is their beginning and primal origin; **they shall be evil spirits on earth, and evil spirits shall they be called.** [As for the spirits of heaven, in heaven shall be their dwelling, but as for the spirits of the earth which were born upon the earth, on the earth shall be their dwelling.] And the spirits of the giants afflict, oppress, destroy, attack, do battle, and work destruction on the earth, and cause trouble: they take no food, but nevertheless hunger and thirst, and cause offences. **And these spirits shall rise up against the children of men and against the women, because**

they have proceeded from them. From the days of the slaughter and destruction and death of the giants, from the souls of whose flesh the spirits, having gone forth, shall destroy without incurring judgement. (I Enoch 15:8–12, 16:1; R. H. Charles, trans.; emphasis added; brackets in original)

The church today doesn't deal much with the topic of demons, but it's clear the early church understood that they were real and distinct from angels. The term "angel" implies a mission, but those who live within the unseen realm are generally called *elohim*, written with a small *e* to distinguish them from the uppercased *E* in *Elohim*, one of the names of Yahweh. Whenever the *elohim* appear in the Bible as messengers from God, they are described as looking like men. Other classes of *elohim*, like the *nachash*, *cherubim*, and *seraphim*, are entities of a different kind; these also possess a "nonhuman" physicality—that is, an outward appearance that can be observed and described by the prophets.

Demons, on the other hand, have no innate physical presence. They are spirits only, but they seek physicality through possession. The consensus view among Jews and Christians until the time of Augustine (the late third/early fourth centuries) was that demons are the spirits of the dead Nephilim, who now roam the earth (boldface added for emphasis in the excerpts below):

PHILO: "And when the angels of God saw the daughters of men that they were beautiful, they took unto themselves wives of all of them whom they chose." Those beings, whom **other philosophers call demons**, Moses usually calls angels; and they are **souls hovering in the air**."

—PHILO, *ON THE GIANTS* 6

ORIGEN: "In my opinion, however, **it is certain wicked demons, and, so to speak, of the race of Titans or Giants, who have been**

guilty of impiety towards the true God, and towards the angels in heaven, and who have fallen from it, and who haunt the denser parts of bodies, and frequent unclean places upon earth, and who, possessing some power of distinguishing future events, **because they are without bodies of earthly material**, engage in an employment of this kind, and desiring to lead the human race away from the true God."

—ORIGEN, *AGAINST CELSUS 4.92*

JUSTIN MARTYR: "**God…committed the care of men and of all things under heaven to angels whom He appointed over them. But the angels transgressed this appointment, and were captivated by love of women, and begot children who are those that are called demons;** and besides, they afterwards subdued the human race to themselves, partly by magical writings, and partly by fears and the punishments they occasioned, and partly by teaching them to offer sacrifices, and incense, and libations, of which things they stood in need after they were enslaved by lustful passions; and among men they sowed murders, wars, adulteries, intemperate deeds, and all wickedness.

—JUSTIN MARTYR, *2 APOLOGY 5*

Justin Martyr not only understood that the Nephilim were the source of the demons that plague mankind; he also clearly knew that the rebellious members of the divine council were the false gods of the pagan world.

Takeaways here are:

- Rebellions lead to judgments, which then lead to rebellions, leading to judgments, and so on.
- Prisoner Zero's first rebellion caused the earth to become "void."
- The Nachash's temptation of Eve and Adam led to their expulsion from Eden and the judgment upon the Nachash.

- The Watchers descended to Hermon, taking human wives and creating the Nephilim.
- The inevitable judgment came again through a worldwide Flood.
- Next came Babel, where the humans once again fell victim to the lies of fallen entities.

MORE LYING REBELS:
THE APKALLU, GILGAMESH, AND THE
SEVENTY SONS OF EL

Ugaritic mythology plainly states that the head of its pantheon, El (who, like the God of the Bible, is also referred to as El Elyon, the "Most High") fathered seventy sons.
—DR. MICHAEL S. HEISER[31]

The ancient records are rife with references to pantheons that imitate the true Divine Assembly of our LORD and Savior. Baal, El, and El's seventy sons are one example. Each pantheon is said to dwell upon a sacred mountain—whether natural or man-made (Babel being one such example). These precipitous and lofty throne rooms could be found across the globe, including Mount Zaphon (abode of Baal-Zaphon), Mount Olympus (abode of the Olympians), Mount Kailash (abode of Shiva), Mount Koubrou (abode of Launingthou Koubrou), Mount Carmel (abode of Melqart), Mount Etna (sacred to Vulcan), and Mount Meru (sacred to Brahma)—to name but a few. But as we study the long spiritual war between Yahweh and the Fallen Realm, we also find ourselves returning to Mount Hermon, the place where the Watchers descended and took an oath before cohabiting with human women and producing giant offspring—for it is also where El held court with his consort Asherah and his "seventy sons."

Who is El? First of all, "El" was a title that came to be used in Hebrew as a generic term for "god" or "lord." We also see it in proper names like El, Elohim, El Elyon, etc. Some scholars contend that the epithet El Shaddai, meaning "god of the mountain," was first applied to El.

"Bel" and "Baal" are titles that have also come to be used as proper names. "Bel" and "Baal" (the plural is *baalim*) are, respectively, East Semitic and Northwest Semitic words that mean the same thing: "Lord." The Mesopotamian god Amurru was called Bel Šade, or "lord of the mountain." (The š sounds like "sh.") These titles and names are used intentionally by the rebels to confuse truth with lies by appropriating names by which Yahweh identified Himself. I imagine the Fallen Realm sees this as clever, but it's the Lord of Armies who will decide that—just before He casts them into the Lake of Fire.

In the book of Exodus, Yahweh introduces Himself to Moses by the name *El Shaddai*, usually rendered "God Almighty" in our English Bibles, which He'd used with Abraham, Isaac, and Jacob (Exodus 6:3). Hence, after Jacob's contentious encounter with the "Angel of the Lord," the patriarch is renamed Isra-*el* ("he who wrestled with God"), not "Isra-*yahu*."

Of course, skeptics take this to mean that Jews and Christians are confused about which deity we worship, saying it's actually El we revere, and that the followers of Yahweh are so dense we've gotten it wrong for the last 3,500 years. But make no mistake: El of the Canaanites was not Yahweh of Israel, and Yahweh was not El. In the Canaanite pantheon, El was a figurehead who was rarely involved in the action. It was Baal who reigned as king of the gods. In fact, if you had to pick a word to describe El, it would be "indifferent" or perhaps "semi-retired."

That is *definitely* not the God of the Bible, who is Lord of Armies, Savior of all who will call upon Him, Creator of every molecular and subatomic particle in the universe—the only Being without a beginning and without an end.

El's symbol is the bull, and he is often equated with Kronos (Greece), Saturn (Rome), and Anu (Mesopotamia). El's consort is Asherah or Anath, and like most pagan gods, he sires many children, including Yam, Mot, Anat, Ashtar, Shahar, Shalim, Shapash, Athtart, and Hadad (Baal). He is also hailed as the father of seventy sons. In the Ugaritic Baal Cycle, the story is told of how Baal built his beautiful temple or house on Mount Zaphon, which is on the Syrian border with Turkey, and is also spelled Mount "Sapan," but is currently known as Jabel al-Aqra.

Once the house is finished, Baal invites the seventy sons of Athirat/Asherah (presumably all of them sired by El) to see his new digs. The number seventy here is important, for it may refer to the seventy *elohim* (sometimes called angels) who were sent to the earth by Yahweh to rule over the seventy nations. If so, then El is claiming to be Yahweh and taking credit for the Creator's deeds. How egotistic can one god get, eh?

There's another group of small-*g* gods who form a pantheon, and they echo the idea of the Watchers who descended to Mount Hermon. Long before Abraham was called by the LORD, the Mesopotamians knew about these "godlike" beings but called them *apkallu*. The *apkallu* were supposedly created by the god Enki to bring knowledge and the gifts of civilization to mankind, a bit like the Greek myth of the Titan Prometheus.

According to Mesopotamian myth, there were seven *apkallu* before the Flood and four afterward. The word *apkallu* comes from the Sumerian *ab* ("water"), *gal* ("big"), and *lu* ("man"). They were considered only *partly* evil—occasionally dangerous and capable of malicious witchcraft. They were chimeric in appearance, usually depicted as humanoid with wings, or sometimes as hybrid "bird-man" or bizarre "fish-man" creatures.

The antediluvian *apkallu* were divine, just like the Watchers. According to one story from the Babylonian period, the *Epic of Erra* (Erra was the god of pestilence and plague—we'll be covering plague and pestilence later), Marduk banished the *apkallu* to the *Abzu*, the freshwater aquifer below the temple of Enki, as punishment for provoking him to send the Flood.

Hmm. Supernatural beings linked to a global flood, who are afterward banished to the abyss? Sound familiar? Interestingly, the four *apkallu* who appeared after the flood were only partly divine and could mate with humans—again, like the Watchers.

The last of the post-flood *apkallu*, Lu-Nanna, was "two-thirds *apkallu*." This matches the status of Gilgamesh, who was described as being two-thirds divine and one-third human. On one cylinder seal, Gilgamesh is called "lord of the *apkallu*," and is elsewhere credited with bringing back great knowledge that existed before the flood.

Scholars who have made the connection between the *apkallu* and the Watchers tend to interpret the way the Watchers are portrayed in Jewish literature from the Second Temple period, like the Book of Enoch, at least partly as a Jewish response to the Babylonian captivity.[32] It was believed that the *apkallu*, though potentially dangerous, had preserved secret pre-Flood knowledge prized by the pagan wizards of Babylon. To the Jews, however, such knowledge was evil, and the Watchers were portrayed accordingly in Enochian texts.

But such modern scholars evaluate the situation in a secular context, analyzing the texts apart from any spiritual reality. Looking back through more than five thousand years, we can only make educated guesses about what happened, but we can assume that Noah and his family knew about the Watchers and the horrors they'd unleashed on the world. It's no surprise, then, that memories of the Watchers survived the Flood, though the stories have obviously changed over time. This was due in part to the confusion of languages after Babel, but also to justify a return to the occult practices the Watchers taught humanity before the Flood.

One of the fascinating aspects of the story of Gilgamesh is that most archaeologists consider him a real, historic character. In 2003, a German archaeological team digging at the site of ancient Uruk announced that they believed they'd found the tomb of Gilgamesh[33] beneath what was the former course of the Euphrates River. Sadly, their discovery came a month after the United States invaded Iraq in 2003, which put a stop to the dig.

Scholars have known for years that there are parallels in Mesopotamian legend and the biblical accounts of the patriarchs. Enoch is similar to an antediluvian king named Enmeduranki, and Noah is variously called Utnapishtim (Babylon), Ziusudra (Sumer), and Atra-Hasis (Akkad), depending on which culture wrote the story. But even those accounts are part of a Fallen Realm military campaign, a supernatural PSYOP.

For example, the accounts from Mesopotamia portray Gilgamesh as a mighty warrior, a hero, two-thirds god and one-third man. He has adventures and slays monsters, notably Humbaba (also called Huwawa), the defender of the faraway cedar forest who'd been assigned to terrorize humans by the god Enlil (Enki's brother).

In the Second Temple Jewish account known as the Book of Giants, Gilgamesh was, himself, one of the gigantic offspring of the Watchers—as was Humbaba, the monster Gilgamesh set out to kill. This is how Gilgamesh was viewed by Jews between the time of the Babylonian captivity and the birth of Jesus—basically, he was one of the Nephilim.

As mentioned above, some scholars tell us that Humbaba might also have been pronounced "huwawa." Dr. David Livingston, the founder of Associates for Biblical Research, points out that "Huwawa" sounds a lot like "Yahweh." If he's right, then it's possible we've discovered another enemy PSYOP: The *real* mission of Gilgamesh was to destroy the guardian of the secret home of the gods—Yahweh![34]

In the Apkallu myths, Adam's story is told with a twist. In the Mesopotamian accounts, Adapa (Adam) is one of the *apkallu*, the son of the great god Enki. One day, in a rage, Adapa breaks the wings of the south wind for overturning his fishing boat. As a result, he is called to the home of the gods by the sky-god Anu to explain himself. Before his journey, Enki warns Adapa not to accept any food or drink because Anu cannot be trusted. Adapa follows these instructions, accepting only a robe and anointing oil, and then misses his chance at immortality because he refuses to eat the food of the gods.

Of course, in the Bible, the story is reversed: Adam is *created as an immortal* by Yahweh. But then Adam and Eve *lose* their immortality by choosing to eat from the tree of the knowledge of good and evil.

The Babylonian account of the Flood is quite different, too. The hero, Utnapishtim (Noah), who reigned from the city of Shuruppak as the last king of Sumer before the flood, is secretly warned about the coming of a great deluge by Enki. Now the flood is coming because Enki's brother, Enlil, is angry and can't sleep because humans make so much noise, so he's decided to solve the problem by killing them all. Though commanded to say nothing about the flood to any human, cunning Enki does an end-run around this rule by revealing Enlil's plan to a wall (one that Utnapishtim just happens to be standing behind), thus holding to the "letter of the law" while warning Utnapishtim.

Of course, the biblical account is much different. Yahweh flooded the earth because of humanity's evil. Man had become corrupted in body and spirit by the Watchers. But Yahweh spared Noah, who was "perfect in his generations," along with his family, to repopulate the earth.

After the Flood, the civilization that had developed in what is today southeastern Iraq, a culture based around cities and irrigation agriculture, was forced to start over. You'd think that an event that epic would leave a lasting impression on people. After all, the eight people in the ark had just seen everyone and everything they knew literally washed out of existence.

But no. Within three generations, Yahweh would find it necessary to personally intervene in human affairs again.

The ark likely landed somewhere in what is modern-day, far-eastern Turkey, near where it borders northwestern Iran and western Armenia. The mountains of Ararat are located within the borders of the ancient nation of Urartu (same name, different language), which covers a lot of the territory occupied by today's Kurds. From there, many of the descendants of Noah, mainly the offspring of Shem and Ham, moved south and east, back down the Tigris and Euphrates to start over.

Interestingly, and probably not coincidentally, scholar Edward Lipiński concluded that the mountains of Armenia were probably where the abode of El was to be found. Hermon was El's mount of assembly.

Dating the Flood is not an easy task, and there is no date we can present here that will make everybody happy. A more recent date, somewhere around 2300–2200 BC, will annoy archaeologists and historians, who can point to ruins and tablets that show life continuing pretty much as usual in Mesopotamia throughout the period in spite of evidence of localized flooding here and there. Choosing an earlier date may anger Bible literalists, who prefer to stick with a date calculated by adding the ages of the patriarchs.

Resolving that conflict is a bigger task than we're going to tackle here. By looking at the historical evidence and lining up biblical events with what is attested in Mesopotamian literature and archaeological evidence of big cultural changes, our best guess puts the Flood somewhere around 4000 BC. That roughly coincides with the transition from the Ubaid period to the Uruk period. This date isn't likely to please anyone with a passionate belief in a particular year, archaeologist or biblical literalist, but at least it puts the event at a point in history that more or less fits the timeline of the Sumerian King List.

There are still problems with the date that won't ever be resolved. For example, Gilgamesh is usually placed in the early third millennium BC, around 2800 or 2700 BC. If that's correct, and if there is truth to the Sumerian legend that Gilgamesh visited his ancestor, Utnapishtim (the Mesopotamian Noah), then the timing just doesn't work. It was more than a thousand years between the date we've assigned to the Flood and the time of Gilgamesh, and the Bible tells us Noah only (only—ha!) lived another three hundred and fifty years after the biblical event.

And scholars will say they haven't found evidence of a flood during that time period. Archaeologists believe the most likely candidates for Noah's Flood were events that left heavy deposits of silt and clay up to eleven feet thick at Ur, Uruk, Kish, and Shuruppak, which is where Utnapishtim—the Akkadian version of Ziusudra, the name recorded in the Sumerian King List—was the last king and lustration priest (lustration is the act of making something ritually pure) before "the flood swept over." Unfortunately, those silt layers are dated to different times, ranging from about 3100 BC to 2500 BC. Not only do they contradict one another, but the archaeological evidence shows there were obviously survivors who rebuilt and carried on with life at each of those sites as soon as the waters receded.

Our theory—and without hard proof (other than the biblical account) it will never be accepted as more than a theory—is that Noah's descendants returned from the north very soon after the Flood and repopulated the plains of Sumer. Eridu was apparently rebuilt fairly quickly, as were other pre-Flood cities such as Kish, Ur, and Uruk.

Skeptics may argue that Mesopotamia of the fourth millennium BC was resettled far too quickly to have been depopulated by a global flood. But that's looking backward with a twenty-first century, Western mindset, one that's based on a culture where the average family has 2.1 children and parents hold off having them until their late twenties or early thirties. That was *not* the perspective of people in the thirty-ninth century BC, who needed all hands on deck as quickly as possible to build houses, bring in crops, and tend the herds.

Besides, a little math makes it clear that a few centuries were all that was needed to repopulate the Fertile Crescent. In Derek's family tree, it's been calculated that the patriarch and matriarch of the clan, who married in the 1750s, produced more than one hundred thousand living descendants by the year 2000. And that's a low number. Our eighteenth- and nineteenth-century ancestors often had six to ten children per family. The last few generations in the twentieth century generally had one or two.

While it's impossible to know who had how many children as the descendants of Noah spread out from the mountains of Ararat (for one thing, the Bible doesn't usually name daughters), it's mathematically possible that his three sons could have produced a couple million descendants within a few hundred years of the Flood.

At some point during this period, we learn of an odd incident between Noah and his youngest son, Ham:

Noah began to be a man of the soil, and he planted a vineyard. He drank of the wine and became drunk and lay uncovered in his tent. And Ham, the father of Canaan, saw the nakedness of his father and told his two brothers outside. Then Shem and Japheth took a garment, laid it on both their shoulders, and walked backward and covered the nakedness of their father. Their faces were turned backward, and they did not see their father's nakedness. When Noah awoke from his wine and knew what his youngest son had done to him, he said,

"Cursed be Canaan;

a servant of servants shall he be to his brothers."

He also said,

"Blessed be the LORD, the God of Shem;

and let Canaan be his servant.

May God enlarge Japheth,

and let him dwell in the tents of Shem,

and let Canaan be his servant." (Genesis 9:20–27)

Noah's curse seems harsh by modern standards. Even in the Law given to Moses a couple of thousand years later, there are no rules about seeing your father without his clothes. While the actions of Shem and Japheth suggest that the sin of Ham was voyeurism, what he did was probably much, much worse.

To "see" or "uncover" someone's "nakedness" is an Old Testament euphemism that refers to illicit sexual relations—in this case, incest. Deuteronomy 22:30 and 27:20 are specific prohibitions against a man lying with his father's wife, because that uncovers "his father's nakedness."

There are examples of this among the patriarchs. Reuben went in to Jacob's concubine, Bilhah, the mother of Dan and Naphtali. King David's son, Absalom, after running David and his supporters out of Jerusalem, "went in to his father's concubines in the sight of all Israel" (2 Samuel 16:22).

Why? In that time and place, that was how a son declared himself the new head of the household. Reuben was Jacob's firstborn. Now, it's possible he just found Bilhah attractive and seduced her. But on the other hand, sleeping with Bilhah may have been Reuben's way of claiming his inheritance early. Instead, for desecrating his father's bed, Jacob gave Reuben's share to the sons of Joseph.

Absalom, though, knew *exactly* what he was doing. David's counselor, Ahitophel, who had deserted to Absalom's cause, advised the would-be king to pitch a tent on the roof of David's house so all of Israel would know that the young man had taken the kingdom. The message to the nation was clear: David was powerless to stop Absalom from doing this outrageous thing, and so he was no longer fit to rule.

Absalom's action was, at the risk of being crude, like a dog marking his territory.

Likewise, Ham may have thought that "uncovering his father's nakedness"—having sex with his mother while Noah was too drunk to notice—was a bold move to bypass his brothers and forcibly take a bigger share of inheritance for himself and his children. That could explain why Noah declared the curse on Ham's son, Canaan, rather than on Ham. At that time, the three sons of Noah were basically dividing the world between them.

It may also explain some of the historical-spiritual events that have shaped the world since that day. The descendants of Ham have played a key role in the spiritual and historical events that followed.

In fact, we might go so far as to say they've been used as a special weapon by the fallen realm in their long-running rebellion against God.

PART II

THE TIMES OF THE GENTILES & OUR PRESENT AGE

Now the last age of the Cumaean prophecy begins:
The great procession of the ages begins anew:
Now the Virgin returns; the reign of Saturn returns:
and the new child is sent down from high heaven.
—*ECLOGUE IV*, LINES 4–7
BY PUBLIUS VIRGILIUS MARO (VIRGIL)

You might call it the secret formula to Ordo ab Chao. If we recite the proper words on the winter solstice, then we can summon the Keeper of the fragment. He knows the locations of all the book's other pieces. With his knowledge, we can find them and reassemble the Book of First Words. Don't you see it? It is the end of the beginning! The true Omega to the Alpha! The snake shedding its accursed skin to regain its magnificent wings. The Golden Age returned! Surely, that is a laudable goal, is it not?
—ALBUS LUCIUS FLINT TO LORD SALTER,
CHAPTER 22 OF *REALMS OF FIRE* BY SHARON K. GILBERT

THE SEVENTY WEEKS TIMELINE

Return to the LORD your God, for he is gracious and merciful, slow to anger, and abounding in steadfast love; and he relents over disaster.

—JOEL 2:13

We've now studied the first rebellion of Leviathan, the chaos-dragon; the subtle Nachash's temptation of Adam and Eve in the garden; the Mount Hermon Watcher rebellion, the post-Flood Babel event (which may have occurred in a city built by Cain); and Gilgamesh's revival of pre-Flood sins. In this section, we investigate the spiritual war as it's presented in three prophecies. These are central to the spiritual war. God Almighty is Lord of Armies, but He is not slow to anger. He has vowed to repay all the fallen realm rebels in full for their crimes, but He is patient. A thousand years are to Him as a day, and every battle occurs in its proper time. In Daniel, the LORD offers several clues as to when He will finally end this long spiritual war.

The book begins with the prophet's arrival in Babylon as a captured youth, circa 604 BC. Daniel, whose name means "God is my judge" (a prophetic name indeed), is considered one of the wisest men in all the Bible. In fact, the Talmud (Yoma 77a) says Daniel was endowed with such wisdom that if you measured his mind against the combined weight of all other wise men in history, Daniel's would outweigh them all. That is some intellect!

One can only imagine what it must have been like for this descendant of Judah. Daniel may have heard the screams of his friends and family as Nebuchadnezzar's soldiers sacked their homes. He could smell the fires, perhaps even the stench of burning flesh. These marauders would have ordered this handsome youth to gather up anything important and prepare for the long march to Babylon, the capital city of the Neo-Babylonian Empire.

He may have suffered from hunger, thirst, and weariness. Perhaps, the soldiers teased him, prodding him to move more quickly on that long journey, or maybe they made him serve them as a slave. It's impossible to know, this side of heaven, just how much this far-seeing prophet endured, but he describes his first duties in the king's court thusly:

> In the third year of the reign of Jehoiakim king of Judah, Nebuchadnezzar king of Babylon came to Jerusalem and besieged it. And **the LORD gave Jehoiakim king of Judah into his hand**, with some of the vessels of the house of God. And he brought them to the land of Shinar, to the house of his god, and placed the vessels in the treasury of his god. Then the king commanded Ashpenaz, his chief eunuch, to bring some of the people of Israel, both of the royal family and of the nobility, **youths without blemish, of good appearance and skillful in all wisdom, endowed with knowledge, understanding learning, and competent to stand in the king's palace,** and to teach them the literature and language of the Chaldeans. (Daniel 1:1–4; emphasis added)

Daniel specifically tells us that the LORD allowed the invasion of Jerusalem. Also, from this brief introduction, we can glean that Daniel was young, that he was of "good appearance," "skillful in wisdom," and "endowed with knowledge, understanding, and learning." But also we learn that Daniel would be expected to learn Chaldean literature and language (Aramaic) as he served in the king's palace.

It's likely that Nebuchadnezzar wanted to show off his captives to important guests by having these handsome young men serve at his table. Certainly, insisting that only the best and brightest were educated as Chaldeans helped to secure the king's foothold in conquered lands, particularly if those young men were "princes" as Daniel was. Raising a boy to speak your language and worship your gods rewired them from the inside out and destroyed the conquered nation's future.

The famous prophecy of seventy weeks is not the first important vision to appear in the book of Daniel, but it's a good starting place when studying eschatology, for it provides a crucial timeline to all other end-times prophecies.

Starting, therefore, in chapter 9, we learn that Daniel has come to the latter years of his life, possibly as old as eighty, and he has been studying and meditating over the Jewish scrolls of Jeremiah. Here, Daniel discovered the reason for the exile from Jerusalem and just how long Israel would be beneath the yoke of Babylon:

> Therefore thus says the LORD of hosts: **Because you have not obeyed my words,** behold, **I will send for all the tribes of the north,** declares the LORD, **and for Nebuchadnezzar the king of Babylon, my servant**, and I will bring them against this land and its inhabitants, and against all these surrounding nations. I will devote them to destruction, and make them a horror, a hissing, and an everlasting desolation. Moreover, I will banish from them the voice of mirth and the voice of gladness, the voice of the bridegroom and the voice of the bride, the grinding of

the millstones and the light of the lamp. This whole land shall become a ruin and a waste, and **these nations shall serve the king of Babylon seventy years. Then after seventy years are completed, I will punish the king of Babylon and that nation, the land of the Chaldeans, for their iniquity, declares the LORD, making the land an everlasting waste.** I will bring upon that land all the words that I have uttered against it, everything written in this book, which Jeremiah prophesied against all the nations. For many nations and great kings shall make slaves even of them, and I will recompense them according to their deeds and the work of their hands. (Jeremiah 25:8–14; emphasis added)

The cause for the invasion of Jerusalem is simple: disobedience. "Because you have not obeyed my words." The fallen realm seeks to separate us from the LORD and entice us into sin. Sadly, many living within Judah (the southern kingdom) had failed to learn from their northern neighbor's plight. Israel had fallen to Assyria in 732 BC and again in 720 BC.

And the LORD sent against him [Jehoiakim] bands of the Chaldees, and bands of the Syrians, and bands of the Moabites, and bands of the children of Ammon, and sent them against Judah to destroy it, according to the word of the LORD, which he spake by his servants the prophets. (2 Kings 24:2)

And how long would it last?

This whole land shall become a ruin and a waste, and these nations **shall serve the king of Babylon seventy years.** (Jeremiah 25:11; emphasis added)

Daniel, who came to Babylon as a youth, had resided in captivity for nearly seventy years. Imagine his joy when he read Jeremiah and realized their banishment from Jerusalem was nearing its end.

Ever the intercessor, and knowing Jerusalem's fall was due to sin, Daniel fell to his knees and petitioned the LORD for mercy. Perhaps, he prayed that Yahweh would shorten the seventy-year sentence and bring a miracle. Instead, Daniel received an alarming vision of an extended sentence: Yes, Israel would return to their homeland, but because of their sins, they would remain beneath the yoke of foreigners until the "times of the Gentiles" reached its end.

Just what does this phrase "the times of the Gentiles" mean? Before we unpack this important prophetic answer to prayer, let's review the reasons God condemned Israel, including both the Northern and Southern Kingdoms, and sent them into captivity. Several obvious ones spring to mind:

- Idol worship
- Sacrificing to the stars of heaven
- Building asherah poles (probably as part of ritualistic sex rites to Astarte)
- Eating food sacrificed to idols

In other words, both the northern and southern kingdoms joined with the wrong side of the spiritual war; they broke faith with YHWH the Creator in favor of created beings (fallen angels) and their offspring (the demon spirits of the drowned Nephilim). These inferior gods enticed them into sexual immorality and human sacrifice.

Surely, this is why God exiled them to Babylon, right?

Actually, there is one other reason for the exile that often goes unnoticed: The nation had failed to observe the *shmitas*, or Sabbath, years. The word *shmita* literally means "release," and it meant the land was to be left fallow every seven years and allowed to go to seed. No agricultural activity was permitted:

When you come into the land that I give you, the land shall keep a Sabbath to the LORD. For six years you shall sow your field, and for six years you shall prune your vineyard and gather in its fruits, but **in the seventh year there shall be a Sabbath of solemn rest for the land,** a Sabbath to the LORD. You shall not sow your field or prune your vineyard. You shall not reap what grows of itself in your harvest, or gather the grapes of your undressed vine. **It shall be a year of solemn rest for the land.** The Sabbath of the land shall provide food for you, for yourself and for your male and female slaves and for your hired worker and the sojourner who lives with you, and for your cattle and for the wild animals that are in your land: all its yield shall be for food. (Leviticus 25:1–7; emphasis added)

As with the manna in the wilderness, the LORD promised to provide a bounty of blessings with plenty for all, providing the people obeyed this simple rule: Let the land rest every seven years. But He made it clear that they would never lack for food:

Therefore you shall **do my statutes and keep my rules and perform them, and then you will dwell in the land securely.** The land will yield its fruit, and you will eat your fill and dwell in it securely. And if you say, "What shall we eat in the seventh year, if we may not sow or gather in our crop?" **I will command my blessing on you in the sixth year, so that it will produce a crop sufficient for three years.** When you sow in the eighth year, you will be eating some of the old crop; you shall eat the old until the ninth year, when its crop arrives. (Leviticus 25:18–22; emphasis added)

Year six would be a bumper crop, so long as the people obeyed God. They would never go hungry, and there would be plenty of seeds to sow after the Sabbath year was done.

But what of those who disobeyed? He also made that clear:

But if you will not listen to me and will not do all these commandments, if you spurn my statutes, and if your soul abhors my rules, so that you will not do all my commandments, but break my covenant, then I will do this to you: I **will visit you with panic**, with **wasting disease and fever** that consume the eyes and make the heart ache. And you shall **sow your seed in vain**, for **your enemies shall eat it. I will set my face against you**, and **you shall be struck down before your enemies. Those who hate you shall rule over you**, and you shall flee when none pursues you.

And take special note of this part:

And if in spite of this you will not listen to me, then I will discipline you again sevenfold for your sins, and I will break the pride of your power, and I will make your heavens like iron and your earth like bronze. And your strength shall be spent in vain, for your land shall not yield its increase, and the trees of the land shall not yield their fruit. Then if you walk contrary to me and will not listen to me, **I will continue striking you, sevenfold** for your sins. (Leviticus 26:14–21; emphasis added)

To make it perfectly clear, the LORD added this very important caveat:

But if in spite of this you will not listen to me, but walk contrary to me, then I will walk contrary to you in fury, and **I myself will discipline you sevenfold for your sins.** You shall eat the flesh of your sons, and you shall eat the flesh of your daughters. And I will destroy your high places and cut down your incense altars and **cast your dead bodies upon the dead bodies of your idols**, and my soul will abhor you. **And I will lay your cities waste and will make your sanctuaries desolate**, and I will not smell your pleasing aromas. **And I myself will devastate the land, so that**

your enemies who settle in it shall be appalled at it. And I will scatter you among the nations, and I will unsheathe the sword after you, and your land shall be a desolation, and your cities shall be a waste. Then the land shall enjoy its Sabbaths as long as it lies desolate, **while you are in your enemies' land; then the land shall rest, and enjoy its Sabbaths.** (Leviticus 26:27–33; emphasis added)

This is exactly what happened. The people of Israel worshiped other idols and refused to heed the LORD's law. Note the verse regarding "the dead bodies of your idols" (verse 30). Why are the idols "dead"? Often times, the Fallen Realm gods are presented as "Lords of the Dead" or "Lords of the Underworld," but also the Avarim (or "Travelers") live in the underworld and are able to cross from one realm to the other. These are the Rephaim, the demons and fallen angels who convinced the people to worship them as their "dead ancestors."

The writer of 2 Chronicles says this regarding the penalty for continued sin:

The LORD, the God of their fathers, sent persistently to them by his messengers, because he had compassion on his people and on his dwelling place. But they kept mocking the messengers of God, despising his words and scoffing at his prophets, until the wrath of the LORD rose against his people, until there was no remedy.

Therefore he brought up against them the king of the Chaldeans, who killed their young men with the sword in the house of their sanctuary and had no compassion on young man or virgin, old man or aged. He gave them all into his hand. And all the vessels of the house of God, great and small, and the treasures of the house of the LORD, and the treasures of the king and of his princes, all these he brought to Babylon. And they burned the house of God and broke down the wall of Jerusalem and burned all its palaces with fire and destroyed all its precious vessels. He took into exile in Babylon those who had escaped from the sword, and they became servants to him and to his sons until the establishment of the kingdom of Persia, **to fulfill the word of the LORD by the mouth of Jeremiah, until the land had enjoyed its Sabbaths. All the days that it lay desolate it kept Sabbath, to fulfill seventy years.** (2 Chronicles 36:15–21; emphasis added)

The scroll of Jeremiah indicated a seventy-year exile for not celebrating the land's *shmita* year, but the scroll of Leviticus added a caveat: Extended sin and refusal to repent would see the sentence multiplied by seven, meaning a total of 490 years.

Daniel must have trembled as he read these words. Having trusted in Yahweh to protect him in that foreign environment, the aging prayer warrior hoped his people might avoid the dire consequence of their intransigence. And so, he fell to his knees and fasted:

I, Daniel, perceived in the books the number of years that, according to the word of the LORD to Jeremiah the prophet, must pass before the end of the desolations of Jerusalem, namely, seventy years. Then I turned my face to the Lord God, seeking him by prayer and pleas for mercy with fasting and sackcloth and ashes. (Daniel 9:2–3)

While he "was speaking in prayer, the man Gabriel, whom I had seen in the vision at the first, came to me in swift flight at the time of the evening sacrifice" (Daniel 9:21).

Isn't that wonderful? As Daniel fell to his knees, the LORD dispatched the answer. Daniel described Gabriel's trip as "swift flight":

The man Gabriel, whom I had seen in the vision at the first, came to me in **swift flight** [the word here is *yeaph*, which implies fatigue, even faintness; Gabriel had come with great speed] at the time of the evening sacrifice.

And here's why the angel had come:

O Daniel, I have now come out to give you insight and understanding. At the beginning of your pleas for mercy a word went out, and I have come to tell it to you, for you are greatly loved. Therefore consider the word and understand the vision.

Seventy weeks are decreed about your people and your holy city, **to finish the transgression, to put an end to sin,** and **to atone for iniquity, to bring in everlasting righteousness, to seal both vision and prophet,** and **to anoint a most holy place.** Know therefore and understand that from the going out of the word to restore and build Jerusalem to the coming of an anointed one, a prince, there shall be **seven weeks.** Then for **sixty-two weeks** it shall be built again with squares and moat, but in a troubled time. And after the sixty-two weeks, an anointed one shall be cut off and shall have nothing. And the people of the prince who is to come shall destroy the city and the sanctuary. Its end shall come with a flood, and to the end there shall be war. Desolations are decreed. And he shall make a strong covenant with many for one week, and for half of the week he shall put an end to sacrifice and offering. And on the wing of abominations shall come one who makes desolate, until the decreed end is poured out on the desolator. (Daniel 9:22–27; emphasis and commentary added)

First of all, the purpose of the angel is to reveal the LORD's battle plans for the remainder of the spiritual war. Boom. Wow. The Fallen Realm must have listened at the door, hoping to determine all of their enemy's future devices, but our LORD is the best general ever, which is why He doesn't reveal *everything* in prophecy.

The angel tells Daniel specifics on how the seventy weeks would be divided, but he also tells the prophet *why* these events would happen. Seven items on are on this list:

1. To finish the transgression
2. To put an end to sin
3. To atone for iniquity
4. To bring in everlasting righteousness
5. To seal up vision
6. To seal up prophet
7. To anoint a most holy place

Seventy weeks would achieve all of this.

Now, this is how Gabriel tells us these seventy weeks would be broken down:

First, seven weeks (49 years) would see the declaration that the exiles could return to Jerusalem (remember that the exiles returned in two groups: one led by Ezra, the other by Nehemiah. Then, sixty-two weeks of sevens would lead to "messiah be[ing] cut off."

When added together, sixty-two weeks and seven weeks equal sixty-nine weeks (or sixty-nine "sevens," understood as 69 x 7 years, equaling 483 years). We know that, as with the Jews, the Chaldeans used a lunar calendar of twelve months, equaling 360-day year. One of the hints that God's prophetic years are the same length may be found in the book of Revelation, where 1,260 days equals three and a half years. Therefore, we can safely surmise that the prophetic year is 360 days long, which means the phrase "until messiah be cut off," can be calculated by multiplying 483 years by 360. After this, the people of the "prince that shall come" would enter Jerusalem to destroy both the city and the sanctuary—which the Romans certainly did.

A STRANGE CONFLUENCE OF EVENTS

Sir Robert Anderson served as assistant police commissioner of London's Metropolitan Police during the 1888 Jack the Ripper investigations. While it may seem incongruent to bring a nineteenth-century policeman into our discussion of Daniel's prophetic visions, it is actually quite enlightening. Sharon's research into police departmental structure during the Ripper investigation forms the bedrock for *The Redwing Saga* series of novels. During that research, she discovered a marvelous connection between these serial murders and, of all places, Mount Hermon: the very mountain where the Watchers of Enoch descended and dared to take human women as their "wives."

We'll return to Anderson in a moment, but first, let's consider his superior in the Metropolitan Police Department, Commissioner Sir Charles Warren.

Before his appointment as police commissioner, mathematics "nerd" Warren served his native England as an army surveyor in Egypt, South Africa, and the Levant—including the ancient sites of Jericho and Jerusalem. As part of his duties, Warren surveyed the Old City and the

Temple Mount. In 1867, he discovered and documented the details of "Warren's Shaft," a vertical channel next to Gihon Spring that provided fresh water to Bronze Age and Iron Age Jerusalem.

In 1869, on behalf of the Palestine Exploration Fund, Sir Charles climbed up the forbidding sides of Mount Hermon to determine its true height and describe any archaeological sites found there. As such, Warren explored, measured, and sketched an ancient temple known as Qasr Antar. Here, the visitor passed through a temple, but was then forced him to continue upwards along the peak, in a peculiar anti-clockwise spiral pattern, in order to reach the summit.

The southern peak's rocky terrain had been scooped out to receive ritual libations to the god or gods of the mount. In confirmation of this theory, Warren discovered within the area a strange *stele* (alternatively spelled *stela*; a stone pillar or marker), engraved on one side in ancient Greek. Once translated, the text is chilling to anyone who's read of the Watchers' descent onto Hermon and the vow each had to make to satisfy their leader Semjâzâ:

> According to the command of the greatest and Most Holy God, those who take an oath, proceed from here.[35]

After leaving the summit, Warren chose to remove the marker from Hermon's slopes and carry it down the nine thousand-foot height for transfer to London. But being twelve inches thick and far heavier than his team could manage, the surveyor ordered the stone to be sliced longitudinally to reduce its thickness. Though the lighter weight did make the trip down the mountain

This stela is currently housed at the British Museum, listed as Item 1903,0422.1 (Image in public domain)

easier, the ancient stone suffered as a result, cracking horizontally along its midsection.

The marker is currently housed at the British Museum, listed as Item 1903,0422.1.[36] While visiting the museum in 2019, we tried to find the marker, but were told it is no longer displayed to the public.

In a strange coincidence and through a series of personal life changes that only our wonderful Lord might contrive, Sir Charles Warren eventually found himself working alongside a fellow Bible archaeology enthusiast. During the 1888 Jack the Ripper investigation, Warren's assistant commissioner for crime was Sir Robert Anderson—mentioned earlier. Besides holding a degree in law, this erudite gentleman also held a degree in divinity; it was in this capacity, as a clergyman, that he published many treatises on the prophet Daniel. With the doggedness of a trained policeman and prosecutor, Sir Robert approached the study of Daniel's seventy-week vision and dared to calculate the clues of its possible timing.

Remember, the angel Gabriel told Daniel this:

Know therefore and understand that from the going out of the word to restore and build Jerusalem to the coming of an anointed one, a prince, there shall be **seven weeks**. Then for **sixty-two weeks** it shall be built again with squares and moat, but in a troubled time. And after the sixty-two weeks, an anointed one shall be cut off and shall have nothing. (Daniel 9:25–26a; emphasis added)

As mentioned earlier, seven weeks added to sixty-two gives us sixty-nine total weeks until "an anointed one shall be cut off." Believing this sixty-nine-week period must have ended sometime during Christ's lifetime, Anderson endeavored to follow every clue at hand. He lists his thoughts in *The Coming Prince,* a powerful and insightful book (which we highly recommend reading.)[37]

Beginning on page 52, we read a summary of Anderson's calculations. (All emphasis is added.)

1. The **scepter of earthly power which was entrusted to the house of David, was transferred to the Gentiles in the person of Nebuchadnezzar,** to remain in Gentile hands "until the times of the Gentiles be fulfilled." The blessings promised to Judah and Jerusalem were postponed till after a period described as "seventy weeks"; at the close of the sixty-ninth week of this era the Messiah should be "cut off."

2. These seventy weeks represent seventy times seven prophetic years of 360 days, to be reckoned from the issuing of an edict for the rebuilding of the city—"the street and rampart," of Jerusalem. The edict in question was the decree issued by Artaxerxes Longitmanus in the twentieth year of his reign, authorizing Nehemiah to rebuild the fortifications of Jerusalem.

3. The date of Artaxerxes's reign can be definitely ascertained—not from elaborate disquisitions by biblical commentators and prophetic writers, but by the **united voice of secular historians and chronologers.**

4. The statement of St. Luke is explicit and unequivocal, that our Lord's public ministry began in the fifteenth year of Tiberius Caesar. It is equally clear that it began shortly before the Passover, The date of it can thus be fixed as between August A.D. 28 and April A.D. 29. The Passover of the crucifixion therefore was in A.D. 32, when Christ was betrayed on the night of the Paschal Supper, and put to death on the day of the Paschal Feast.

5. If then the foregoing conclusions be well founded, we should expect to find that **the period intervening between the edict of Artaxerxes and the Passion was 483 prophetic years.** And accuracy as absolute as the nature of the case permits is no more than men are here entitled to demand. There can be no loose reckoning in a Divine chronology; and if God has; deigned to mark on human calendars the fulfillment of His purposes as foretold in prophecy, the strictest: scrutiny shall fail to detect miscalculation or mistake.

6. The Persian edict which restored the autonomy of Judah was issued in the Jewish month of Nisan. It may in fact have been dated the 1st of Nisan, but: no other day being named, the prophetic period must be reckoned, according to a practice common with the Jews, from the Jewish New Year's Day. **The seventy weeks are therefore to be computed from the 1st of Nisan B.C. 445.**

7. In B.C. 445 the new moon by which the Passover was regulated was on the 13th of March at 7h. 9m. A. M. And accordingly the 1st Nisan may be assigned to the 14th March. But the language of the prophecy is clear: "From the going forth of the commandment to restore and to build Jerusalem unto Messiah the Prince shall be seven weeks and threescore and two weeks." **An era therefore of sixty-nine "weeks," or 483 prophetic years reckoned from the 14th March, B.C. 445, should close with some event to satisfy the words, "unto the Messiah the Prince."**

8. No student of the Gospel narrative can fail to see that the Lord's last visit to Jerusalem was not only in fact, but in the purpose of it, the crisis of His ministry, the goal towards which it had been directed. After the first tokens had been given that the nation would reject His Messianic claims, He had shunned all public recognition of them. But now the twofold testimony of His words and His works had been fully rendered, and His entry into the Holy City was to proclaim His Messiahship and to receive His doom. Again and again His apostles even had been charged that they should not make Him known. But now He accepted the acclamations of "the whole multitude of the disciples," and silenced the remonstrance of the Pharisees with the indignant rebuke, "I tell you if these should hold their peace, the stones would immediately cry out." (Luke 19:39, 40)

9. **The time of Jerusalem's visitation had come, and she knew it not.** Long ere then the nation had rejected Him, but this was the predestined day when their choice must be irrevocable,—the day so distinctly signalized in Scripture as the fulfillment of Zechariah's

prophecy, "Rejoice greatly, O daughter of Zion! shout, O daughter of Jerusalem! behold thy King cometh unto thee!" (Zechariah 9:9) Of all the days of the ministry of Christ on earth, no other will satisfy so well the angel's words, unto Messiah the Prince.

10. And the date of it can be ascertained. In accordance with the Jewish custom, the Lord went up to Jerusalem upon the 8th Nisan, "six days before the Passover." But as the 14th, on which the Paschal Supper was eaten, fell that year upon a Thursday, the 8th was the preceding Friday. He must have spent the Sabbath, therefore, at Bethany; and on the evening of the 9th, after the Sabbath had ended, the Supper took place in Martha's house. Upon the following day, the 10th Nisan, He entered Jerusalem as recorded in the Gospels.

11. The Julian date of that 10th Nisan was Sunday the 6th April, A.D. 32. What then was the length of the period intervening between the issuing of the decree to rebuild Jerusalem and the public advent of "Messiah the Prince,"—between the 14th March, B.C. 445, and the 6th April, A.D. 32? **THE INTERVAL CONTAINED EXACTLY AND TO THE VERY DAY 173,880 DAYS, OR SEVEN TIMES SIXTY-NINE PROPHETIC YEARS OF 360 DAYS**, the first sixty-nine weeks of Gabriel's prophecy.

If you wonder at the precision of these statements and calculations, Anderson goes on to explain that he was:

…indebted to the courtesy of **the Astronomer Royal**, whose reply to my inquiry on the subject is appended:

"ROYAL OBSERVATORY, GREENWICH."
June 26th, 1877.

"SIR, —I have had the moon's place calculated from Largeteau's Tables in Additions to the *Connaisance des Tems* 1846, by one of my assistants, and have no doubt of its correctness. The place being calculated for—444, March 12d. 20h., French reckoning, or March 12d. 8h. P. M., it appears that the said time was short of New Moon by about 8h. 47m., and therefore the New Moon occurred at 4h. 47m. A. M., March 13th, Paris time."

I am, etc.,

"(Signed,) G. B. AIRY." (all emphases to above quotes are added)

What a mind Sir Robert Anderson possessed! Again, we strongly recommend *The Coming Prince* to you, for it is filled with incredible insights and scholarly exposition. Sharon certainly found Sir Charles Warren's connection to Mount Hermon fascinating; but then to discover a second man, Sir Robert Anderson—who served side by side with Warren during that pivotal crime spree—had studied biblical archaeology and prophecy and composed entire volumes on both positively made her shout for joy!

Even today, Jack the Ripper remains a mystery; his identity is now synonymous with evil: a bogeyman embodiment of the ancient Chaos Dragon, who would destroy all humans just to spite the Creator.

We now turn to one of the men who hunted Ripper to compute the timing of Christ's entry into Jerusalem. Instead of welcoming Him as their Messiah, most in the city saw Him as an invader—even a charlatan. And so, He would be "cut off" and become a substitutionary sacrifice in our place.

As Paul says in Hebrews 2:14–15:

Since therefore the children share in flesh and blood, he himself likewise partook of the same things, **that through death he might destroy the one who has the power of death, that is, the devil,** and deliver all those who through fear of death were subject to lifelong slavery. (Emphasis added)

By taking on flesh, the LORD provided a release from the curse of spiritual death, placed on us in the Garden. And it returns us to our original positions as members of the divine council. That is what this current battle is all about, and it is a continuation of the original war, the *Chaoskampf.*

Sir Robert Anderson's calculations give us the very day when the first sixty-nine weeks ended.

And, according to the angel (most likely Gabriel), there is one more "seven" of years remaining until Israel is finally redeemed and released from bondage to the enemy. If we can rely upon this nineteenth-century master detective's calculations—and many scholars do—then Christ literally fulfilled the first sixty-nine weeks *to the very day*; therefore, we may assume the final week of the seventy-week prophecy will proceed the same way—in literal fashion.

Today, dear friends, we stand today in a parenthetic space between the last day of week sixty-nine and the first of week seventy, the next phase of prophecy. And we who live at this moment in time—in fact, all who've lived since the day when Messiah was "cut off" in Jerusalem—await that pivotal second when the final week begins.

Remember that Israel's captivity was due not only to sin, but to a failure to keep the *shmita*; the Sabbath years when the land must be allowed to rest. The seventy-year captivity allowed the land to recapture all of those lost Sabbaths. Daniel would have been familiar this idea; therefore, when he heard the prophecy of "sevens," it must have struck him as a stark reminder of his people's failings. But the same God who works all things together for good according to His purposes also promises to reverse those failings. Daniel knew that in seventy "sevens" (490 years), Israel would be redeemed and the true Messiah would restore the world to rights.

What Daniel may not have understood was the great length of time that would pass between the sixty-ninth and seventieth years. When Jesus was "cut off" on that Palm Sunday, the prophetic pause button was pressed, and ever since then, the world has waited for the timeline's clock to resume ticking.

8

THE FOUR BEASTS OF GENTILE RULE

My soul is in the midst of lions;
I lie down amid fiery beasts—
the children of man, whose teeth are spears and arrows,
whose tongues are sharp swords.
—Psalm 57:4

The seventy-weeks vision covers the total period of Gentile rule over the land of Israel. But if Jerusalem is considered the location of the Lord's mount of assembly, then it is the true center—the *omphalos*—of the world, and the prime target for the Fallen Realm's plots. Is it any wonder that the small-*g* gods want to blind us to this prophetic truth? The seventy-weeks timeline is a countdown to their final doom!

To forestall this inevitability, these rebel angels and their demonic offspring try to convince human governments to invade, or, failing that, to redraw the borders of Israel—even erase all history of the nation ever having lived there. But archaeological evidence is mounting that refutes that claim, meaning it will take a very big eraser if the Fallen Realm wish to maintain control of the Temple Mount through the Gentile nations.

But a day is coming when the LORD will judge these rebels, and it is our belief that the Day of the Lord is close at hand. The people of Israel have yet to establish true autonomy. Despite becoming a supposedly sovereign nation in 1948, Israel is not permitted to exist or make foreign policy without United Nations' oversight and input. The leaders of the West constantly act as though it is *they*, not her own people, who determine Israel's future. This Gentile rule is just what Daniel foresaw all those centuries ago: Israel would live beneath the yoke and oversight of the Gentiles until the seventy weeks were complete.

To understand which nations would achieve this, we turn again to Daniel, who was shown these future periods of Gentile rule by the angel Gabriel. It was in the first year of Belshazzar king of Babylon that Daniel experienced "a dream and troubling visions" as he lay in his bed. As soon as awoke, he wrote down the dream, recorded for us in Daniel 7:

> I saw in my vision by night, and behold, **the four winds of heaven were stirring up the great sea.** [Note: The four winds are also mentioned in Revelation 7, and the "great sea" could mean the Mediterranean, which gave rise to these beasts, but it might also represent *yam* or Chaos; see our earlier discourse on the Chaoskampf]. And four great beasts came up out of the sea, different from one another. The first was **like a lion and had eagles' wings.** Then as I looked its **wings were plucked off,** and **it was lifted up from the ground and made to stand on two feet like a man, and the mind of a man was given to it.**
>
> And behold, another beast, a second one, like a **bear.** It was **raised up on one side.** It had **three ribs in its mouth between its teeth;** and it was told, "Arise, devour much flesh."
>
> After this I looked, and behold, another, like **a leopard, with four wings of a bird** on its back. And the beast had **four heads,** and dominion was given to it.
>
> After this I saw in the night visions, and behold, a **fourth beast, terrifying and dreadful and exceedingly strong.** It had **great iron**

teeth; it devoured and broke in pieces and stamped what was left with its feet. It was **different from all the beasts that were before it, and it had ten horns.**

I considered the horns, and behold, there came up among them another horn, a little one, before which three of the first horns were plucked up by the roots. And behold, in this horn were eyes like the eyes of a man, and a mouth speaking great things. (Daniel 7:1–8; emphasis added)

In these verses, Daniel is shown present and future Gentile kingdoms *on the earth*, but then he sees a vision of the *true* King in the Divine Assembly as He enters the throne room, a scene that is echoed in Revelation 5. (One wonders if John and Daniel were present at the same future moment.)

As I looked, **thrones were placed and the Ancient of Days** [God the Father] **took his seat;** his clothing was white as snow, and the hair of his head like pure wool; his throne was fiery flames; its wheels were burning fire. A stream of fire issued and came out from before him; a thousand thousands served him, and ten thousand times ten thousand stood before him; the court sat in judgment, and the books were opened.

I looked then because of the sound of the great words that the horn was speaking. And as I looked, the beast was killed, and its body destroyed and given over to be burned with fire. As for the rest of the beasts, their dominion was taken away, but their lives were prolonged for a season and a time.

I saw in the night visions, and behold, with the clouds of heaven there came **one like a son of man** [Christ, the slain Lamb of God, arrives in heaven and is given the scroll as shown in Revelation 5], and **he came to the Ancient of Days and was presented before him.** And **to him was given dominion and glory and a kingdom,** that all peoples, nations, and languages should serve him; his dominion is an everlasting dominion, which shall not pass away, and his kingdom one that shall not be destroyed. (Daniel 7:1–14; emphasis added)

This is an amazing vision with loads of stuff to unpack, so let's jump in. Here, we see the prophet Daniel, taken to the throne of God and allowed to see the future coronation of Christ (Messiah) as the rightful heir to earth and ruler of humanity (and the universe) by His father, "the Ancient of Days." And we see the divine council members are surrounding the throne as witnesses of this coronation.

Belshazzar, the king mentioned in the first verse of Daniel 7, was the eldest son of Nabonidus, the last king to reign over the Neo-Babylonian (Chaldean) Empire. His name means "Bel protects the king." It's unclear just which Bel (a generic term meaning "lord") is meant here, but it most likely refers to Marduk; if so, Belshazzar's very name disputed his absent father's decision to remove Marduk as head of the Chaldean pantheon in favor of the moon-god, Sin.

It should also be mentioned that, as with his three friends, Meshach, Shadrach, and Abednego, Daniel had received a new Chaldean name, Belteshazzar, meaning "the prince whom Bel (the lord) favors." An ironic name, for it was the real LORD who favored Daniel, not Marduk or Bel. But also, Daniel's name means "God is judge."

Prince Belshazzar never ascended the throne on his own, but ruled as regent during his father's ten-year absence, during which Nabonidus served the moon-god at the oasis of Teima, where he even rebuilt Sin's temples. One assumes, therefore, that the "first year" of Belshazzar refers to the first year of his regency. Most historians put this at 553 BC. To add context for those who love history, 553 BC also marked:

1. Two hundred and one years since the founding of Rome
2. The year that Cyrus II of Persia invaded Astyages of the Medes
3. The period when Amasis II of the Twenty-Sixth Dynasty was Pharaoh in Egypt
4. The 56th Greek Olympiad

Now, with this in mind, let's take a look at the vision itself. First, Daniel tells us that the dream occurs in the night. Night is obviously a time for sleep, but the hours of darkness are favorites for Fallen Realm activity. Oftentimes, people who suffer from night terrors do so between midnight and 3 a.m. Both of us have awakened many times during the night, only to notice that it's three in the morning. And we've both been awakened periodically by an as-yet unseen "roof walker" who strolled across the top of our house at night, generally performing his mysterious activity near this same hour.[38]

Daniel also states that he experiences a "dream and troubling visions," so it may be that the night brought him close to the spiritual battlefield, and that both sides—good and evil—vied for his attention. Of course, this is speculation, but as we'll see in the next chapter, the Enemy certainly tried to stop the angel from delivering the visions recorded in chapters 10 through 12. Perhaps, the Enemy tried to prevent this one as well.

The vision of the beasts is a tantalizing one revealing four great, specific animals:

1. Lion with wings
2. Bear with ribs in its mouth
3. Leopard with four heads and four wings
4. A terrible beast with iron teeth, claws of bronze, and ten horns (then a little horn arises out of these ten and plucks up three of the ten)

Understandably, Daniel is greatly disturbed by these visions, and he approaches one of the entities surrounding the throne. It's possible that this is an angel, or it might be one of the cherubim who will later direct the apostle John to "come and see" the Four Riders of Revelation chapter 6. Whatever his identity, this heavenly being informs Daniel that the beasts he saw are four kings who will arise in the earth, but that these Gentile kingdoms are temporary, for it is the "saints of the Most High"—not human kings—who will rule forever.

Isn't that amazing? Not only will Christ be crowned King of all kings, but *we will rule with him!* Hallelujah!

Daniel then adds this:

> As I looked, **this horn** [i.e., the little horn that had arisen last and plucked up three of the ten] made war with the saints and prevailed over them, until the Ancient of Days came, and judgment was given for the saints of the Most High, and the time came when the saints possessed the kingdom. (Daniel 7:21; emphasis added)

The prophet is told that the fourth kingdom will be different; it will trample the earth beneath its feet. The ten horns represent ten kings, but these will give rise to an eleventh, one who is different from the others, and he will put down three kings. The saints of the Most High will be given into this king's hand for "a time, times, and half a time."

This phrase, "a time, times, and half a time," is important, as it is generally interpreted as representing three and one-half years, or half of seven years. In other words, this future prophecy will be fulfilled during *one-half of Daniel's seventieth week*. However, this is not the end. Praise God, dear readers, the enemy does not win!

> But the court [the divine council as revealed in Revelation 5] shall sit in judgment, and his dominion shall be taken away, to be consumed and destroyed to the end. And the kingdom and the dominion and the greatness of the kingdoms under the whole heaven **shall be given to the people of the saints of the Most High**; his kingdom shall be an everlasting kingdom, and all dominions shall serve and obey him.
>
> **Here is the end of the matter.** As for me, Daniel, my thoughts greatly alarmed me, and my color changed, but I kept the matter in my heart. (Daniel 7:26–28; emphasis added)

Looking back through the entire section, we can see how history fulfilled all the elements of Daniel's vision.

1. THE LION represents the Neo-Babylonian Empire, whose founder, Nebuchadnezzar, might be described as the fearless lion. Jeremiah refers to this kingdom as a lion in Jeremiah 49:19, and a visit to the British Museum will allow you to see the enormous statues of the *lamassu*, throne guardians from ancient Assyria represented as winged bulls with human heads and the feet of lions. Compare those statues to the cherubim described by the prophet Ezekiel (remember, each with faces of man, eagle, lion, and ox/cherub), and it's clear that the cherubim looked a lot more like this than the graceful, feminine angels artists place atop their concepts of the Ark of the Covenant, or the chubby, winged babies of Renaissance paintings! We had the honor to visit this museum in 2019. You can see the photo of Derek standing beside one of these giant *lamassu* (throne guardians).

Derek Gilbert with a throne guardian, or *lamassu*, at the British Museum. Photo by Sharon K. Gilbert

Note that the statue includes all four aspects of the cherubim described by Ezekiel: Man (face), ox (body), eagle (wings), and lion (feet).

2. THE BEAR represents the cruel and voracious Medo-Persian empire. Their clever Persian general, Cyrus the Great, conquered Belshazzar's capital city by digging beneath the Tigris River and entering the city with the help of insiders—possibly priests of the chief god Marduk, who may have resented the loss of prestige that would follow the demotion of Marduk in favor of the moon-god Sîn, the favorite deity of King Nabonidus. The famous "writing on the wall" inscribed by the finger of God sealed Belshazzar's fate, because the foolish regent chose to hold a pagan celebration using the plates and other items taken from the Temple in Jerusalem. As Derek showed in his book *Bad Moon Rising*, it's almost certain that the meal for which God's vessels were used was an annual festival called the *akitu*, held in honor of Sîn.[39]

3. Alexander the Great is THE LEOPARD, and the four wings and four heads are the four generals who inherited the young conqueror's kingdom after Alexander died at just thirty-three years old. According to Adam Clarke: "Nothing in the history of the world, was equal to the conquests of Alexander, who ran through all the countries from Illycrium and the Adriatic Sea to the Indian Ocean and the River Ganges; and in twelve years subdued part of Europe, and all Asia."[40] The four heads are the generals who replaced Alexander as rulers, becoming the Seleucids of Mesopotamia and Central Asia, Ptolemaic Egypt (yes, Cleopatra was Greek), Attalid Anatolia, and Antigonid Macedonian empires.

4. The FINAL BEAST is two phases, representing the ancient Roman Empire and a revived consortium of countries built from the remnants—somewhat like a phoenix rising from its own ashes. Rome's iron teeth and fierce claws chomped and tore their way to domination, destroying and taking dominion.

If you doubt this interpretation, let's examine another of Daniel's prophecies: an interpretation of a king's dream.

9

THE MAGNIFICENT IDOL
OF GENTILE HISTORY

You saw, O king, and behold, a great image. This image, mighty
and of exceeding brightness, stood before you, and its appearance
was frightening.

—DANIEL 2:31

Then I saw another beast rising out of the earth. It had two horns
like a lamb and it spoke like a dragon…. And it was allowed to
give breath to the image of the beast, so that the image of the beast
might even speak.

—REVELATION 13:11, 15A

Daniel is written in Aramaic, not Hebrew, probably because the language
of the Chaldeans was Aramaic. As we study chapter 2 of Daniel's
prophecies, we come across a dream with a central theme: a statue or
image. The Aramaic term translated "image" in this chapter is *tselem*, and
it implies an idol. Again, we see a parallel with the book of Revelation,
for we find the False Prophet of Revelation 13 is given power to erect an
image and make it speak.

In Revelation, the original Greek is *eikon,* which can mean a "likeness," "image," or "statue." In the Orthodox churches of Greece and Russia, icons (also spelled "ikons") are as common as statues of saints in Catholic churches. Despite the LORD's command to worship no "graven image," modern Christians find it difficult to worship without something tangible to "look upon." Though we as believers find it difficult to imagine, those living beneath the dominion of the Antichrist may clamor to build his image and worship it. The final seven years of Daniel's prophecy will be like nothing that has ever gone before.

And so, in chapter 2, we come to a great and disquieting image of a king's vision. During his second year as king, Nebuchadnezzar suffered a troubling dream that required interpretation. Deciding to test his soothsayers and "wise men," the wily king insisted that he'd only hear an interpretation from the first man who would relate the facts of the dream to him. Failure was not an option.

> The word from me is firm: if you do not make known to me
> the dream and its interpretation, you shall be torn limb from
> limb, and your houses shall be laid in ruins. But if you show the
> dream and its interpretation, you shall receive from me gifts and
> rewards and great honor. Therefore show me the dream and its
> interpretation. (Daniel 2:5–6)

Now, if you're one of the king's insiders, this command is both tempting and terrifying. After all, the promised reward is great, but then so is the consequence if one fails. So the magicians and soothsayers plead with the king to reveal the dream's details, promising to provide an answer in return. Needless to say, the clever king is not persuaded—in fact, his reply indicates that he's keenly aware of their apparent lack of insight and fear:

> The king answered and said, "I know with certainty that you are
> trying to gain time, because you see that the word from me is

firm—if you do not make the dream known to me, there is but one sentence for you. **You have agreed to speak lying and corrupt words before me till the times change.** Therefore tell me the dream, and I shall know that you can show me its interpretation." (Daniel 2:8–9; emphasis added)

Imagine being in their shoes. The magicians are stymied, but what's worse, it's clear that the king knows their thoughts. He accuses them of plotting to speak lies to him, and insists they're stalling until he changes his mind (which, of course, they are).

But what can they do? If they confess their inability to reveal another man's dream, then they admit that they're just ordinary men. However, if they try and then *get it wrong*, the king will have them all killed.

It's a tough spot, but their quibbling only makes the king angry. Realizing they're frauds, he orders that all the magicians be executed.

Now, it has to be remembered that Daniel the prophet was brought to the city of Babylon as a boy, then placed with the magicians for training. Despite this, Daniel remained faithful to his own God (YHWH), but he used his time to learn all about Babylon's rules and beliefs. As a member of this "wise men" class, he, too would have been killed.

So we read this:

So the decree went out, and the wise men were about to be killed; **and they sought Daniel and his companions, to kill them.** Then Daniel replied with prudence and discretion to Arioch, the captain of the king's guard, who had gone out to kill the wise men of Babylon.

He declared to Arioch, the king's captain, "Why is the decree of the king so urgent?" Then Arioch made the matter known to Daniel. **And Daniel went in and requested the king to appoint him a time, that he might show the interpretation to the king.** (Daniel 2:13–16; emphasis added)

Now, we've emphasized that final line because Daniel's choice to go directly to the king was, in itself, a very bold move. He might easily have been slain on the spot, but relying upon the protection of YHWH, the prophet dared to ask for an audience. Most of you Bible scholars are already leaping ahead in your heads to the next event, for it's a much-studied topic. But for those who don't know, here's the skinny:

Before leaving to see the king, Daniel asked his friends, Hananiah, Mishael, and Azariah (the Hebrew names of Shadrach, Meshach, and Abednego) to pray for him. He did not jump ahead without petitioning God for guidance and protection. He asked them to "seek mercy from the God of heaven concerning this mystery, so that Daniel and his companions might not be destroyed with the rest of the wise men of Babylon" (verse 18). After making this request, Daniel decides to get some sleep, and it's during this period of rest that the LORD makes the king's dream known to the young prophet. Did Daniel expect God to use a dream to reveal a dream? Maybe. But Daniel's response is beautiful, and these are verses which we should all take to heart:

> Blessed be the name of God forever and ever, to whom belong wisdom and might. He **changes times and seasons; he removes kings and sets up kings; he gives wisdom to the wise and knowledge to those who have understanding; he reveals deep and hidden things; he knows what is in the darkness, and the light dwells with him.** To you, O God of my fathers, I give thanks and praise, for you have given me wisdom and might, and have now made known to me what we asked of you, for you have made known to us the king's matter. (Daniel 2:20–23; emphasis added)

Once again, we've made some of these lines bold, because they have such importance for prophecy students—in fact, for everyone in the Body of Christ. As we write this chapter, the country stands divided on the handling of the current COVID-19 crisis, but it's a division that has long, bloody roots. All Christians long for a political leader who honors Christ: one who allows us to speak freely and preach freely, who trusts in the God of the Bible and uses His wisdom to lead. But trying to elect a "pastor-in-chief" is a fool's errand. Anyone who runs for high political office usually gets there by compromise and a willingness to play ball with those who rig the system. And we end up with a man or woman who ultimately disappoints.

Our reactions are human, aren't they? They're based on our position as members of a society made of sinful, mortal humans. Daniel's plight was just the same. Though he'd had no voice in an election, he lived beneath a leader who claimed allegiance to a wide variety of gods—a man who would soon erect a great statue of himself and insist that everyone bow down to it to prove loyalty or be thrown into a fiery furnace. But instead of whining and crying out to God to change things, Daniel goes to sleep. He literally rests in the LORD!

And after he awakens, Daniel thanks the LORD for His reply. In verses 21–23, we read the prophet's confession that *only YHWH had the right to set up kings and the right to remove them*—at His will; only God knows the truth that lurks within the darkness, but He will one day reveal it all to us.

This beautiful sacrifice of praise reveals Daniel's true heart and serves as an example to each of us regarding our own responses when a king, prime minister, or president disappoints us. God has the right to set them up, and He has the right to remove them.

After the dream and prayer, Daniel seeks an audience with King Nebuchadnezzar, but he doesn't use it to toot his own horn and claim to be the best prophet in the land. No! Daniel uses this golden opportunity to witness. He declares to the most powerful man in the known world that *only YHWH could reveal the king's dream*—not the moon-god Sîn, not Marduk, not Enlil or Nabu or Shamash or Ishtar.

Only YHWH.

Then, the young prophet relates the details of the king's troubling dream:

You saw, O king, and behold, a great image. This image, mighty and of exceeding brightness, stood before you, and its appearance was frightening. The head of this image was of fine gold, its chest and arms of silver, its middle and thighs of bronze, its legs of iron, its feet partly of iron and partly of clay. As you looked, a stone was cut out by no human hand, and it struck the image on its feet of iron and clay, and broke them in pieces. Then the iron, the clay, the bronze, the silver, and the gold, all together were broken in pieces, and became like the chaff of the summer threshing floors; and the wind carried them away, so that not a trace of them could be found. But the stone that struck the image became a great mountain and filled the whole earth. (Daniel 2:31–35)

It must have startled the king when Daniel relayed the dream to him in detail and without error. As Daniel gives his interpretation, we learn that the elements within the statue's order and metallic composition reveal a timeline of great kingdoms—Gentile kingdoms—that would rule most of the region, but more importantly, would rule over Jerusalem.

As we studied in the previous chapter, this succession of kingdoms parallels the revelations shown to Daniel and related to us in Daniel 9. This repetition makes the king's vision even more important. Because the LORD used two separate visions—one to a king, the other to a prophet—this timeline must mean that these Gentile kingdoms have relevance to us today.

The statue's elements are as follows:

- Head of gold (Nebuchadnezzar is the head—the "lion" in Daniel's vision)
- Chest and arms of silver (this is the Medo-Persian Empire—the "Bear")
- Middle and thighs of bronze (the Greek Empire—the "Leopard")
- Legs of iron (Roman Empire—the terrible fourth beast with ten horns; its fierce imagery continues with the toes of iron and clay)

- Toes of iron mixed with "miry clay" (continuation of Roman Empire into today's Euro-Amero-centric globe, led by the United States; and this may also represent an echo of the Roman Empire, which we'll cover in detail later).

Lastly, Daniel tells us that a stone uncut by human hands destroys the statue by striking at its hybrid feet, and that all the kingdoms become nothing more than chaff, which is blown away in the wind. After this, the uncut stone becomes a great mountain and fills the earth.

Wow! What a promise! Our Lord Jesus Christ is *the* Stone, and when He returns, He will destroy the Antichrist kingdom forever. Then, He'll fill the whole earth with His new, eternal kingdom.

As we've mentioned several times now, Daniel's prophecies help us understand what is happening in Revelation. This final kingdom, made from the hybrid toes, is a revived Roman Empire led by the Antichrist. But the LORD is returning to destroy it.

We may not yet know the identity of the "Man of Sin," but we can already see his kingdom as it takes shape. Globalism is led by human politicians and fallen angel spirits. It is a sickness built on sin and greed, a message that's being slickly packaged as "unity" and "common purpose," and pressed between the metaphorical pages of "bleeding-heart" causes that sound egalitarian and just, like "human rights," "global climate change," and "diversity."

But don't be fooled, dear friends. Platitudes and political promises are clever lures meant to entice us into joining the Antichrist's side.

The Beast's platform of peace and inclusion are but a pale and deception imitation of the TRUE CHRIST, the TRUE PEACE, the TRUE KINGDOM, which can only be found in Christ the LORD.

THE FOUR CORNERS OF THE EARTH

He will raise a signal for the nations
and will assemble the banished of Israel,
and gather the dispersed of Judah
from the four corners of the earth.

—ISAIAH 11:12

The "Four Corners" designation in ancient Mesopotamia refers to the extent of a king's reign. Many rulers laid claim to the title "king of the Four Corners": Naram-Sîn, Hammurabi, Tiglath-Pileser, Ashurnasirpal II, Sargon II, Sennacherib, Ashurbanipal, and Cyrus the Great, to name but a few. It's similar to the idea of ruling "the world island" to European monarchs. In other words, the more territory you control, the greater and safer you are.

Eventually, the Four Corners will include all the earth.

For the purposes of this chapter, we'll consider the Mesopotamian idea of the Four Corners. As with most of the book of Daniel, chapters 10 through 12 are foundational to Christian eschatology. Remembering that our current chapter-and-verse divisions didn't exist when these scrolls were written, we'll begin our study with chapter 10.

Daniel dates this vision to the third year of King Cyrus the Great, founder of the Achaemenid Empire. (Yes, that Cyrus, the one who would later give permission for the Jews to return to Israel. Therefore, this would be about two years after Ezra led the first group of exiles back to Jerusalem.)

The image below illustrates just how extensive the Achaemenid Empire actually was, and because Cyrus the Great claimed to be king of the Four Corners of the world, it's especially interesting that Daniel's vision specifically mentions contenders that arise from two of these cardinal points: North and South.

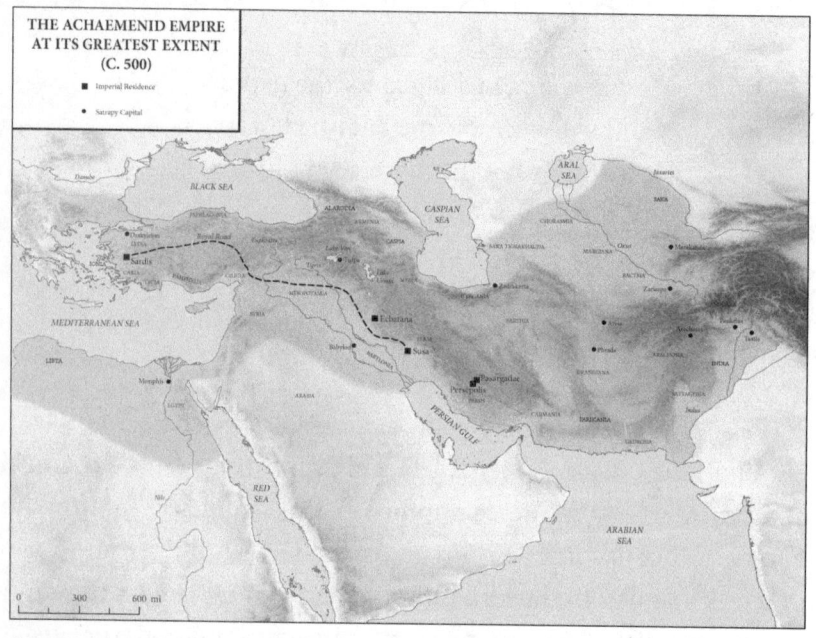

Controlling the World Island: The Persian or Achaemenid Empire at its height. (Image courtesy of Wikimedia.)

This vision begins just as Daniel has spent three weeks fasting and praying. With some of his people already in Jerusalem, it may be that Daniel sought enlightenment as to when the remainder might be given permission to return home. We find the prophet standing on the bank of the Tigris, and he dates the vision with great precision: Cyrus's third year—the twenty-fourth day of the first month.

Nisan is the first month, and Daniel may have been fasting because he had just celebrated the Passover, or it could be that he was fasting to seek God's wisdom. It's also possible that Daniel had been counting the Omer (the forty-nine days or "seven sevens" after the day of First Fruits). Regardless of the reason, Daniel is clearly praying earnestly seeking God— just as all of us should.

Verse 7 tells us that Daniel's not alone, for he mentions that his companions could not see the vision. This is how he describes this miraculous encounter with a heavenly messenger. It's a lengthy excerpt, but we'll interrupt the flow now and then to offer a comment. And when we've completed the quote, we'll take a close look at this very meaty section of prophetic Scripture and explain how it gives us clues to our present situation. All verses are from the English Standard Version, as we've quoted primarily from throughout the rest of the book, and the emphases are our own.

Beginning at Daniel 10:4:

On the twenty-fourth day of the first month, as I was standing on the bank of the great river (that is, the Tigris) I lifted up my eyes and looked, and behold, **a man clothed in linen, with a belt of fine gold from Uphaz around his waist. His body was like beryl, his face like the appearance of lightning, his eyes like flaming torches, his arms and legs like the gleam of burnished bronze, and the sound of his words like the sound of a multitude.** And I, Daniel, alone saw the vision, for the men who were with me did not see the vision, but a great trembling fell upon them, and they fled to hide themselves. So I was left alone and saw this great vision, and no strength was left in me. My radiant appearance was fearfully changed, and I retained no strength. Then I heard the sound of his words, and as I heard the sound of his words, I fell on my face in deep sleep with my face to the ground.

First of all, this otherworldly being is described as having the appearance of a man. The angels who visited Sodom had a human appearance, as have many other messengers sent by God. It might be that archangels, like Gabriel and Michael, were created with humanoid features (though they certainly have a magnificence which we presently lack), or perhaps *elohim* (citizens of the divine realm) must assume a human appearance when speaking to humans in the material world.

Regardless, this is an extraordinary entity. Note that his face is like lightning, his eyes are like flame, and his limbs are like bronze. All these elements indicate an inner glow, which is hardly earthly. Daniel is terrified, and indeed he falls to his knees and passes out with his face to the ground. The being, however, shows infinite compassion:

> And behold, a hand touched me and set me trembling on my hands and knees. And he said to me, "O **Daniel, man greatly loved**, understand the words that I speak to you, and stand upright, for now **I have been sent to you**."

The visitor has "been sent," indicating that he is not the Angel of the LORD (the preincarnate Christ), but a messenger sent by the LORD.

> And when he had spoken this word to me, I stood up trembling. Then he said to me, "Fear not, Daniel, for from the first day that you set your heart to understand and humbled yourself before your God, your words have been heard, and I have come because of your words. The prince of the kingdom of Persia withstood me twenty-one days, but Michael, one of the chief princes, came to help me, for I was left there with the kings of Persia, and came to make you understand what is to happen to your people in the latter days. For the vision is for days yet to come."

Here, we have a verse that clearly speaks of spiritual warfare. The angel sent by God is detained for three weeks by the "prince of the kingdom of Persia." The Hebrew word translated "prince" is *sar*. Gesenius defines this word as a "leader or commander," but in this usage, he insists it is "a prince" or "archangel" sent by God to intercede for a particular nation.

Compare this with the promise in Daniel 12:1, where we read, "At that time shall arise Michael, the great prince who has charge of your people." If the prince of Persia worked against God's representative in this case, then it implies an adversarial relationship between the two *elohim* or "angels," if you will. Hence, we see spiritual warfare. And the archangel Michael must be quite a warrior—perhaps, stronger than the Prince of Persia—for he was able to rescue his brother and allow him to fulfill his mission.

> When he had spoken to me according to these words, I turned my face toward the ground and was mute. And behold, **one in the likeness of the children of man touched my lips.** Then I opened my mouth and spoke. I said to him who stood before me, "O my lord, by reason of the vision pains have come upon me, and I retain no strength. How can my lord's servant talk with my lord? For now no strength remains in me, and no breath is left in me."

Again, Daniel reminds us that this heavenly being looks like a human, but seeing such a radiant image is terrifying.

> Again **one having the appearance of a man** touched me and strengthened me. And he said, "**O man greatly loved,** fear not, peace be with you; be strong and of good courage." And as he spoke to me, I was strengthened and said, "Let my lord speak, for you have strengthened me." Then he said, "Do you know why I have come to you? But now I will return to fight against the prince of Persia; and when I go out, behold, the prince of Greece will come. But **I will tell you what is inscribed in the book of truth: there is none who contends by my side against these except Michael, your prince.**

Daniel is greeted as a "man greatly loved." How comforting are these words! This terrifying being (possibly Gabriel), though he is in the general conformation of a human, shines like a flaming fire; yet, he takes the time to speak these loving words. He also mentions that he must return to relieve Michael as soon as he's delivered the prophecy to Daniel. Remember, the spirits of the Nephilim giants (i.e., demons) are still with us, but also the seventy sons or *elohim* placed in charge of the nations are also here, and this "Prince of Persia" might be one of the latter.

The angel also mentions a tantalizing object: The Book of Truth. Just what might this be? We know that when the judgments commence in the final days (both the bema seat and the great white throne), books will be opened, but what might this be? The apostle John is given a "little book" in Revelation 10, which tastes like honey in his mouth but is bitter in his stomach. What is the Book of Truth?

The two words translated here are *kathab 'emeth*, which refer to written instructions or edicts of truth or faithfulness. Might there be a heavenly book that contains God's pronouncements? It's a theme Sharon explores in *The Redwing Saga* using a book called the *Sefer Raziel*, a collection of God's spoken words as inscribed by a recording angel—in this case, Raziel. The book is referred to in ancient Jewish writings, many of them somewhat mystical, but there appears to be some basis for the idea of heavenly books.

The story continues in chapter 11. Again, this is the ESV translation, and all emphases are our own.

And as for me, in the first year of Darius the Mede, I stood up to confirm and strengthen him. [NOTE: Remember, there were no chapter divisions in the original scrolls, so this is actually a continuation of 10:21; therefore, it can be assumed here that "him" means the archangel Michael.] And now I will show you the truth. Behold, three more kings shall arise in Persia, and a fourth shall be far richer than all of them. And when he has become strong through his riches, he shall stir up all against the kingdom of Greece. Then a mighty king [Alexander the Great] shall arise, who shall rule with great dominion and do as he wills. And as soon as he has arisen, his kingdom shall be broken and **divided toward the four winds of heaven, but not to his posterity**, nor according to the authority with which he ruled, for his kingdom shall be plucked up and go to others besides these. [Alexander died at age thirty-two with no heir, and his empire was divided among his generals; see below for more.]

Now, let's see if we can unravel some of these verses. First of all, as we mention in our note above, the angel (possibly Gabriel) refers to an earlier time, when he assisted Michael, indicating the ongoing spiritual war. Remember, that whatever happens in the natural world is very likely to be a consequence caused by events in the supernatural world.

The messenger tells Daniel that a fourth king of Persia would arise who would outshine them all. This was fulfilled in the person of Xerxes the Great, son of Darius I and Cyrus the Great's daughter, Atossa, who dared to invade Greece and Sparta. Anyone who's seen Frank Miller's 2006 film *300* is now picturing the moment when Xerxes and his army of "Immortals" challenge Leonidas's tiny force of Spartans at the narrow pass of Thermopylae. The movie portrays Xerxes as almost supernatural in form and size—practically one of the Nephilim, wearing lots of jewels and a nose ring—but it is a visual representation of his loyalties in the spirit realm. Xerxes rose to power, at least in part, because of his devotion to the gods. Known as the "King of Kings" of the Persians, he worshiped Ahura Mazda, the creator deity of the Zoroastrianism religion.

By attacking Greece, Xerxes feeds the vengeful desires of a future prince: none other than Alexander, son of King Philip II, who would march his men across the Four Corners region until he became the first king of Asia.

Alexander died in June of 323 BC, at the age of just thirty-two years, leaving no heir. His empire was then divided amongst his four generals, becoming the Ptolemaic (called the "king of the south" in Daniel), Seleucid (the north), Pergamon, and Macedonian empires.

Now, continuing with the prophecy:

> Then the king of the south [Ptolemy] shall be strong, but one of his princes shall be stronger than he and shall rule, and his authority shall be a great authority. After some years they shall make an alliance, and **the daughter of the king of the south shall come to the king of the north to make an agreement.**

This happened when Antiochus II, a Seleucid, married Berenice, the daughter of Ptolemy II.

> But she shall not retain the strength of her arm, and he and his arm shall not endure, but she shall be given up, and her attendants, he who fathered her, and he who supported her in those times.

After Ptolemy II died, Antiochus II divorced Berenice in favor of his former wife, ruthless Laodice, who was reputed to be quite a schemer. In fact, Queen Laodice was such a schemer that she devised a joint plan to poison her husband in Asia Minor while her co-conspirators murdered Berenice and her infant son in Antioch. Then Laodice placed *her* son, Seleucus II, on the throne. Nice family.

This remarkable and very detailed prophecy goes on:

> And from a **branch from her roots one shall arise** in his place. He shall come against the army and enter the fortress of the king of the north, and he shall deal with them and shall prevail. He shall also carry off to Egypt their gods with their metal images and their precious vessels of silver and gold, and for some years he shall refrain from attacking the king of the north. Then the latter shall come into the realm of the king of the south but shall return to his own land.

The branch of Berenice's roots is Ptolemy III, her brother, who invaded Syria to avenge his sister's murder. It's starting to sound a bit like a soap opera now, isn't it?

> His sons [of the northern king] shall wage war and assemble a multitude of great forces, which shall keep coming and overflow and pass through, and again shall carry the war as far as his fortress. Then the king of the south, moved with rage, shall come out and fight against the king of the north. And he shall raise a great multitude, but it shall be given into his hand. And when the multitude is taken away, his heart shall be exalted, and he shall cast down tens of thousands, but he shall not prevail. For the king of the north shall again raise a multitude, greater than the first. And after some years he shall come on with a great army and abundant supplies.

Here, we see the fine details of the six Syrian Wars, as waged by the Seleucids against the Ptolemies.

> In those times many shall rise against the king of the south, and the violent among your own people shall lift themselves up in order to fulfill the vision, but they shall fail. Then the king of the north shall come and throw up siege works and take a well-fortified city. And the forces of the south shall not stand, or even his best troops, for there shall be no strength to stand. But he who comes against him shall do as he wills, and none shall stand before him. And he shall stand in the glorious land, with destruction in his hand.
> He shall set his face to come with the strength of his whole kingdom, and he shall bring terms of an agreement and perform them. **He shall give him the daughter of women to destroy the kingdom,** but it shall not stand or be to his advantage.

In 195 BC, Antiochus III gave his daughter Cleopatra to Ptolemy V of Egypt, and she became the first Syrian queen of Egypt. Antiochus, "king of the north," did this hoping to gain permanent influence, and eventually control, in Egypt. To the great disappointment of Antiochus III, the plan did not succeed because Cleopatra was unfaithful.

By the way, this Cleopatra is but the first in a long line of princesses with the same name. The famous Cleopatra who loved Mark Antony ruled about a hundred years after this one.

Afterward **he shall turn his face to the coastlands** and shall capture many of them, but **a commander shall put an end to his insolence.** Indeed, he shall turn his insolence back upon him. Then he shall turn his face back toward the fortresses of his own land, but he shall stumble and fall, and shall not be found.

Antiochus III invaded Asia Minor and Greece, receiving help from Hannibal, the infamous Carthaginian general. But this northern king's success was short lived, for another famous general, the Roman Lucius Cornelius Scipio, defeated Antiochus in Greece. So, tucking his metaphorical tail twixt his legs, Antiochus III returned to his home base, having lost nearly all that he'd gained, dying shortly after, killed by a mob of local citizens.

Then shall arise in his place one who shall send an **exactor of tribute** [referring to Seleucus III, who raises taxes—war is expensive] for the glory of the kingdom. But within a few days he shall be broken, neither in anger nor in battle. [Seleucus III was assassinated.] In his place shall arise a contemptible person [Antiochus IV, called Epiphanes] to whom royal majesty has not been given. He shall come in without warning and obtain the kingdom by flatteries.

According to Adam Clarke's 1831 Bible commentary,[41] Antiochus:

...flattered Eumenes, king of Pergamus, and Attalus his brother, and got their assistance. He flattered the Romans, and sent ambassadors to court their favour, and pay them the arrears of the tribute. He flattered the Syrians, and gained their concurrence.

We will stop here, but you get the point. Every prophecy given to Daniel regarding the coming Gentile rulers came true—right down to the intrigues and schemes. But this begs the question: Since God's prophecies to Daniel and others are often somewhat generic in scope, why is this one so very specific?

Daniel didn't live to see most of this happen, which means it wasn't to convince him of the words' authenticity. He didn't know Xerxes or Alexander or Ptolemy. Yet, he faithfully wrote all of the angel's words for us.

Perhaps that is why this section contains such fine detail, so that history could record immediate or very soon fulfillment of parts of it—making the portions not yet fulfilled reliable and truthful.

All that occurs in our natural world has a source in the spirit world. The archons who direct the actions of the generals and foot soldiers in the Fallen Realm's demonic army looked upon Jerusalem with envious eyes and wanted to destroy the Temple and control the Mount.

The devil and his minions are fully aware of all prophecy, but even they don't completely understand *when* God's promises will be fulfilled. Seeing any chance, they can't help rushing in to desecrate God's Holy of Holies. We see this throughout the prophecies of the Gentile nations that have ruled and continue to oversee matters within Israel.

But God allows the fallen realm only so much rope before He yanks it taught and strangles their efforts. Antiochus Epiphanes *almost* fulfilled the prophecy of Daniel 11, but not completely. Remember that he set up a statue of Zeus—not a statue of Antiochus, but the Greeks' chief deity. When the future Antichrist does arise, he will set up an image of himself as the god in the Temple, and he will command that all the world should worship *him*—not Zeus.

As we near the return of the True Christ, our world is becoming more and more paganized, and it won't take much of a push to convince many to worship a prideful "god" who pretends to be inclusive and generous. The Antichrist may even claim that he is Zeus, or Odin, or any number of ancient deities. He might convince the world that he fulfills *all* end-times prophecies, no matter the origin, no matter the nation.

The language of the angel in Daniel 11:40 is explicit; he tells us that:

> At the time of the end, the king of the south shall attack him, but the king of the north shall rush upon him like a whirlwind, with chariots and horsemen, and with many ships. And he shall come into countries and shall overflow and pass through.

"The time of the end" refers to the very last days of God's prophetic timeline, and as we write this book, it is in our future—but probably our immediate future. Perhaps, this verse means that we will see a revision of the Syrian Wars: the king of the North versus the king of the South. If so, then expect to see Rome—or rather the revived Roman Empire—become involved again. And if we're right in our theory that the hybrid toes of iron and miry clay in the king's statue dream of Daniel 2 refer to those countries inspired and populated by "Rome," then the US and England will most likely enter a Middle East war very soon.

Or maybe we've been there for years waging a proxy war. This future war might even be cyber.

But there are clues, if you know where to look.

Those paying attention to news from the Middle East have noticed that Turkey's President Recep Tayyip Erdogan is attempting to restore the Ottoman Empire to its former glory, with himself as the new caliph. Syria is suffering from a crippling internal war and sees Turkey as an enemy. The internationally recognized government in the chaotic, failed state of Libya has just asked Egypt to come to its aid to fend off hegemonial advances from Turkey; all of this is happening as Israel claims sovereignty over the Golan Heights.

This last is important, because the Golan includes the fertile area at the foot of Mount Hermon, as well as a huge necropolis of ancient dolmans. These stone markers once served a part in rituals involving the Avarim, or "Travelers," of the underworld.

As with the kings and queens of the Syrian Wars, the Fallen Realm are staking claims to Bible lands and lining up both their human and spirit armies in preparation for one last invasion of the "glorious land."

The book of Daniel is central to understanding end-times prophecy and the plans of the giants, whom we now battle as demons; the small-*g* gods, those fallen spirits once worshiped by adulterous Israel and her neighbors; and the dragons, an upper-echelon class of *elohim* that probably includes the *nachash* and archons, who rule over the lessers in the spirit realm.

Is it any wonder that the Fallen Realm dispatched the prince of Persia to prevent the angel (possibly Gabriel) from delivering such a vital message? You can just picture the battle that must have ensued! Gabriel against the archon of Persia, swords clashing in multiple dimensions—a battle that continued for twenty-one days in the natural realm but may have lasted much longer in the supernatural domain. Only Michael's arrival allowed Gabriel to complete his mission. And after doing so, the angel returned to relieve Michael, called the "prince of Israel."

And every almost word of the prophecy has been fulfilled—to the letter. Those that haven't yet found fulfillment await the arrival of the Man of Sin.

Daniel had been praying for wisdom regarding the ending of his people's banishment from the land of Israel. Seventy years had been decreed, and the prophet realized this period was nearing its end. Therefore, the opening of Daniel 12:1 presents tantalizing clues as to when the "times of the Gentiles" would finally be concluded, and it's a thrilling, action-packed portion of Scripture, worthy of any hero film:

At that time shall arise Michael, the great prince who has charge of your people. And there shall be a time of trouble, such as never has been since there was a nation till that time. But at that time your people shall be delivered, everyone whose name shall be found written in the book. And many of those who sleep in the dust of the earth shall awake, some to everlasting life, and some to shame and everlasting contempt. And those who are wise shall shine like the brightness of the sky above; and those who turn many to righteousness, like the stars forever and ever. But you, Daniel, shut up the words and seal the book, until the time of the end. Many shall run to and fro, and knowledge shall increase.

Then I, Daniel, looked, and behold, two others stood, one on this bank of the stream and one on that bank of the stream. And someone said to the man clothed in linen, who was above the waters of the stream, "**How long shall it be till the end of these wonders?**" And I heard the man clothed in linen, who was above the waters of the stream; he raised his right hand and his left hand toward heaven and swore by him who lives forever that it would be for **a time, times, and half a time**, and that when the shattering of the power of the holy people comes to an end all these things would be finished. I heard, but I did not understand. Then I said, "O my lord, what shall be the outcome of these things?" He said, "Go your way, Daniel, for the words are shut up and sealed until the time of the end. Many shall purify themselves and make themselves white and be refined, but the wicked shall act wickedly. And none of the wicked shall understand, but those who are wise shall understand. And from the time that the regular burnt offering is taken away and the abomination that makes desolate is set up, there shall be 1,290 days. Blessed is he who waits and arrives at the 1,335 days. But go your way till the end. And you shall rest and shall stand in your allotted place at the end of the days.

PART III

UNVEILING THE FUTURE AND THE END OF TIME

They have as king over them the angel of the bottomless pit.
His name in Hebrew is Abaddon,
and in Greek he is called Apollyon.

—REVELATION 9:11

And I saw a beast rising out of the sea,
with ten horns and seven heads,
with ten diadems on its horns and blasphemous
names on its heads.

—REVELATION 13:1

"And this spell, as you call it, will unlock some doorway? Is that it?" asked Salter, his hands trembling.

"Not only a doorway, but a sealed portal. I shall speak the words, and the Stone King and his mighty Dragon will arise once more to set the world aflame."

—SHARON K. GILBERT, *REALMS OF FIRE*, CHAPTER 22

THE SEVEN SEALS

And one of the elders said to me, "Weep no more; behold, the Lion of the tribe of Judah, the Root of David, has conquered, so that he can open the scroll and its seven seals."
—REVELATION 5:5

And now, we leave Daniel to follow the promises given to John in the latter part of the first century AD, *Anno Domini*, the "Year of Our Lord." Daniel longed for the day when his people would no longer be under the control of Gentiles, and he prayed that he'd see the conclusion of their seventy-tear exile, but to his shock, was told that the sentence had been multiplied by another seven, on account of continued sin.

Since that time, Christ has been born, lived, and died—but He also arose! Hallelujah! The empty tomb is proof of His identity as God Incarnate. The Avarim and Rephaim may hope to arise from their dusty graves, but God's word promises this:

They are dead, they shall not live; they are deceased, they shall not rise. (Isaiah 26:14, KJV)

Christ has inherited the earth as His kingdom, and those shining dragons, the small-*g* gods and demons, and all the Watchers of Enoch's day have an appointment with judgment in the divine assembly. And they will never control the earth again.

Most prophecy students love the book of Revelation, Sharon began studying it at just nine years old and hasn't stopped since. But even she admits that humans cannot understand all of the prophecies within its pages this side of heaven. Why? Because God Almighty is the greatest General in the entirety of Creation, and He reveals His plans couched in coded language.

Due to this, we humans differ on many aspects of eschatology (the study of end times). Some are pre-Trib, while others are mid- or post-Trib. Some believe all prophecy has been fulfilled and call themselves preterists, while others say we've not yet experienced the final things, and that the millennial reign lies before us.

For the record, we are staunchly premillennial, but only *mostly* pretribulational regarding the timing of the Rapture. Why do we say "mostly"? Because we see that pivotal moment when the Church is raptured to heaven as happening very soon, but believe its timing is shrouded in some of that coded language. We therefore leave it to the Lord's timing, rather than our own. However, we look for Him at any moment.

Since the focus of this book is to examine the spirits behind world events, especially as regards prophecy, let's look at some of the most tantalizingly mysterious beings in all of the Bible: the Four Horsemen of the Apocalypse.

The word "apocalypse" is merely the transliteration into English of the Greek word *apocalypsis*, meaning "unveiling." We get "Revelation" from the Latinized form. But before we discuss the infamous riders of Revelation 6, we need context. Why are they riding? On whose authority? What kind of document are these seals attached to, and why is it important?

Revelation 5 opens with God sitting on His throne, holding a document in His right hand:

Then I saw in the right hand of him who was seated on the throne a scroll written within and on the back, sealed with seven seals. And I saw a mighty angel proclaiming with a loud voice, "Who is worthy to open the scroll and break its seals?" And no one in heaven or on earth or under the earth was able to open the scroll or to look into it, and I began to weep loudly because no one was found worthy to open the scroll or to look into it. And one of the elders said to me, "Weep no more; behold, the Lion of the tribe of Judah, the Root of David, has conquered, so that he can open the scroll and its seven seals." (Revelation 5:1–5)

We can guess pretty easily who John meant by those in heaven or on earth—presumably, the prophet was talking about humans in the natural realm and the spirits in heaven. But who are those who exist "under the earth"?

Satan comes to mind, and it should be obvious why he wasn't considered worthy. However, to the ancient world mind, there were other inhabitants of the spirit realm believed to occupy the space under the earth. John isn't specific in identifying who, exactly, is under the earth, but it's our view that these are the Rephaim spirits who plagued Israel at least from the time of Moses and probably much earlier.

Isaiah depicts them as kings of a bygone era now confined to Sheol, marveling that the rebel from Eden has been humbled like them.

Sheol beneath is stirred up
to meet you when you come;
it rouses the shades [the *Rephaim*] to greet you,
all who were leaders of the earth;
 it raises from their thrones
all who were kings of the nations.
All of them will answer
and say to you:

"You too have become as weak as we!
You have become like us!"
Your pomp is brought down to Sheol,
the sound of your harps;
maggots are laid as a bed beneath you,
and worms are your covers. (Isaiah 14:9–11)

In his lamentation over the king of Egypt, Ezekiel depicts these long-dead leaders of the earth as denizens of the netherworld, although they appear to occupy a place of honor, separate from the run-of-the-mill dead:

They shall fall amid those who are slain by the sword. Egypt is delivered to the sword; drag her away, and all her multitudes. **The mighty chiefs shall speak of them, with their helpers, out of the midst of Sheol**: "They have come down, they lie still, the uncircumcised, slain by the sword."…

And they do not lie with the mighty, the fallen from among the uncircumcised, who went down to Sheol with their weapons of war, whose swords were laid under their heads, and whose iniquities are upon their bones; for the terror of the mighty men was in the land of the living. (Ezekiel 32:20–21, 27; emphasis added)

The term "mighty chiefs" in verse 21 is derived from the Hebrew *'êlê gibbōrîm*. They're located in the "midst of Sheol"; this is apparently a position of status, since the graves of the hated Assyrians "are set in the uttermost parts of the pit." These mighty *'êlê* appear to be the underworld small-*g* gods, venerated by the pagan neighbors of ancient Israel, called in the Ugaritic dialect the *ilm ars* ("gods of the earth"). This is confirmed by the Septuagint translation, which shows that Jewish religious scholars, three hundred years before the birth of Jesus, connected the "mighty chiefs" with the legendary giants of old, the Rephaim (i.e., the spirits of the ancient giants, the Nephilim):

And the giants will say to you, "Come in the depth of clamor! Than whom are you mightier? And descend and sleep with the uncircumcised in the midst of those wounded by swords!" (Ezekiel 32:21, Lexham English Septuagint)

Verse 27 is even more interesting. The first portion reads thus in Hebrew:

Chz velo yishkevu et-gibborim, **nofelim** *me'arelim, asher yaredu-she'ol bichlei-milchamtam...* (Emphasis added)

Some scholars believe that *nofelim* ("the fallen") has a mispointed vowel and should read *nephilim* instead. That would transform the phrase into this:

They do not lie with the uncircumcised mighty ones, the Nephilim, who went down to Sheol with their weapons of war... (Emphasis added)

Once again, the translators of the Septuagint had this connection in mind:

And they were laid with the giants, who had fallen long ago, who descended into Hades with weapons of war... (Ezekiel 32:27, Lexham English Septuagint; emphasis added)

The "mighty chiefs" of verse 21 and the "mighty" of verse 27 are linked in Ezekiel's mind with the ancient giants of Genesis 6, the Nephilim, who, after death, became the Rephaim spirits venerated by the pagan Amorites of Canaan. In turn, as we demonstrated in our book *Veneration* and in Derek's previous book, *Last Clash of the Titans,* the Rephaim of Canaan became the ἥρως, transliterated as *heros,* of Greek religion—demigods like Herakles, Theseus, Perseus, and Dionysus.

This identification was well known to Jews of the first century AD, who'd been living in a world dominated by Greek and Roman religion and philosophy for about four hundred years by the time John wrote the book of Revelation. In addition, John was clearly familiar with the prophecies of Ezekiel; the destruction of Babylon the Great in Revelation 18 draws on the prophecy of the destruction of Tyre in Ezekiel 27. And since Ezekiel 28's condemnation of the prince of Tyre is a parallel to Isaiah 14's taunt of the king of Babylon, it's clear that John knew the prophecies of Isaiah, too.

We've written elsewhere at length about the origin of demons, especially in our book *Veneration*. It was understood by the Jews of Jesus' day that demons were the spirits of the Nephilim who'd been destroyed in Noah's Flood. This is described in the non-canonical book of I Enoch, which is alluded to in the New Testament by Peter and Jude (and quoted by Jude). This was the belief among leading early church theologians such as Irenaeus, Origen, Clement of Alexandria, Tertullian, Justin Martyr, Commodian, Lactantius, and Sulpicius Severus; in fact, it was the consensus among Christians until Augustine put forward his arguments in favor of the Sethite view—the idea that righteous male descendants of Seth were corrupted by wicked women of the line of Cain.

Now, just how the union of two human lineages produced giants is still unclear, but the Sethite view is the standard teaching on Genesis 6:1–4 in seminaries today, so that's probably what you've heard from the pulpit (if you've heard those verses preached at all!).

It's too bad; for as we show in *Veneration*, the demons created by the unions of angels and humans play a much larger role in Christian theology and end-times prophecy than we've been taught.

However, the point here is not that John wrote specifically about the destruction of demons, but to demonstrate that even what may appear to be a throwaway line in Revelation 5:3 ("under the earth") *was based on John's understanding of the spirit realm*. Under the earth is where the demonic Rephaim lived, those who were worshiped as gods by the pagan

Amorites, Canaanites, Phoenicians, Greeks, and Romans. And contrary to what most people in John's day thought of Herakles (known as Melqart to the Phoenicians), Dionysus, or the healing demigod Asclepius, not one of them was found worthy to open the scroll.

Continuing in Revelation 5, we encounter more supernatural entities that we need to discuss:

> And between the throne and the four living creatures and among the elders I saw a Lamb standing, as though it had been slain, with seven horns and with seven eyes, which are the seven spirits of God sent out into all the earth. (Revelation 5:6)

The Lamb is obviously Jesus Himself, newly arrived in heaven. The concept of the Messiah as a sacrificial lamb was first expressed by Isaiah, who described God's anointed one as "a lamb led to slaughter." This is expressed numerous times in the New Testament, most directly by John the Baptist, who said, "Behold, the Lamb of God, who takes away the sin of the world!" (John 1:29).

The seven horns and seven eyes represent power and wisdom. The seven spirits of God are mentioned earlier, in Revelation 1:4 and 4:5. Interestingly, these seven spirits are actually named in the Messianic prophecy of Isaiah 11:

> There shall come forth a shoot from the stump of Jesse,
> and a branch from his roots shall bear fruit.
> And the **Spirit of the** Lord shall rest upon him,
> the Spirit of **wisdom** and **understanding,**
> the Spirit of **counsel** and **might,**
> the Spirit of **knowledge** and the **fear of the** Lord. (Isaiah 11:1–2;
>   emphasis added)

These seven spirits are also hinted at in the prophecy of Zechariah:

And the angel who talked with me came again and woke me, like a man who is awakened out of his sleep. And he said to me, "What do you see?" I said, "I see, and behold, a lampstand all of gold, with a bowl on the top of it, and seven lamps on it, with seven lips on each of the lamps that are on the top of it….

"These seven are the eyes of the LORD, which range through the whole earth." (Zechariah 4:1–2; 10b)

The question is whether these spirits represent God's omnipresence and omniscience—being everywhere and knowing everything—or if they're angelic beings tasked with watching over humanity and reporting back on what they observe. This second interpretation is hinted at in the Divine Council scenes of Job 1 and 2, where Satan tells the LORD that he's back from "going to and fro on the earth, and from walking up and down on it."

More relevant to our study here, Zechariah is shown a *vision of horsemen* who report that "we have patrolled the earth, and all the earth remains at rest." We'll examine the horsemen of Zechariah more closely in an upcoming chapter.

The "four living creatures" are another call-back to Ezekiel, this time to chapter 1 and the famous vision of the wheels within wheels that modern UFO enthusiasts like to mischaracterize as alien spaceships:

As I looked, behold, a stormy wind came out of the north, and a great cloud, with brightness around it, and fire flashing forth continually, and in the midst of the fire, as it were gleaming metal. And from the midst of it came the likeness of four living creatures. And this was their appearance: they had a human likeness, but each had four faces, and each of them had four wings. Their legs were straight, and the soles of their feet were like the sole of a calf's foot. And they sparkled like burnished bronze. Under their wings on their four sides they had human hands. And the four had their faces and their wings thus: their wings touched one another. Each one of them went straight forward, without turning as they went. As for the likeness of their faces, each had a human face. The four had the face of a lion on the right side, the four had the face of an ox on the left side, and the four had the face of an eagle. (Ezekiel 1:4–10)

These creatures return in Ezekiel 10, but described in a slightly different way:

And every one had four faces: the first face was the face of the cherub, and the second face was a human face, and the third the face of a lion, and the fourth the face of an eagle. (Ezekiel 10:14)

As you've guessed by now, these creatures were cherubim. They were the throne guardians of the ancient world, and anyone reading Ezekiel's description of his vision in the sixth century BC would have known immediately what he'd seen—a heavenly throne, not a flying saucer.

The one difference in the descriptions of the creatures is in the faces: Ezekiel equates the face of an ox in chapter 1 with the face of a cherub in chapter 10. The other three faces—human, lion, eagle—are mentioned in both chapters. In other words, the face of the cherub was bull-like, which means those classical paintings depicting cherubs as chubby babies with wings could not be more wrong!

Cherubim stood guard at the entrance to Eden. Their wings shadowed the mercy seat on the Ark of the Covenant, upon which God was enthroned when He spoke to Moses in the tent of meeting. Two cherubim of olive wood, each fifteen feet tall and with a fifteen-foot wingspan, stood side by side in the inner sanctuary, with their outspread wings spanning the width of the chamber, touching in the middle—guarding the very throne of God.

This is not a job for pudgy infants, winged or not. Cherubim are dangerous creatures who probably look like winged, bull-like sphinxes. You wouldn't dare try to get past them to approach God Almighty without receiving permission—which speaks to the status of the Lamb in Revelation 5. He stands *between* the throne and the cherubim, at the right hand of God, a position of supreme authority that confirms His status as the Messiah and His identity as Jesus.

The twenty-four elders with Him are a bit of a mystery. Their identity is unclear. They may represent the tribes of Israel and the twelve apostles, but that's still debated, even after two thousand years. However, from the context, it appears that the elders are angels. When Jesus took the scroll from the right hand of God, they "sang a new song":

> Worthy are you to take the scroll
>   and to open its seals,
> for you were slain,
>   and by your blood you ransomed people for God
>   from every tribe and language and people and nation,
> and **you have made them** a kingdom and priests to our God,
> and **they shall reign** on the earth. (Revelation 5:9–10; emphasis added)

It seems logical that if the elders were the souls of humans, they'd sing, "You have made *us* a kingdom and priests to our God, and *we* shall reign on the earth."

To be fair, that's exactly how the King James Version is translated. However, the elders are singing alongside the four cherubim, who are clearly *not* human, and thus not ransomed by Christ's blood. Since the cherubim could not sing "us," it follows that the correct translation would be as we've shown above, using the English Standard Version. Hebrews 2:14–17 makes it clear that Jesus died to redeem humanity, not the angels. No, the twenty-four elders are counted among the "ministering spirits sent out to serve for the sake of those who are to inherit salvation."

Now, let's turn our attention to the two most important figures in Revelation 5—the One seated on the throne and the Lamb who arrives in verse 6. Clearly, John was describing God the Father and Jesus the Messiah. And the arrival of the Lamb in the throne room of God is an important clue to the timing of the opening of the seals and the ride of the Four Horsemen.

A futurist view of prophecy, which is that the end-times events foretold in the Bible haven't happened yet, would typically be that the seven seals of Revelation chapter 6 have yet to be opened. That seems to make sense; after all, you'd think that events worthy of being described in the book of Revelation would be so big that they'd be impossible to miss.

But John is caught up to heaven in time to see the mighty angel ask, "Who is worthy to open the scroll and break its seals?" Enough time has passed since the Resurrection so that no one in heaven, on the earth, or under the earth is deemed worthy to break the seals and reveal the contents of the scroll. Then, in Revelation 5:6, a Lamb that looks "as though it had been slain" appears between the throne and the four living creatures—i.e., Jesus arriving in heaven after the Resurrection.

If we are still waiting for the first seal to be opened, then nearly two thousand years have passed with no one in heaven knowing where to find the Messiah! Does that seem logical? No, it does not. Especially when the Bible plainly tells us that Jesus, the Lamb, was at the right hand of God decades before John wrote Revelation.

So then the Lord Jesus, after he had spoken to them, was taken up into heaven and sat down at the right hand of God. (Mark 16:19)

But [Stephen], full of the Holy Spirit, gazed into heaven and saw the glory of God, and Jesus standing at the right hand of God. (Acts 7:55)

If then you have been raised with Christ, seek the things that are above, where Christ is, seated at the right hand of God. (Colossians 3:1)

He is the radiance of the glory of God and the exact imprint of his nature, and he upholds the universe by the word of his power. After making purification for sins, he sat down at the right hand of the Majesty on high. (Hebrews 1:3)

Jesus Christ, who has gone into heaven and is at the right hand of God, with angels, authorities, and powers having been subjected to him. (1 Peter 3:21b–22)

Clearly, Jesus was in the throne room of God by about AD 35, when Stephen was martyred—more than fifty years before John was exiled to the island of Patmos.

Our view is not typical of futurists. We believe that Revelation 5 shows us that Jesus took the scroll upon His arrival in heaven, forty days after the Resurrection, in or around AD 32. Therefore, the most logical interpretation of history is that He began opening the seals immediately after taking the scroll from the right hand of God.

It's our belief that the Four Horsemen of the Apocalypse are riding now. In fact, they've most likely been loose in the world for nearly two thousand years, their effects felt by humans in waves of growing intensity.

Now, at this point, it would be understandable if you asked, "Why would God allow such destructive forces to run loose on the earth?" The fact is that the Bible shows us He's done such a thing before. Flip back to Genesis 11 in your Bible.

The first nine verses of that chapter describe the odd story of the Tower of Babel. As we explained in an earlier chapter, God's judgment against the people of Sumer for building the Tower wasn't to teach them a lesson about pride. Nor were the people of ancient Sumer primitive rubes who thought they could somehow build a structure that would literally reach into heaven. It's a good bet that people five thousand years ago had already figured out that you couldn't stack mud bricks high enough to reach the throne of God.

No, the answer is simpler. Babel was built as an artificial mountain, meant to be an "abode of the gods." Not surprisingly, the name is based on the Akkadian words *bab* + *ilu*, meaning "gate of God" or, more likely, "gate of the gods."

And archaeological evidence points not to Babylon, but to the ancient temple of the god Enki at Eridu, which the Sumerians believed was their oldest city,[42] as the location of Babel. The temple was called the *E-Abzu*, or "House of the Abyss." It was a ziggurat, and the oldest and largest Sumerian ziggurat ever found by archaeologists.

The time frame for the construction of the Tower was almost certainly what scholars called the Uruk period, between about 4000 and 3100 BC, when the Sumerian city-state controlled the Fertile Crescent from the Persian Gulf to what is now southern Turkey. Nimrod was the second king of Uruk—spelled *Erech* in the Bible—after the Flood of Noah, just as the Sumerian King List records a man called Enmerkar as the second king of Uruk, after "the flood had swept over."[43]

Enmerkar is remembered as the greatest epic hero in Sumerian history, excepting only Gilgamesh. Enmerkar's conflict with the neighboring kingdom of Aratta is preserved in an epic poem that contains the main points of the Babel story, including the confusion of languages.[44]

What's even more interesting, however, is that archaeologists who excavated at Eridu in 1946 found that the period of Uruk's dominance ended in a truly biblical way:

This was the situation at Eridu during the first half of the Uruk period, which appears to have been brought to a conclusion by no less an event than the total abandonment of the site.... In what appears to have been an almost incredibly short time, drifting sand had filled the deserted buildings of the temple-complex and obliterated all traces of the once prosperous little community.[45]

Hmm. What could have caused "the total abandonment of the site"?

So the LORD dispersed them from there over the face of all the earth, and they left off building the city. (Genesis 11:8)

But that wasn't the end of it. Not by a longshot.

The consequences of the rebellion at Babel were immediate and intense. Not only did Yahweh scatter the people "over the face of all the earth," He told humanity that we'd have to deal with His subordinates—the lesser *elohim*—from then on.

It's not immediately obvious in the text of Genesis, but Moses reminded the Israelites of what went down in the aftermath of Yahweh's divine intervention at Babel:

When the Most High gave to
the nations their inheritance,
when he divided mankind,
he fixed the borders of the peoples
according to the number of the sons of God.
(Deuteronomy 32:8)

Most English translations render the last words of that verse "sons of Israel." The translators of the English Standard Version, who followed existing copies of the Septuagint and the texts of Deuteronomy found among the Dead Sea Scrolls, rendered it "sons of God."

But on logic alone, "sons of God" makes more sense. Israel wasn't around when God divided mankind after Babel. Jacob, whose name was changed to "Israel" by God, wouldn't be born for at least another fifteen hundred years.

Why does it matter? Because, after the sin of Babel, God gave us—fallen humanity—just what we wanted: access to the small-*g* gods. But He warned Moses that these gods were not to be worshiped by the children of Israel.

And beware lest you raise your eyes to heaven, and when you see the sun and the moon and the stars, all the host of heaven, you be drawn away and bow down to them and serve them, things that the LORD your God has allotted to all the peoples under the whole heaven. (Deuteronomy 4:19)

After Babel, the world was divided ethnically, geographically, and spiritually "according to the number of the sons of God," and those sons of God, spirit beings we generally call angels, were given the responsibility of overseeing God's precious creation, humanity.

This was not a reward. This was punishment. Those angels chose to set themselves up as gods in their own right, and this led to many of the conflicts we read in the Bible as these rebellious spirits inspired their human followers to try to destroy Israel—the people of God who are reserved as *His* allotted heritage.

The *bene ha'elohim* failed God's test. And because of their sin, He has judged them and passed sentence:

God has taken his place in the divine council;
in the midst of the gods he holds judgment:
"How long will you judge unjustly
and show partiality to the wicked?" *Selah*...
I said, "You are gods,
sons of the Most High, all of you;
nevertheless, like men you shall die,
and fall like any prince."
Arise, O God, judge the earth;
for you shall inherit all the nations! (Psalm 82:1–2, 6–8)

The judgment that is coming to the earth on the Day of the Lord is not just against an unbelieving world of humans, it is also for those sons of God who abused the responsibility that He delegated to them.

So, you see, setting loose the Four Horsemen of the Apocalypse—freeing rebellious and destructive spirits on the earth—is not without precedent. Nor is it the first time God has used war, famine, and pestilence to convince people to change their ways. Although Jeremiah didn't write about supernatural horsemen *per se*, he prophesied that these very perils would afflict the people of Judah if they failed to heed the word of Yahweh.

It's fitting that, just as Babylon brought sword, famine, and pestilence to Judah in Jeremiah's day, it will be Babylon the Great, the "great prostitute" of Revelation 17, who will torment the earth in the last days.

God created all of us with free will, even the angels who chose to rebel. Jesus called Satan "the ruler of this world."[46] If we're going to question whether God would release the apocalyptic riders of Revelation 6, then, to be fair, we also have to ask why He ever allowed Satan the freedom to walk up and down on the earth.

Understand, the purpose of this section is not to get lost in details about the history of the spirit realm on earth. Our purpose is to show the cultural context—*what John had in mind*—when he described the heavenly court of the unseen realm and the creatures who live there. This is not imagination. It's not a film or a novel. The twenty-four elders and the cherubim who surround the throne are as real as Christ Himself. Therefore, it's only logical to conclude that the Four Horsemen of the Apocalypse are likewise real entities.

Which begs the question: Who are they? We'll explore that in the next chapter.

12

THE SOUND OF HOOFBEATS

The kings of the earth set themselves,
and the rulers take counsel together,
against the LORD and against his Anointed, saying,
"Let us burst their bonds apart
and cast away their cords from us."
—PSALM 2:2–3

Horses, horses, horses, horses
Coming in in all directions
White shining, silver studs with their nose in flames,
He saw horses, horses, horses,
horses, horses, horses, horses, horses.
—"HORSES" BY BYRON GAY AND RICHARD WHITING,
PERFORMED BY PATTI SMITH (1975)

Scholars have tried to identify the main characters in end-times prophecy since the prophets first wrote them down. Gog, Magog, the Antichrist, the False Prophet, Babylon the Great, the two witnesses, and the Four Horsemen of the Apocalypse have intrigued men and women for millennia. That's only natural; everybody has an interest in the future.

That we haven't reached an absolute consensus on who will fill the roles described by Daniel, Ezekiel, Paul, John, and Jesus is a testament to the wisdom of God. If we understood end-times prophecy perfectly, the rebellious principalities and powers at war with God would also know exactly what He's got planned, giving them an edge in coming up with a deception even more ingenious than the one Jesus warned would "lead astray, if possible, even the elect."[47]

God is called LORD of Hosts ("Yahweh of Armies") more than 260 times in the Bible, and this is intentional. He is the greatest military commander in history, and He won't reveal His plans to the enemy until they see them unfold on the field of battle.

Many modern interpretations of end-times prophecy seek naturalistic explanations for the often-confusing visions given to the prophets. For example, these scholars see attack helicopters in the evil locust-like beings that emerge from the abyss in Revelation 9 or read "Russia" into Ezekiel's prophecy of Gog and Magog.

Now, if you hold the view that "the uttermost north" must be a reference to Russia—which seems logical when you look at a globe— please bear with us, because we were brought up believing that, too. Russia will certainly play a role in the final battle of the ages, as will the rest of the world. Ezekiel had a supernatural location in mind when he wrote the words translated into English as "uttermost north"—a sort of *cosmic north*, if you will.

If we look for Gog in the Kremlin, then we're not seeing the world through the eyes of Ezekiel's readers in the sixth century BC. That's what we need to do, as far as we're able, if we are to understand what he wrote. The same holds true for John. Since he drew on the Hebrew prophets of the Old Testament, we need to look there to make sense of Revelation.

The Holy Spirit guided the Hebrew prophets in their war of words against the principalities and powers—the fallen angels who were worshiped as gods in the ancient world. But translators have all but removed them from our Bibles, through an anti-supernatural bias that's clouded the vision of Christians for the last sixteen hundred years.

Around the beginning of the fifth century AD, the brilliant theologian Augustine of Hippo popularized a view first put forward about a hundred years earlier by Julius Africanus,[48] the notion that the Hebrew phrase *bene ha'elohim* in Genesis 6:1–4 should be translated as "godly male descendants of Seth; not divine beings." By shifting Christian thought away from taking the text at face value, Augustine put Christians on a new path, one that, to this day, leads us away from preaching and teaching that the pagan gods of the ancient world were real. It de-supernaturalizes the Bible. This is a very strange thing to do, when the core of Christian belief is that the Creator of the universe became a human, died, and then rose again. Hardly natural at all.

Ironically, this de-supernaturalization shift commenced with Jewish scholars roughly a hundred years before Julius Africanus.

> …the Fall of the Watchers was the dominant Jewish interpretation of Gen 6:1-4 from the second century BCE until the middle of the second century CE. It should be noted that, despite the prevalence of this interpretation for hundreds of years, in the second century CE there was a "widespread reaction in Judaism against the interpretation of bene Elohim as angels."…R. Simeon b. Yohai cursed anyone who thought the *bene Elohim* were actually "sons of God": in his view, the expression meant "sons of judges."[49]

Rabbi Simeon ben Yohai was a student of the famed Rabbi Akiva, considered one of the most learned Jewish scholars and sages in history. Akiva was executed by the Romans in 135 AD, following the Bar Kokhba Revolt, which might have something to do with Rabbi Simeon's new direction. Akiva's declaration that Simon bar Kokhba was the Messiah caused a split between Jews and Christians. Prior to this, the Nazarenes were considered a sect of Judaism and lived as part of the Jewish community. Because of the doctrinal split, Christians withdrew their support of Akiva. Rome crushed the rebellion, killing more than half a million Jews and destroying all hope for an independent Jewish state.

Thereafter, the split between Jews and Christians became irrevocable. To that end, teachings that had previously been accepted among rabbis were reversed. Most significantly, they denied the existence of a second power in heaven, usually named in the Old Testament as the Angel of YHWH. Christians understand these appearances as *Christophanies*—a reference to the preincarnate Jesus in the Old Testament. After the failure of Bar Kokhba's rebellion and the perceived treason of Jewish Christians, their claim that Jesus of Nazareth was the second power in heaven could not be tolerated.

Taken further, the existence of other divine beings called "sons of God" (not to be confused with *malakim*—"angels") was also deemphasized in rabbinic teaching. Rabbis feared such a teaching might offer a persuasive argument for the existence of a second power in heaven.

When the old gods are mentioned at all, they're dismissed as mere idols—nothing more than lifeless blocks of wood and stone. Often, their names are translated into English as forces of nature. Instead of deities who were well known to the Hebrew prophets, we read about plague, pestilence, hail, terror, fortune, death, the dead, and the sea. It's rare to find a Bible commentary that interprets "Leviathan" as a literal sea dragon; teachings on Job 41 often conclude that the mighty and terrible creature with a back "made of rows of shields," whose "breath kindles coals" because "a flame comes forth from his mouth," striking fear into the hearts of the *elim*—"the gods"—is just a crocodile.

Seriously? A crocodile?

We recognize that poetic language is sometimes used by the Bible's writers; that allegory, metaphor, even hyperbole is employed to make points in Scripture. But again and again in the Bible, we find stories that make more sense—and in some cases, *only* make sense—when we acknowledge that when God called these entities "gods," He meant exactly what He said. Small-*g* gods. Baal, Molech, Chemosh, and the Queen of Heaven *are real*. And they have their own assembly. In fact, Lucifer's "mount of the congregation" was named in Isaiah 14:13, and it just happens to be a mountain in Turkey that's sacred to Baal, Zeus, and several other storm-gods of the ancient world. It is the "remote parts of Zaphon."

The Hebrew prophets knew what their pagan neighbors believed. It shouldn't surprise us that John named two of their gods in his prophecy of the Four Horsemen of the Apocalypse. Or is it five? Hades rides with the spirit on the pale horse, Thanatos, translated as "Death." Unless they're sharing a mount, we may have to recount the horsemen. But if these two are named, and both are clearly identified as supernatural entities in the ancient world, then it follows that the first three likewise have names and are listed among the gods known to the Hebrews and their pagan neighbors.

Identifying these characters who play such an important role in the prelude to Armageddon is useful to get a better understanding of what John was shown and why.

To put it more succinctly, you won't understand end-times prophecy if you don't know what the prophets knew. You need to study Genesis to make sense of Revelation, which is why we commenced this study with the Chaoskampf: *that which was*. Using recently unearthed manuscripts and other archaeological finds, we begin to see the Four Horsemen with greater clarity.

RIDER ONE: CONQUEST

Now I watched when the Lamb opened one of the seven seals, and I heard one of the four living creatures say **with a voice like thunder, "Come!"** And I looked, and behold, a white horse! And its rider had a bow, and a crown was given to him, and he came out conquering, and to conquer.

—REVELATION 6:1–2; EMPHASIS ADDED

The sixth chapter of Revelation begins the process of opening the seven seals of the scroll first shown to John in Revelation 5:1. And may we just point out how silly it would be for the cherubim to have voices like thunder if they truly looked like chubby-winged babies?

Now, there are a couple of ways to interpret the living creature's command. The ESV translation may read a little differently than the way you've heard or read this verse. The King James Bible renders the cherub's cry as, "Come and see." This gives the sense that the cherub is speaking to John: "Come and see the seals and the horsemen." This is the traditional understanding of the verse, and it's the view that Sharon holds.

This is one of the few occasions where the two of us agree to disagree over a particular verse. Derek believes that the words "and see" (Greek *kai ide* or *kai blepe*) are probably a gloss, a later addition to clarify that the statement was directed to John, not in the most reliable manuscripts.[50]

That being the case, Derek feels the command is more likely addressed to the rider on the white horse: "Come!"

This gives the verse, and the similar commands to the next three riders, a different flavor. However, the larger point here, on which we do agree, is that the Horsemen of Revelation 6 *only ride when God allows it.* They are not given free rein to plunder the earth at will. They are, in a sense, like dogs on chains, allowed to go this far and no farther.

Of course, this means that the rider on the white horse is not Jesus. Yes, Christ will return riding a white horse to the Battle of Armageddon as described in Revelation 19, but the evidence here points to this rider as a deliberate, but rather poor, imitation of the Messiah.

First, let's examine his weapon: The first rider of Revelation 6 carries a bow—in Greek, a *toxon*. This is the only place in the Bible where the word is used, which means it's weird, and as our friend, respected Bible scholar Dr. Michael Heiser, says, "If it's in the Bible and it's weird, it's important."

Toxon is the etymological root of our English word "toxic." It came the long way around; *toxikón* in Greek refers to an arrow dipped in poison. That's actually the shortened form of *toxikón phármakon* ("bow poison"). The Romans imported the word as *toxicus* ("poisonous"), derived from *toxicum* ("poison"), and by the middle of the seventeenth century it made its way into the King's English.[51]

The *toxon* is not the weapon Jesus wields in Revelation 19: "From his mouth comes a sharp sword with which to strike down the nations."[52] John also mentions that "sharp, two-edged sword" in Revelation 1:16, 2:12, and 2:16. This archer on the white horse does not wield that weapon.

The second clue that we're looking at someone other than Jesus on the white horse in Revelation 6 is the crown. Don't assume it's a symbol of royalty, because not all crowns are alike. This rider's crown is a *stephanos*, a "crown of victory" given to winners in public games in the Greek world.[53] It can also signify political power, which certainly fits this rider and his mission "to conquer."

But a *stephanos* does not necessarily indicate that the wearer is of royal blood. It differs from the type of crown called a *diadema*—the source of our English word "diadem." Christ, the rider on the white horse in Revelation 19, wears "many diadems,"[54] distinguishing Him from the rider called forth at the opening of the first seal.

It's true that Jesus wore a *stephanos* during His time on earth, but that wasn't a crown you or I would ever want. His *stephanos* was the crown of thorns, placed on His head at the cross in mockery.[55]

Like *toxon*, *diadema* is rarely used in the Bible, occurring only in the book of Revelation. Interestingly, there are two other entities in Revelation who wear diadems: The "great red dragon"[56] of Revelation 12—i.e., Satan, who has "seven heads and ten horns, and on his heads seven diadems." Then, in the following chapter, we meet "a beast rising out of the sea, with ten horns and seven heads, with ten diadems on its horns and blasphemous names on its heads."[57] This is the Antichrist.

Why Satan and the Antichrist are given multiple diadems (but not "many," you'll notice) is unknown. Nor do we know why they get diadems, and the rider on the white horse of Revelation 6 only gets a *stephanos*. It suggests that these spirit beings are of different rank and maybe a different type. The spirit realm is full of strange creatures—four-faced, six-winged cherubim, fiery serpents[58] (*saraph nachash*, which suggests that seraphim may be reptilian), seven-headed dragons and other fantastic beasts, and even Ezekiel's wheels with eyes all around are described as having the "spirit of the living creatures" (or "spirit of life") in them.[59]

By comparison, the Four Horsemen of the Apocalypse seem rather boring, at least in appearance.

We conclude, then, that the two white-horse riders in Revelation are not the same. This leads us to a major question: If, as we believe, the rider on the white horse in Revelation 6:1 is a literal entity and not just a symbol representing the spirit of Antichrist, the Roman emperors, war, or some other type or shadow that allows us to read a naturalistic explanation into this character, then just *who is he*?

Now, please understand that this is not a theological hill we'll defend to the last. Our theory is admittedly speculative, but we think the evidence supports this approach to identifying the riders of Revelation 6. Texts found at an archaeological site in northern Syria called Tell Mardikh, the ancient city of Ebla, tell us of a god worshiped as one of the most important deities of the local pantheon. He was called *Resheph*, a plague-god and gatekeeper of the netherworld. Resheph is also equated to the underworld god of Akkad and Babylon, Nergal. We think this entity is a good fit for the first rider, and there is evidence that suggests his return, later in Revelation.

Resheph makes a number of appearances in the Bible. The Hebrew prophets knew this character very well. Habakkuk's prayer in chapter 3 summarizes God's battles on behalf of Israel, and the prophet refers to several rebellious "sons of God."

> God came from Teman,
> and the Holy One from Mount Paran. *Selah*
> His splendor covered the heavens,
> and the earth was full of his praise.
> His brightness was like the light;
> rays flashed from his hand;
> and there he veiled his power.
> Before him went **pestilence**,
> and **plague** followed at his heels.
> (Habakkuk 3:3–5; emphasis added)

"Pestilence" (Deber) and "plague" (Resheph) were pagan deities in the days of the prophets. We should therefore assume that the prophets knew about them, too, as they obviously had contact with the people who lived around them. In the passage above, Habakkuk describes Deber and Resheph as subservient to Yahweh. They may even have been prisoners of war from an earlier conflict, as God marched off from Mount Sinai ("Paran" is an alternate name for "Sinai") to do battle against the gods of Canaan.

Although Deber was a relatively minor character among the pagan gods of the ancient Near East, he is mentioned about fifty times in the Bible. However, his name is usually translated "pestilence" or "plague." Only scholars who spend their lives studying this kind of thing have noticed it.

The most obvious reference to Deber as an entity rather than a natural disaster is the Scripture above, but back in the third millennium BC, Deber was a big deal. At Ebla, an ancient city that was located near modern Aleppo, Deber was called *dingir-eb-la*^{ki}, the "god of Ebla."[60] In other words, a demonic creature named Pestilence was the patron god of the earliest known political power in northern Syria.

Why is this relevant? Because Habakkuk named the pestilence-god Deber as a colleague to Resheph, the plague-god, when he told the story of the Exodus and the attack on Canaan. And he described them as either servants or prisoners of Yahweh.

How did God convince Pharaoh to let His people go? Yep. Plagues and pestilence.

Before the showdown at the Red Sea, which was directed at Baal, the ruler of the Canaanite pantheon,[61] God subdued two other West Semitic deities: Deber and Resheph. He either compelled them to do His bidding, or He simply demonstrated that they were powerless to protect the people holding Israel captive.

Now, what do we know about Resheph? Even though you may not have heard his name, Resheph was one of the most popular gods in the ancient Near East for about three thousand years. He was a warrior, a divine archer, who spread plague with his arrows. This is a description that fits well with the first rider of Revelation 6, whose bow is a *toxon*—a bow with poisoned arrows.

At the Amorite kingdom of Ugarit, located on the Mediterranean coast of northwest Syria, Resheph served the sun-goddess Shapash as gatekeeper of the underworld. This is why Resheph is identified with the

Babylonian god Nergal, who was likewise an archer, a plague-god, and the gatekeeper of the netherworld.

As Nergal, the god was considered a fierce and terrible warrior. He was sometimes called Erra, who, in this guise, was an agent of chaos and destruction, responsible for political and social instability. He was a "warrior," "lord of plague and carnage," and "lord of affray and slaughter."[62] Based on the great number of copies found by archaeologists, a poem called the "Epic of Erra" must have been one of the most popular pieces of literature in the ancient world, even though it's not nearly as well known today as the Gilgamesh epic.[63] The "Epic of Erra" describes how Erra/Nergal nearly wiped out humanity with plague after gaining temporary control of the world.

The root word behind Resheph's name appears to mean "flaming," "burning," or even "lightning"—possibly a metaphorical reference to the fever that accompanies plague. An intriguing biblical reference to Resheph comes from the Psalms, where God's punishment of the Egyptians for their treatment of Israel is described.

> He gave over their cattle to the hail and their flocks to thunderbolts.
>
> He let loose on them his burning anger, wrath, indignation, and distress, a company of destroying angels.
>
> He made a path for his anger; he did not spare them from death, but gave their lives over to the plague. (Psalm 78:48–50)

"Plague" in verse 50 is actually the pestilence-god Deber, not Resheph. But here's the interesting part: The "thunderbolts" in verse 48 are connected to Resheph rather than to the storm-god, Baal. Even more interesting, the verse literally reads, "He gave over their cattle to the hail and their flocks to the *reshephim*"—that is, "to the Reshephs."

Consider this: Since the root word behind the type of angelic beings called *seraphim* and *saraph* also means "burning," thus making the seraphim "burning ones," is it possible that the *reshephim* are another class of angel? It's speculative but not impossible. An inscription from the

Phoenician city of Sidon in the fifth century BC names one of the city's quarters "Land of the Reshephs."[64]

The takeaway from Psalm 78 is that the judgments against Egypt were carried out by "a company of destroying angels," which included Deber, Barad ("hail"), and Resheph (or the "reshephs"). It would seem, then, that those destroying angels accompanied God when He led Moses and Israel to Canaan—and, in our view, these entities have been allowed to roam the earth in the years since.

But the story of Exodus is even more amazing than we've been taught. The cult of Resheph extended south into Egypt, probably carried there by the Amorites, who took over Lower (northern) Egypt as the Hyksos kings in the seventeenth century BC, either around the time Joseph was brought there as a slave or shortly thereafter. Egyptians continued to worship Resheph for centuries, past the time of Ramesses the Great, who ruled Egypt about two hundred years after the Exodus.[65]

A native Egyptian king in the fifteenth century BC adopted Resheph as one of his personal gods and his special protector in battle,[66] probably because of Resheph's warrior aspect as a god of horses and chariots. That king was Amenophis II, also known as Amenhotep II.[67] Scholar Douglas Petrovich has made an excellent case that Amenhotep II, devotee of Resheph, was the Pharaoh of the Exodus.[68]

Think about that for a minute: The Pharaoh whose special supernatural protector was the plague-god, a divine warrior who was also a god of horses and chariots, was compelled to release the Israelites because his personal god couldn't stop the *devastating plagues* sent by Yahweh—including the final plague that claimed the life of the pharaoh's first-born son.

And then, to top it off, Pharaoh's elite chariot battalion was destroyed, drowned beneath the waves of the Red Sea.

But wait—there's more!

The texts from Ebla reveal another tantalizing detail about this ancient god. According to one tablet, Resheph was the patron god of several cities in the Levant, including Shechem,[69] modern Nablus in Israel. Why is this important?

And Abram took Sarai his wife, and Lot his brother's son, and all their possessions that they had gathered, and the people that they had acquired in Haran, and they set out to go to the land of Canaan. When they came to the land of Canaan, **Abram passed through the land to the place at Shechem**, to the oak of Moreh.

At that time the Canaanites were in the land. Then the Lord appeared to Abram and said, "To your offspring I will give this land." So he built there an altar to the Lord, who had appeared to him. (Genesis 12:5–7; emphasis added)

Did you catch that? Yahweh personally confirmed to Abraham that he was doing the right thing on a hill overlooking a city that was sacred to the plague-god, Resheph.

Shechem was also where Joshua reconfirmed the covenant with God immediately after Israel destroyed Jericho.[70] Mount Gerizim and Mount Ebal, where the Israelites recited blessings and curses to celebrate their arrival in the Holy Land according to God's command,[71] rise above Shechem—Mount Gerizim to the south and Mount Ebal to the north.

In 1980, Israeli archaeologist Adam Zertal found what appears to be a large altar of uncut stones on Mount Ebal, the location described in the Bible. While other archaeologists agree that it appears to be a religious site, dated to the early Iron Age, not all agree with Zertal's conclusion that this is the altar of Joshua.[72]

We believe it is. The location is right, the ruins are dated to the right time, and there's no evidence of other cultic activity earlier or later at the site. It is Joshua's altar.

And it's on a mountain overlooking a city sacred to the god who just happened to be the personal protector of the pharaoh from whom the Israelites escaped forty years earlier.

The favorite weapon of Resheph/Apollo, the arrow, was employed by Yahweh in the battle on Joshua's Long Day. Even the "glittering spear"— the lightning bolt—is described in pagan texts as a weapon of Resheph. The point is that the ancient world saw this entity as a warrior and death-dealer who could spread plague indiscriminately with his supernatural arrows.

Here's why we've taking this detour into the history of Resheph: Not only was this god equated with Nergal of the Babylonian pantheon, he was also identified as the divine archer and plague-god of the Greeks and Romans—none other than Apollo.[73]

While you may not be familiar with Resheph/Nergal, you've certainly heard of Apollo. He was the Greek god *par excellence*: god of music, oracles, and poetry; the ideal athlete; the beardless youth; the god who hitched the team of heavenly horses to the solar chariot that carried the sun-god Helios across the sky each day. His role as a warrior and god of plagues is downplayed these days, especially in popular fiction marketed to teens and preteens. But in ancient Greece and Rome, where he was one of only a few deities called by their Hellenic names, Apollo was a god to be feared.

The Greeks believed Apollo and his twin sister Artemis were the children of Zeus and Leto, daughter of the Titans Coeus and Phoebe. Zeus' wife Hera, displeased that her husband had fathered children by another woman (he had a habit of doing this), had threatened to curse any land that offered refuge to Leto. Only the small, rocky island of Delos was willing to offer Leto a place to give birth, in a shaded spot beneath its only palm tree.

Thus, the island became one of two major shrines to Apollo,[74] the other being the site of the famous oracle, Delphi.

Apollo's status as a god of oracles sets him apart from his older incarnations Resheph and Nergal. Foretelling the future was not among their attributes. The role of oracle in Mesopotamia was held in tandem by the storm-god, Adad (Baal in the Bible), and the sun-god, Shamash.[75] Their Greek counterparts, Zeus and Helios, generally didn't answer questions about the future. But as the center of the world's political power shifted westward from Mesopotamia towards Greece and Rome, Apollo—the Greek form of Resheph/Nergal—became the primary source of divine revelation.

Delphi was settled just before the Exodus, around 1500 BC. Its religious importance as the site of Apollo's oracle dates to about 800 BC,[76] around the time of King Joash in Judah. The Greeks believed that Delphi was quite literally the center of the world, as evidenced by the *omphalos* outside the entrance to the oracle's cave. The omphalos was a rounded stone that represented the navel of the earth and, oddly enough, was believed to be the stone the Titaness Rhea gave to her husband, Kronos, in place of the infant Zeus. Rhea, being observant, had not failed to notice that Kronos had swallowed her six previous children shortly after they were born. Thinking quickly, Rhea swapped a rock for her newly born seventh child. Fortunately for Zeus, Kronos was obviously not a picky eater.

Delphi was previously called Pytho, so named because it was the home of Python—not (as you might guess) a really long snake, but the *dragon* son of the earth-goddess, Gaia. As the story goes, jealous Hera sent Python after Leto to prevent her from giving birth to Apollo and Artemis. The god Apollo later sought payback for the distress this caused his mother, so he cut down Python with his arrows on Mount Parnassus, next to the oracle of Gaia at Delphi.

You can't help but notice the parallel between Python's pursuit of Leto and this section of Revelation chapter 12:

And a great sign appeared in heaven: a woman clothed with the sun, with the moon under her feet, and on her head a crown of twelve stars. She was pregnant and was crying out in birth pains and the agony of giving birth. And another sign appeared in heaven: behold, **a great red dragon**, with seven heads and ten horns, and on his heads seven diadems. His tail swept down a third of the stars of heaven and cast them to the earth. **And the dragon stood before the woman who was about to give birth, so that when she bore her child he might devour it.** She gave birth to a male child, one who is to rule all the nations with a rod of iron, but her child was caught up to God and to his throne, and the woman fled into the wilderness, where she has a place prepared by God, in which she is to be nourished for 1,260 days. (Revelation 12:1–6; emphasis added)

We learn later in Revelation 12 that the dragon is Satan, but in Revelation 13 *another* seven-headed monster emerges from the sea. This appears to be a composite of the beasts seen by the prophet Daniel (Daniel 7:2–8). Mesopotamia was home to a long tradition of warrior gods battling serpents or dragon with multiple heads, usually seven. As we learned earlier, scholars call this the *Chaoskampf*, or "chaos struggle," and depending on the culture, the tale is connected to either a creation story and/or the ascension of the storm-god to kingship among the gods.

The point here is that the Greek myth, by framing the confrontation with the dragon as Apollo's revenge for Python's attempted infanticide, appropriates John's description of the birth of Messiah (typical of the fallen realm). In truth, the male child in Revelation 12 is Christ, the woman represents Israel, and the 1,260 days point to a future three-and-a-half year period during which the remnant of Israel is protected from the fury of Satan and his commander-in-chief, the Antichrist—the seven-headed chimera that emerges from the sea in Revelation 13.

By establishing his authority over the oracle at Delphi, Apollo became one of the most important gods of the Greco-Roman world. Kings and commoners alike consulted the god for guidance on everything from military matters to the mundane for more than a thousand years. The high priestess of Apollo's temple was called the Pythia, possibly because it was thought that her visions came from the noxious vapors emitted by the corpse of Python, rotting beneath the earth. Oddly enough, these vapor-induced visions were discovered by a goatherd who noticed the ecstatic behavior of one of his flock after it fell into a crack in the earth. When his story was verified by nearby villagers, who visited the site to share in the prophetic trances, a shrine was erected and a cult center was born.[77]

The connection between Apollo, the dragon Python, and oracles isn't as strange as it might seem. The Hebrew word translated "serpent" in Genesis 3 is *nachash*. That word appears thirty-one times in the Old Testament, usually describing a snake—but not always. In Deuteronomy 8:15 and Numbers 21:6, we read about the *saraph nachash* ("fiery serpents"), sent by God as a punishment for the complaints of the Israelites. *Saraph*, which, as we've noted, roughly means "burning one," is the singular form of seraphim, the six-winged supernatural throne guardians seen by the prophet Isaiah. We also see *saraph* and *nachash* used interchangeably in Isaiah 14:29.

The root word behind *nachash* adds some important context here. As a verb, it means to practice divination or fortunetelling.[78] Putting this together, it appears that what the word conveys is a radiant, winged, supernatural entity, possibly of serpentine (dare we say dragon-like?) appearance, connected to the forbidden practice of divination.

So, the character of the "serpent" who led Adam and Eve astray in Eden is much more complex than we've been taught. It was *not* a talking snake or a snake possessed by Satan. It does, however, sound a lot like Python, the dragon that Apollo killed (if we believe the story), to become the preeminent god of oracles, between about 800 BC and AD 300.

Interestingly, Apollo's oracles fell silent when the worship of Jesus Christ spread across the Mediterranean world. The Pythia at Delphi went quiet after the second century AD,[79] and in the third century, the other major oracles at Didyma and Clarus in western Asia Minor ceased to prophesy as well, but not before a couple of oracles that reflected the growing tension between the old culture dominated by the pagan gods and the emerging culture founded on the worship of Jesus Christ.

It is well known that the longest and most intense persecution of Christians by the Roman Empire was rolled out in the early, fourth century AD under the emperor Diocletian. During the first fifteen years of his rule, which began in AD 284, the emperor barred Christians from the army and surrounded himself with men hostile to the faith.

But that wasn't enough for Diocletian's Caesar (junior emperor),

Galerius, who pushed Diocletian to expand the punishments for Christians to all who refused to return to the old pagan ways.

What is less well known is that a pair of Apollo's oracles convinced the emperor to go along.

In AD 299, Galerius reportedly heard an oracle from the temple of Apollo at Daphne, near Antioch, complain "that the righteous men on earth were a bar to his speaking the truth."[80] This prompted Diocletian's purge of Christians from the army.[81] Then in the winter of 302, Diocletian, apparently at the urging of Galerius, sent a soothsayer to the oracle at Didyma on the west coast of Asia Minor. The early Christian author Lactantius wrote that the "answer was such as might be expected from an enemy of the divine religion."[82]

The answer, whatever it was, prompted an extended period of persecution that lasted through 311.[83] Christians were stripped of titles and property, churches were destroyed, Scriptures were burned, and leaders were imprisoned.[84]

By AD 311, however, Diocletian had retired and Galerius apparently decided enough was enough. Although Constantine usually gets credit for ending the persecution of Christians with the Edict of Milan in 313, it was Galerius who did so two years earlier with the Edict of Toleration.[85] This appears to have been either an acknowledgment that the crackdown wasn't working, or it was a straight-up desperation move by the frightfully ill Galerius to curry favor with the God of the Christians, since his own pantheon had failed him. Either way, Galerius died less than a week later of a horribly painful and gruesome disease,[86] possibly the same one that killed Herod the Great[87] and his grandson Herod Agrippa.[88]

We might be tempted to dismiss all of the accounts of the oracles' messages if we didn't have a biblical basis for believing that contact from the spirit realm was possible. Why else would God forbid contacting spirits through mediums and necromancers? Who would invent "doctrines of demons" other than, you know, demons?

One of the last known messages from Apollo came through the oracle at Clarus in the late second or early third century. This is preserved on a wall at Oenoanda, an ancient Greek city in what is now southwestern Turkey. If the writing is genuine, it is truly remarkable, considering what the god seems to admit about the One True God:

> Self-produced, untaught, without a mother, unshaken,
>> A name not even to be comprised in word, dwelling in fire,
>> This is God; and we His messengers [or "angels"]
>> are a slight portion of God.[89]

Lactantius noted that this could not refer to the king of the Roman pantheon, Jupiter, who had both a mother and a name. Only Yahweh, the God of the Bible, could make such a claim—and the oracle, speaking for Apollo, had been compelled to admit it.

Not long after this, Apollo fell silent. An attempt to revive the oracle by the emperor Julian the Apostate (reigned 361–363) failed.[90]

One other point of contact exists between Apollo and the rider on the white horse: The Greeks and Romans credited the god with inventing the *stephanos*—the crown of victory given to the rider on the white horse in Revelation 6:2. According to Greek myth, Apollo, the divine archer, had mocked the god Eros (better known to us as Cupid) for taking up the bow. In revenge, Cupid let fly a couple of arrows—one of gold for Apollo, and one of lead for the river-nymph, Daphne. The golden arrow ignited the god's passion for the nymph. (Eros is the origin of the modern word "erotic," so "love" is probably not the correct word to describe Apollo's emotion here.) The lead arrow had the opposite effect on Daphne, and she fled from Apollo's amorous advances, finally crying out to her father, the river-god Ladon, for rescue. He responded by transforming her into a laurel tree.

Seeing that the object of his desire had turned into a tree, the still-smitten Apollo declared that Daphne's leaves would always adorn his hair; furthermore, he would use his skill as a healer to keep her forever young. This is why, the story goes, the laurel is evergreen, and her leaves crowned the heads of winners at the Pythian Games.[91] These Panhellenic contests were held every four years at Delphi to commemorate Apollo's victory over the dragon, Python.[92] In fact, the four most prestigious games in the Greek world, the Pythian, Olympic, Nemean, and Isthmian, were called *stephanitic*—internationally recognized and awarding only crowns to the winners.[93]

This link between the *stephanos* and Apollo would have been common knowledge among Mediterranean people of the first century AD. By this time, a laurel wreath was the crown given to victorious military commanders at their triumphs. In Rome, the *triumphus* was a civil and religious celebration for a leader who successfully led troops in service of the state.

So, how was it that the Greek god Apollo, inventor of the *stephanos* crown of laurel leaves that adorned the heads of the Caesars, adopted into the Roman pantheon?

Homer's *Iliad* opens with Apollo sending a plague among the cattle and army of the Achaeans with his silver bow. As with his older incarnations, Resheph and Nergal, Apollo was a god who caused or prevented disaster, depending on his mood. As a Greek deity, Romans weren't allowed to build a temple to him inside city limits—although, interestingly, Apollo was one of only a few Greek deities known by the same name in Rome. Tradition holds that during an epidemic that ravaged Italy in 433 BC, a temple was promised for Apollo as thanks for "averting the plague from the people."[94] It was constructed shortly thereafter on the Campus Martius, and for four hundred years—from 431 BC to 28 BC—it was the only temple of Apollo in Rome.[95]

This structure was dedicated to *Apollo Medicus* (Apollo the Physician). His reputation may be an extension of the attributes of Resheph, whose worship, as we noted above, is documented in the Levant at least two thousand years before the Romans built a temple in Apollo's honor. Apollo was also credited with fathering a medically minded son, the mythical healer Asclepius, who was called Eshmun at the Phoenician city of Sidon, where he was the patron god. The story of Asclepius's birth is a sordid tale of love, betrayal, and divine murder—all too often the case with the gods of the ancient world.

In this story, Apollo had fallen in love with a mortal woman, Koronis, a princess from a kingdom in Thessaly (eastern Greece). During her pregnancy, Koronis had a fling with a man named Iskhys. A raven, who was then white, tattled on the two, and in his rage, Apollo's intense glare scorched the bird's feathers and turned it black. Apollo's sister, Artemis, who was also handy with a bow, killed the adulterous pair. Apollo, feeling remorse at causing the death of his lover, rescued the baby by removing him from his dying mother's womb, which probably means caesarean births should rightly be called "asclepian." He then gave the boy to the centaur Kheiron (Chiron) to raise.

Thanks to the centaur's instruction, Asclepius grew so skilled in the art of healing that he was able to raise the dead to life. Seeing this act as a crime against nature, Zeus deemed it necessary to destroy Asclepius with a thunderbolt. Maybe Hades feared he'd be out of a job if Asclepius were allowed to continue his work.

Now, we need to follow a complicated thread of languages here for a bit. Trust us—this will be worth it.

One of main healing temples devoted to Asclepius, called an Asclepeion, was on the island of Kos just off the southwest coast of Turkey. In ancient times, the island was called Meropis after its first ruler, Merops. His name is derived from the West Semitic word *merappê'* ("healer"). [96]

As it happens, *merappê* is also behind the term *meropes anthrôpoi*, which appears in Homer's *Iliad*:

Then among them arose Nestor, sweet of speech, the clear-voiced orator of the Pylians, from whose tongue flowed speech sweeter than honey. **Two generations of mortal men [*meropes anthrôpoi*] had passed away in his lifetime**, who had been born and reared with him before in sacred Pylos, and he was king among the third. He with good intent addressed the gathering and spoke among them: "…In earlier times I moved among men more warlike than you, and never did they despise me. **Such warriors have I never since seen, nor shall I see, as Peirithous was and**

Dryas, shepherd of the people, and Caeneus and Exadius and godlike Polyphemus, and Theseus, son of Aegeus, a man like the immortals. Mightiest were these of men reared upon the earth; mightiest were they, and with the mightiest they fought. (Emphasis added)[97]

Here is why we've gone down this rabbit hole: The West Semitic word *merappê*, from which the Greeks derived *meropes*, is based on *rp'*—the root behind the Hebrew word *rephaim*.[98]

Now, it's generally believed by Bible scholars that the name "Rephaim" is based on the Hebrew word *rapha*, a verb that means "to heal."[99] Why is that significant? Because the Rephaim were *never* depicted in the Bible as healers.

They were, however, described as "leaders of the earth," "kings of the nations,"[100] and "other lords" who "have ruled over us"[101]—in other words, spirits of the Nephilim, the "mighty men who were of old"—like the legendary warriors described by Nestor in the *Iliad*.

How the Semitic root *rp'* and its derivatives *merappê*, *rapha*, and Rephaim came to be associated with healing is unclear. We'll offer another explanation for the origin of the name "Rephaim" in an upcoming chapter.

The point is this: Those "men of renown" had been destroyed in the Flood of Noah, but not forgotten. In later years, they were remembered as the deified royal ancestors of the pagan Amorites, neighbors of the ancient Israelites. The cult of the Rephaim was an essential part of Amorite religion, which held that the spirits of the dead could intercede for the living. And that, in turn, became the *heros* worship of the Greeks, who venerated demigods (Nephilim) such as Herakles, Theseus, and Perseus.[102]

As Derek showed in his earlier book, *Last Clash of the Titans*, the *heros* cults of Greece and Rome continued well into the Christian age and eventually entered the church as the veneration of saints. We have Augustine to thank for that,[103] and it all goes back to Genesis 6.

To recap: Asclepius, the demigod son of Apollo, was venerated as a supernatural "healer" across the Mediterranean world. Under the

Phoenician name Eshmun, he was the patron god of Sidon, and worshiped at Cyprus, Sardinia, and Carthage. One of his most famous healing temples was at Kos, earlier called Meropis after its first king Merops, whose name derives from *merappê*', which was based on the Semitic root *rp*' that's behind the Hebrew name for the demonic spirits of the pre-Flood giants, Rephaim.

Oh, and did we mention that the healing ritual at an Asclepeion involved sleeping in the temple while snakes slithered around and over you? It was believed that Asclepius would appear to the patient in a dream-vision with instructions for treatment that would be interpreted by the physician-priests, if they weren't clear enough.[104]

So, where are we?

Asclepius was connected to Apollo, serpents, immortality (and the loss thereof), and to the Rephaim. The Rephaim, in turn, were the spirits of the giant, monstrous Nephilim, the children of the Watchers—angelic beings of high rank.[105]

And, finally, Asclepius plays an uncredited role in the book of Revelation through his famous Asclepeion at Pergamum, the very city that Jesus called the home of Satan.

Back to Apollo: The most important question concerning the entity and whether he fits the description of the rider on the white horse is this: How was Apollo viewed in the Roman world of the first century AD? As it happens, Apollo's status as a second-tier god in Rome changed just before the birth of Jesus, when the nephew of Julius Caesar rose to power after the great man's death.

Octavian credited Apollo with his decisive victory over Mark Antony and Cleopatra at the Battle of Actium on September 2, 31 BC, which was fought under a shrine to Apollo.[106] The win cemented Octavian's control over Rome and its territories, making him master of the world from Britain to the Holy Land. Octavian, soon to be proclaimed Caesar Augustus ("Revered Caesar") by the Roman Senate, built a temple to honor Apollo connected to his own home on the Palatine Hill, centermost of the seven hills of Rome.[107]

Some forty years after the death of Augustus, Nero became emperor upon the death of Emperor Claudius, who was probably poisoned by Nero's mother Agrippina. Modern scholars aren't quite convinced that the negative portrayals of the young man were entirely true, but it's certain that Nero was a patron and performer of the arts—more than was considered proper for his social class.[108] Nero, it seems, believed he was the equal of Apollo as a performer on the *cithara*, a type of lyre. About five years into his reign, the poet Lucan declared the emperor the "New Apollo" during a performance at the Neronian Games in AD 60.[109]

The emperor's story didn't end with his death eight years later. Nero was more popular among the people than with the ruling class, probably because of the heavy tax burden he imposed on the wealthy. That's the problem with governments that soak the rich to raise money—the rich can fight back, and they did. In AD 68, a rebellion led by Galba, the powerful governor of a vast territory that included most of modern Spain, ended with the emperor's death. Nero was supposed to have died as a suicide, in keeping with Roman custom, but he just couldn't bring himself to do it. In the end, his freed-man Epaphroditus stabbed the emperor just as horsemen from Rome approached.

However, like the persistent stories of Elvis faking his own death, the ascension of a new emperor—or four (there was a high turnover in the first year after Nero)—didn't convince every Roman that Nero was well and truly dead. The legend of *Nero Redivivus* ("Nero Reborn") was widely believed towards the end of the first century AD—which, you will have noticed, is precisely when John wrote the book of Revelation. According to the legend, Nero fled east to Rome's old enemy Parthia, an empire that included most of modern Iran and Iraq. There, it was believed, the emperor would raise an army and return to take his revenge on Rome.

This tale is documented in the Sibylline Oracles, a collection of late first century apocalyptic writings in the style of the ancient Greek oracles,[110] but Christian theologian Augustine of Hippo noted that this belief was still popular more than three hundred years later.

Some think that the Apostle Paul referred to the Roman empire, and that he was unwilling to use language more explicit, lest he should incur the calumnious charge of wishing ill to the empire which it was hoped would be eternal; so that in saying, "For the mystery of iniquity does already work," he alluded to Nero, whose deeds already seemed to be as the deeds of Antichrist. And hence some suppose that he shall rise again and be Antichrist.[111]

It's a fair bet that when John's readers in the early second century noted the description of the Beast in Revelation 13:3, it wouldn't have been unusual to see Nero as one of the seven heads—the one that "seemed to have a mortal wound, but its mortal wound was healed."

Frankly, Nero was a more logical candidate for the Antichrist than any recent American president, a couple of whom have been called the Man of Sin by misguided prophecy students. And there are Christians today who view Bible prophecy as either partly or completely fulfilled by the time John wrote Revelation. This view is called *preterism*, and many preterists believe that Nero was the prophesied Antichrist.

But the takeaway for us is not whether Nero was the Antichrist (although he definitely wasn't). What's relevant is that the emperor was closely identified with Apollo, and that Apollo was the symbol of Rome's might, through the use of his laurel-leaf *stephanos* to reward victorious military commanders.

However, we do connect Apollo to the rider on the white horse. To be clear: The first rider of Revelation 6 is *not* the Antichrist. That's the Beast that emerges from the sea in Revelation 13, the creature with seven heads, ten horns, and ten diadems—the crowns of royalty. The white horse rider in Revelation 6 has only one crown, and it's a *stephanos*.

History shows that faith in Jesus Christ gradually replaced the cults of the old pagan gods in the Mediterranean world. As we noted above, Galerius in AD 311 and Constantine in AD 313 legalized Christianity, and in 380, Theodosius made Nicene Christianity the official religion of the empire. He oversaw the destruction of many pagan temples throughout his domain, including Apollo's main temple at Delphi, thus silencing his oracles and the destroying his center of worship.

Wow. Did you get that? The principalities and powers in the spirit realm were totally outmaneuvered by the Resurrection of Christ. As Paul wrote to the church at Corinth, if the rulers (*archons*) of the age had understood what God was doing, "they would not have crucified the Lord of Glory."[112] The fallen realm also recognized that intense persecution made the church stronger by driving out the weak. The countermove, then, was to *legalize* the church, leading grateful Christians to celebrate Constantine as a savior, and then to impose the new religion on all the empire. This transformed ministry into a career instead of a calling, and the bishops who found favor with an emperor could live very comfortable lives indeed.

Meanwhile, the culture of Greece and Rome became the basis for Western civilization. This was how the first rider earned his crown of victory when he went forth "conquering, and to conquer." As the inheritors of Greco-Roman art, literature, philosophy, and political systems, is not the Western world, led by the United States of America, the New Roman Empire?

As of spring 2020, United States military personnel were deployed in more than one hundred fifty countries around the world.[113] Many of those deployments are small, but even so, American forces were actively engaged in counterterrorism operations in eighty nations on six continents,[114] a global reach that Julius Caesar could not have imagined.

The symbols of ancient Rome are all around us. Look at government buildings in our capital cities. Many, especially the older ones, look like temples designed by architects more than two thousand years ago. And they are often topped by pagan idols.

Here, in our home state of Missouri, a bill to block the restoration of the statue of the grain-goddess Ceres, which has adorned the dome of the state capitol in Jefferson City since 1924, went nowhere. In fact, it was treated as something of a joke by local media, who poked fun at closed-minded, rural Christians for objecting that a pagan goddess stood in a place of honor above the seat of Missouri's state government.

So it is in many state and federal capitals of the Western world. The citizens of what used to be called Christendom see nothing wrong with symbols of the old gods adorning our public buildings, for we are ignorant of the rites these rebel gods once demanded—and will demand again, before the end.

Apollo's victory was not military; it was in the corruption of the nations who trace their cultural, philosophical, and political heritage to Rome and Greece—unaware that the epitome of unblemished youth in those cultures, the patron god of music and prophecy, was also a terrifying plague-god with a strong connection to the underworld.

There is one other aspect of Apollo we would call to your attention. Fair warning: This is speculation. Although it's not mentioned in the stories from Greece and Rome, it's possible that the book of Revelation reveals another characteristic that Apollo shared with his older identities in Canaan and Mesopotamia, Resheph and Nergal—gatekeepers of the underworld.

In Revelation 9, a cloud of terrifying, locust-like beings fly out of the abyss, when "a star fallen from heaven to earth" is given "the key to the shaft of the bottomless pit."[115] To complicate things, we're given this detail about the creatures in the abyss:

> They have as king over them the angel of the bottomless pit. His name in Hebrew is Abaddon, and in Greek he is called Apollyon. (Revelation 9:11)

"Apollyon" is Greek for "destroyer," and scholars note that it's a possible reference to Apollo, a god of pestilence and destruction. Thus, "[Apollyon] can be seen as a demon who brings destruction and whose realm is the underworld."[116]

To be honest, it's not clear from scripture that Apollo is the one with the key to the abyss or the king of the beings in it. Nor is it clear that Apollo and Apollyon are one and the same entity. It does seem odd that the angel of the bottomless pit would ride across the earth on a white horse for thousands of years while his minions are stuck in the pit. Resheph ("Plague") and Abaddon ("Destruction") are mentioned separately in the Old Testament, suggesting that the Hebrew prophets didn't recognize them as the same character, and there are no references in the Old Testament, other than in Job 28:22, where Abaddon is unquestionably depicted as an entity rather than a place.

Still, the identification of Apollo with Resheph and Nergal is solid, and his older identities are clearly linked to the underworld. John, guided by the Holy Spirit, would have known this, even if the Greek and Roman poets and priests did not. Since we can't make a strong case, we'll leave the connection of Apollo to Apollyon and the creatures in the abyss in the "undecided" category.

John saw fit to identify the Fourth Horseman of the Apocalypse, the rider on the pale horse, by name. He is called Thanatos ("Death"), an entity known to the pagans of the ancient world with cognates in older religions of Canaan and Babylon. We argue that the first three riders are also entities known to the pagan world, as are the creatures we encounter later in the book of Revelation—the things from the abyss in Revelation 9, the beasts of Revelation 11, and the "great prostitute" of Revelation 17.

In our view, the clues John offers in Revelation 6:2 are enough to identify the First Horseman of the Apocalypse as Apollo, the Greco-Roman god of plagues, art, and prophecy—known in ancient times as Resheph and Nergal. Apollo was an archer and a horseman whose arrows spread plague—a close match for the *toxon* carried by the rider on the white horse. The god's role as the one who hitched the team to the chariot of Helios/Sol, the sun-god, echoed the older belief that the god was the gatekeeper to the netherworld, because in Mesopotamian religion, the chariot was the vehicle that carried the dead to the afterlife. That's why the spirits of the Rephaim were described as chariot warriors in pagan religious texts.[117]

Apollo was believed to be the inventor of the *stephanos*, the symbol of Roman military success and the crown given to the rider on the white horse.

As Resheph, this entity was specifically humiliated by God during the Exodus for failing to protect his devotee, Pharaoh Amenhotep II, from the plagues that devastated Egypt and the destruction of his elite chariot corps. And then God directed Moses and Joshua, even before they crossed the Jordan, to set up an altar on Mount Ebal, overlooking a city that had been sacred to Apollo/Resheph for more than a thousand years.

Why would God allow this entity to ride at all? Our Lord has used sword, famine, and pestilence to get the attention of His people for a very long time. What we see at work in the world today was prophesied to the last kings of Judah by Jeremiah in the sixth century BC.

Sadly, we are slow to listen and even slower to learn. Thus, the hoofbeats of the riders have sounded across the earth for nearly two thousand years.

14

RIDER TWO: WAR

When he opened the second seal, I heard the second living creature say, "Come!" And out came another horse, bright red. Its rider was permitted to take peace from the earth, so that people should slay one another, and he was given a great sword.

—REVELATION 6:3–4

Identifying the rider on the red horse is easy. It's safe to say that there is nearly universal agreement that the second of the Four Horsemen represents war. But just as we put a name to the entity on the white horse, we're going to put forward our best guess at the identity of rider number two.

John wrote Revelation in an age that had been dominated by people from the West for four centuries—first Greece, and then Rome. Until recently, Western scholars denied the influence of Mesopotamian thought, specifically that of Semitic people, on Greco-Roman civilization. That attitude has changed over the last half century or so. Influential studies such as *The East Face of Helicon* by Martin L. West and *Hellenosemitica* by

Michael C. Astour have helped document the Eastern origins of "Western" civilization—so called, ironically, because "the West" was all that was left of Christendom after the armies of Islam exploded out of Arabia in the seventh century AD.[118]

So, it's likely that the war-god you're now picturing, assuming you're trying to guess where we're going with this, is probably correct—but not by the name you imagine.

A war-god worshiped by the pagan neighbors of ancient Israel has been a key player in a long supernatural drama that's unfolded over the last five thousand years. He embodies the destructive, uncontrolled martial aspects of Resheph (AKA Nergal and Apollo), but also Astarte (AKA Ishtar and Inanna). You won't find this god referenced as often in Scripture as Baal or Astarte, but his followers were a thorn in the side of Israel for a thousand years.

What's more, this god's cult is documented in the region at least a thousand years before the Exodus, and he's still active as part of the Fallen Realm's long game to destroy as much of God's creation (and as many of His people) as they can before the end.

We're referring to Chemosh, the national god of Moab.

Surprised?

Old Testament Hebrews fought often with neighbors, but Moab was never an existential threat to Israel in the way Egypt, Assyria, and Babylon were. Despite being called "the abomination of Moab,"[119] you get the sense that Chemosh was a second-tier deity, playing on the infernal realm's junior varsity team. He's mentioned in only eight verses in the entire Bible. That can be somewhat misleading; perhaps Chemosh likes it that way.

This little-known god of Moab was worshiped alongside Resheph and Dagan in Ebla, an ancient city that was the first regional power in northern Syria, emerging around or shortly after 3000 BC. There, "Chemosh" was spelled "Kamish," and he was one of the most important deities in what was the most powerful kingdom in the Levant at the time. Texts from between 2400 BC and 2200 BC show that Kamish/Chemosh was one of six deities for which a month was named:

1. Feast of DAGAN — First month
2. Feast of ASHTABI [war-god; Hurrian name for Athtar]
    — Second month
3. Feast of HADA [Adad/Baal, storm-god] — Third month
4. Feast of ADAMMA [goddess, consort of Resheph] — Ninth
    month
5. Feast of ISHTAR — Eleventh month
6. Feast of KAMISH [Chemosh] — Twelfth month[120]

There's an interesting pattern here. The first month of the year was named for Dagan, called *bēl pagrê* ("lord of the corpse"). The next two were named for warrior gods. Athtar was the male aspect of the ancient, gender-fluid god/dess of sex and war, Inanna/Ishtar. More on him/her shortly. And while Hada, called Baal in the Bible, was the Syrian storm-god, he was usually depicted holding a lightning bolt in one hand with a mace or club in the other, raised in a "smiting" pose.

The next grouping of three months, named for gods, began with the feast month for Adamma, a Hurrian goddess whose name meant something like "soil" or "earth," which is logical for the consort of the gatekeeper of the underworld. Think Persephone, grain-goddess and wife of Hades in Greek mythology. Adamma's feast month was followed by two more months named for warrior deities.

Thus, the pattern of months named for deities in Ebla was:

Underworld god, warrior, warrior.
Underworld goddess, warrior, warrior.

And the city's patron deity was Deber, the god of pestilence! Ebla must have been a fun place to live. *Not.*

We also note that the Ebla texts record dealings with the ancient city of Carchemish, about sixty miles northeast of Aleppo, on the modern border between Syria and Turkey.

The name of that city means "port" or "market of Kamish."[121] It's mentioned several times in the Bible[122] and was the site of a key battle between Egypt and Babylon in 605 BC. More recently, the ruins were near the center of intense fighting for the modern village of Jarabulus, during the Syrian civil war in late August 2016.

The key takeaway here is that the war-god Chemosh was worshiped for about a thousand years before Moab was founded by the oldest son of Abraham's nephew, Lot.[123] The cult of Chemosh isn't well known by scholars, because there haven't been many texts recovered from ancient Moab. Most of what we know about the god comes from two sources—the Bible and the Mesha Stele, also known as the Moabite Stone.

Mesha was the king of Moab in the time of Jehoshaphat, king of Judah, and of Ahab's son Joram, king of Israel, around 850 BC. Moab had been conquered by David more than a century earlier, but the Moabites recovered their independence while Israel was preoccupied with the rebellion of the northern tribes following the death of Solomon. Israel's King Omri reconquered northern Moab, and it had been under Israel's control for several decades by the time of Mesha's rebellion.

Second Kings 3 and the Mesha Stele (discovered by our old friend Sir Charles Warren of the Ripper investigations) record different aspects of this fight, but both shed light on the character of Chemosh. The records agree that while the coalition of Israel, Judah, and Edom routed Mesha and his army, forcing them to take refuge in his capital city of Kir-hareseth, they did not succeed in stripping Moab of its independence.

On his commemorative stone, Mesha described instructions he was given by his patron god.

> And the men of Gad lived in the land of Ataroth from ancient times, and the king of Israel built Ataroth for himself, and I fought against the city, and I captured, and **I killed all the people from the city as a sacrifice for Kemoš** and for Moab....
>
> And **Kemoš said to me: "Go, take Nebo from Israel!"** And I went in the night, and I fought against it from the break of dawn until noon, and I took it, and I killed its whole population, seven

thousand male citizens and aliens, female citizens and aliens, and servant girls; for I had put it to the ban of Aštar Kemoš. And from there, I took the vessels of YHWH, and I hauled them before the face of Kemoš.[124] (Emphasis added)

This account of the slaughter of Nebo, which was probably at or near the place where Moses got his only look at the Promised Land, is similar to the treatment given by Joshua and the Israelites to the Amorite cities declared *khērem* (meaning "under the ban"), a phrase usually translated into English as "devoted to destruction" or "annihilated." The sense of the word is difficult for us in the modern West to grasp, because we aren't taught that things can be so sacred or set apart that we humans possess them on pain of death.

For example, the first use of the word *khērem* in the Bible is in Exodus 22:

Whoever sacrifices to any god, other than the LORD alone, **shall be devoted to destruction**. (Exodus 22:20; emphasis added)

Khērem is the root behind the name of Mount Hermon, the mountain where the Watchers of Genesis 6 began their rebellion and where the pagan Amorites believed their creator-god El held court with his consort and their seventy sons.

The Mesha Stele confirms that Chemosh and his followers understood the concept of *khērem*. And that's not all. Before the slaughter of the Israelites of Nebo, this happened:

When the king of Moab saw that the battle was going against him, he took with him 700 swordsmen to break through, opposite the king of Edom, but they could not. **Then he took his oldest son who was to reign in his place and offered him for a burnt offering on the wall**. And there came great wrath against Israel. And they withdrew from him and returned to their own land. (2 Kings 3:26–27; emphasis added)

This makes it pretty clear: Chemosh accepted child sacrifice. Verse 27 can be a hard pill to swallow for Jews and Christians. Why, after the prophet Elisha told the kings of Judah, Israel, and Edom that God would grant them victory over Moab, was there "great wrath against Israel"? And, more important, was it the wrath of Yahweh or of Chemosh?

There are a couple of possible explanations, but here's the bottom line: This account does not depict a victory by Chemosh over Yahweh. God's anger was most likely directed at Judah and Israel for losing faith in His ability to deliver on His promise.

The practice of child sacrifice was well known in the ancient Near East, even in times of battle. Classical historians record the horror of the mass sacrifice of at least two hundred children in 310 BC, when the people of Carthage were surprised by an army from the city-state of Syracuse on Sicily.[125] Inscriptions from Egyptian temples commemorating military victories of the New Kingdom pharaohs (Eighteenth through Twentieth Dynasties, which covers the period from about a hundred years before the Exodus to about the time of the birth of Israel's first king, Saul) confirm that rituals of child sacrifice like this were not uncommon in exactly the situation described in the Bible.

> The pharaoh [Ramesses II, the Great] attacks the city of Ashkelon; in the city we can see four beseeching men, and three women kneeling below them. The hands of these men are directed toward the sky. The chief, with the brazier, can be clearly made out, and in front of him is depicted a man together with a young child. The hairlock of youth plus the diminutive size of the second figure removes any doubt concerning its age. **The child is definitely being sacrificed as the battle rages on.** Moreover, **the same act is being repeated to the left.** On both occasions, it is clear that the **two children are not being carried up to the citadel, but thrown down**; and from the depiction of the limp arms and legs of the child at the right, we can conclude that one, at least, is definitely dead.[126] (Emphasis added)

It appears that the armies of Judah, Israel, and Edom, after seeing King Mesha slaughter his firstborn son, assumed that Chemosh was about to unleash his fury, and they simply lost heart. As a result, thousands of Israelites in the towns of Ataroth and Nebo later died. Mesha, according to his account, expanded his kingdom northward by capturing territory that had belonged to the Israelite tribes of Reuben and Gad for the better part of five hundred years.

The other point we need to emphasize from the Mesha Stele is the link between Chemosh and Ashtar, an alternate spelling of Athtar, the war-god. It appears that to Mesha and the Moabites, Athtar and Chemosh were the same entity.

How can that be? Both Athtar and Chemosh were worshiped in Ebla about fifteen hundred years earlier. To be honest, trying to pin down precise correlations between the gods and goddesses of the ancient world is a great way to drive yourself mad. They change names and genders over the centuries—and besides, they lie.

It's possible that the names of these deities are, at least in some cases, more like job titles than proper names. For example, in the Hebrew Old Testament, Satan is actually "*the* satan" (for example, in chapters 1 and 2 of the book of Job). And since *ha'šāṭān* means "the accuser" or "the adversary," it would be the equivalent of what we humans would put on the second line of our business cards—an occupation rather than a name. In fact, during the Second Temple period, Jews believed in *multiple* satans,[127] and even named some of them: Gadreel,[128] Mastema,[129] Belial, and Samael.[130]

In the same way, the etymology of some of the names of ancient deities seems to fit this pattern, like "plague," "pestilence," "thunderer," and so on. It may explain why some that we'd assume to be evil characters, like Resheph and Deber ("Plague" and "Pestilence"), are described in the Bible as serving God's purposes, as in Habakkuk 3:3–5 or Psalm 78:48–50, where known Canaanite deities and demons "hail" (Barad), "plague" (Deber), and "thunderbolts" (*reshephim*) are God's "company of destroying angels" who executed His judgment during the plagues sent against the land of Egypt.

This begs the question: Did Chemosh take on the job or mantle of "the *athtar*," the war-god, after Israel established itself in Canaan? At about the same time as the conquest of Canaan, the violent, male side of Astarte, the war-god Athtar/Ashtar, was either deemphasized or entirely split away from her character. By the time she became Aphrodite of the Greeks, Venus of the Romans, and Attarshamain ("Astarte of Heaven") of Arabia, the warlike aspect of Astarte's personality was nearly gone, set aside in favor of emphasizing her identity in the Western world as the Queen of Heaven.[131]

By the way, the Queen of Heaven aspect of Inanna/Ishtar/Astarte has not disappeared. Sadly, it's been folded into the Roman Catholic Church beneath the guise of venerating Mary, the mother of Jesus.[132] Athtar, however, continued his career after Moab faded from history as an independent male war-god elsewhere.

By the time of Muhammad in the early seventh century AD, the worship of Athtar had spread throughout Arabia. The southern part of the peninsula, modern-day Yeman and Oman, had the most developed pantheons in all of Arabia. Scholars have identified more than one hundred gods from pre-Islamic southern Arabia, and Athtar was clearly the most important:

> The difference between the numerous deities of south Arabia seems not to lie in their function, but in their sphere of operation. Thus there was not one dedicated rain-god, but rather there were tutelary deities responsible for the irrigation of the village, patron deities for that of the tribal lands, and Athtar for the whole world.[133]

The popularity of a war-god whose unquenchable thirst for blood is attested as far back as the third millennium BC (for her female Sumerian aspect, we refer you to Inanna) explains much about the nature of Islam to this day.

Chemosh began to fade from history after Nebuchadnezzar conquered the Levant in the early part of the sixth century BC. The last known inscription attesting to the name Chemosh is dated to the fourth century BC.[134] What happened to him? We get a clue from coins issued during the reign of Roman emperor Septimius Severus (AD 193–211) found at Moab's capital city, featuring the emperor on one side and a war-god on the reverse. By that time, Moab's ancient capital, Diban, had been renamed Areopolis in honor of the region's patron god, who had been equated with the Greek war-god, Ares.[135]

Like Chemosh, Ares (Mars to the Romans) wasn't a pleasant god to have around. In his Greco-Roman form, he embodied the unrestrained, destructive aspect of war—the mindless shedding of blood for its own sake. In other words, the character of Ares/Mars was very much like the bloodthirsty war-goddess Anat of the Canaanites and Ishtar/Inanna of Babylon and Sumer. This is consistent with the image of Moab's King Mesha slaughtering his own son the midst of a battle, in full view of all, to appease his bloodthirsty god.

So, Chemosh did *not* disappear; he simply did what other deities of the ancient world have done for thousands of years—changed his identity. And he's been known to the world for the last two thousand years as the god of the red planet, Mars.

In *Bad Moon Rising*, Derek argues that the war-god Chemosh/Ares/Mars/Athtar, or the spirit manifesting as the war-god, has played a key role in the history of the world. It's easy to document that we humans have been fighting one another since before the Flood.[136] We picked up again not long after the waters receded; archaeologists have documented the "earliest evidence of large scale organized warfare" at the ancient city of Hamoukar in far northeastern Syria, dated to about 3500 BC.[137] As we noted in an earlier chapter, this was during the time that Mesopotamia was dominated by Uruk, the city at the heart of Nimrod's kingdom.

This destructive, martial spirit has influenced humanity for millennia. A brief survey of the history of war on earth is, frankly, both disturbing and depressing. At least a dozen major conflicts in recorded history have killed more than ten million people, and about three dozen in all left more than a million dead. Two-thirds of those wars have occurred within the last four hundred years.[138] The deadliest was World War II, for which estimates range from forty to eighty-five million deaths from war-related causes.[139]

That said, and while acknowledging that religious differences have often caused or been used to justify violent conflicts throughout history, only one major religion on earth calls on its followers to use violence to spread their faith. At its current rate of growth, Islam will become the world's largest religion by 2070.[140]

Bad Moon Rising made the case for the influence of the old gods of Mesopotamia, specifically the Amorite pantheon, on Islam. This included the warrior plague-god Resheph, the warlike storm-god Baal, whom Jesus identified as Satan,[141] and Inanna/Ishtar/Astarte, identified with Chemosh/Ares/Mars through her male war-god aspect, Athtar, the chief god for many of the Arab tribes when Muhammad emerged on the world stage. Although Muslim historians have rewritten and whitewashed a great deal of Islam's history, many accounts from its early years survive. From those texts and from the long record of Islam's dealings with the West, we can identify characteristics of the spirits behind the religion in the teachings of Muhammad.

By the time of his "revelation" in AD 610, most of the known world—at least, the world known to us Westerners—had abandoned polytheism for a monotheistic faith.[142] Yahweh was worshiped from Mesopotamia to Britain, the Zoroastrians of Persia followed Ahura Mazda, and Jews had been scattered across the Mediterranean world. Obviously, this analysis doesn't consider the religions of the far corners of Asia, Africa, Australia, and the Americas, but since the supernatural war of rebellion is for control of the *har mô 'ēd*, God's "mount of assembly," the lands closest to Israel are the most relevant.

The Arabian tribes continued to worship the old Mesopotamian gods long into the Christian era, though their names changed and roles sometimes shifted—for example, the split of the dual-gendered god/dess of sex and war Astarte/Attar into the male war-god Athtar, and the female counterpart al-Lat ("the goddess"), alternatively called al-'Uzza, or even both. Worship of the moon-god and sun-god continued under various names, and regional gods never lost their importance to the tribes that lived on their home ground. For example, Qôs, the national god of Edom, was adopted by the Nabataean Arabs as their national god Dushara when they settled in the Edomites' former territory.[143]

Alone among the peoples who lived in and around Israel in the centuries after the Resurrection, most of the Arabian tribes—with the notable exceptions of the Ghassanids and Lakhmids in the north—retained their polytheistic brand of paganism. They also practiced rituals that were later absorbed into Islamic doctrine, such as the annual pilgrimage to a place called the Al-Masjid al-Haram, or the "forbidden gathering place."

But the real question is this: How did this new coalition of pagan gods guide Muhammad and his followers when they brought this new religion to the rest of the world?

It's well established that Muhammad began his ministry around AD 610. His first ten years of preaching met with little success. It was only after his fellow Qurayshi tribesmen, tired of Muhammad's preaching against their polytheistic ways, drove him and his followers away from the *masjid al-haram* and forced them to take refuge in the oasis of Yathrib (later renamed Medina), that Muhammad had an epiphany that changed everything.

Even sympathetic mainstream historians acknowledge his change in tactics, although they tend to try to justify it:

> Muhammad and the emigrants from Mecca had no means of earning a living in Medina; there was not enough land for them to farm, and, in any case, they were merchants and businessmen not agriculturalists. The Medinese, who were known as the *ansar* (the helpers), could not afford to keep them gratis, so the emigrants resorted to the *ghazu*, the "raid," which was a sort of national sport in Arabia, as well as being a rough-and-ready means of redistributing resources in a land where there was simply not enough to go round.[144]

You can spot the holes in this story from miles away. Muhammad's band was made up of merchants and businessmen, so they couldn't farm to support themselves—but somehow they became a military force that conquered the Arabian Peninsula within ten years? And the practice of—let's be honest—*stealing* property that belonged to others, called "piracy" on the high seas, was just "redistributing resources"? The people on the wrong end of the Muslims' sharp swords almost certainly had a different term for it.

The "national sport" Muhammad played so well wasn't waged to keep himself and his ragged band of followers alive. The principalities and powers behind the prophet had a longer game in mind, and his first efforts hadn't worked quickly enough for their plan. The historic fact that Muhammad only won about a hundred followers after a decade of peaceful preaching in Mecca, but "converted" nearly all of Arabia after a decade of raiding—"an average of no fewer than nine campaigns annually"—speaks for itself.[145]

Losers in the caravan raids had two choices: Death or submission. Submission is, after all, what "Islam" means. Submission required reciting the *shahada*, the first pillar of Islam: "There is no god but Allah and Muhammad is the messenger of Allah." Those who refused to submit were killed or enslaved.

However, Muhammad's followers were forbidden from taking the lives or property of those who chose to submit.[146] Needless to say, this was a persuasive argument for conversion. As an added incentive for new converts, Muhammad preached that the rewards of a raider—wealth, slaves, and women—were even better in the afterlife for those who died during *jihad*.

"I guarantee him either admission to Paradise," said Muhammad, "or return to whence he set out with a reward or booty." As for "the martyr"—the *shahid*—he "is special to Allah," said the prophet. "He is forgiven from the first drop of blood [he sheds]. He sees his throne in paradise.... Fixed atop his head will be a crown of honor, a ruby that is greater than the world and all it contains. And he will copulate with seventy-two *Houris*."

The houris are supernatural, celestial women—"wide-eyed" and "big-bosomed," says the Koran—created by Allah for the express purpose of gratifying his favorites in perpetuity.[147]

Let's face it: For hot-blooded young men, this was a win-win situation.

Note that the rewards promised by Muhammad were carnal, things that appeal to the flesh—food, drink, gold, and physical pleasures. This is in sharp contrast with the promises of Jesus. The rewards for Muhammad's potential recruits were couched in terms they could easily understand. Join the army of Allah! Win the fight and take home all the loot and women you can carry! If you die, you get even *more*!

It's no wonder Islam overwhelmed Arabia within a decade. After a few key victories early on, it wasn't hard for any man who could wield a sword to figure out which way the wind was blowing. The dark, violent god of war behind this spirit of bloodshed and conquest inspired an army that swiftly captured Zion and soon marched to the gates of Constantinople— the most powerful city in what remained of the Roman Empire.

Christendom has had its share of war over the centuries, without question. But war as a tool for converting unbelievers, much less for profit, is not sanctioned in the Bible.[148] Rather than spreading the gospel by force, Jesus told His disciples to shake the dust from their sandals of any town that refused to hear their words.[149] Islam, as we noted earlier, only began its explosive growth when Muhammad began pandering to the basest instincts of men who could fight well enough to take what they wanted.

And here is where we detect the influence of the god, or gods, of war. In our view, the mindless, unrestrained violence and bloodshed of the goddess Ishtar/Inanna and the war-god Chemosh/Ares/Mars stand behind the wars of Islamic expansion and modern Islamist suicide bombers. Those spirits have convinced millions over the centuries that shedding blood in the cause of Allah is a holy act.

Whether the war-god was always independent or emerged as a distinct entity in his own right after Moab became an established kingdom during the Israelite sojourn in Egypt is unknown. Evidence is fragmented, so we can only speculate. The violent goddess Inanna/Ishtar was the original transgender icon, and by the time of the patriarchs she was worshiped in Canaan as both the female sex-goddess Astarte and the male war-god Attar. As we noted earlier, Moab's King Mesha called his god "Ashtar Chemosh" on the Moabite Stone, suggesting that the two gods had become one by the ninth century BC.

While Christian missionaries traveled peacefully as far as Ireland and China within a few hundred years of the Resurrection, Islam took a much quicker path to grow its numbers: conversion or death. The tactic yielded many new converts, but it also spilled a great deal of blood. We assume that either outcome was perfectly acceptable to the infernal council, so long as the job got done.

Within half a century of Muhammad's death in AD 632, the armies of Islam had ended the four-century rule of the Sassanid dynasty in Persia (AD 651) and besieged the capital of the Eastern Roman Empire at Constantinople (AD 674–678). A century after Muhammad's death, a Muslim army fought Charles Martel and the Franks at Tours, deep inside what is modern-day France. If the Romans or Franks had lost either of those battles, European history—and thus American history—would be very different from the one we know.

Sadly, the effectiveness of the war-god's approach to spreading the message of Muhammad has been aided by the tendency of modern Christians' failure to recognize the spiritual forces at work in the world around us. Even with fourteen centuries of history as a guide, Western intellectuals still believe that Muslims hate us for our support for Israel or "because of our freedom."[150]

The first reaction to the Brussels massacres [*the bombings of March 22, 2016, that killed thirty-two and wounded three hundred*] among postmodern European intellectuals was predictable: What did we, Europeans, do to them, our Muslims?[151]

The answer is simple: All nations that refuse to acknowledge Allah's authority through Muhammed are to be branded infidels and sinners, and it's the right and duty of Islam to make war upon us, wherever we can be found. If this statement sounds harsh and closed-minded of us, then consider what kind of spirit would inspire devout followers to say things like:

> It is neither hunger nor poverty that has driven us from our land [Arabia]. We, the Arabs, are drinkers of blood and we know there is no blood more tasty than that of the Greeks. That is why we have come, to spill and to drink your blood.
> —KHALID BIN AL-WALID, THE "SWORD OF ALLAH"[152] (AD 636)

Now, compare that to the following statement from the Islamic State, issued nearly fourteen hundred years later:

> Fox News reports that *jihadi* web sites are rejoicing over today's terrorist attacks in Paris. The line we have heard more than once from ISIS-related sites is, "The American blood is best, and we will taste it soon."[153] (2015)

Khalid bin al-Walid was a companion of Muhammad and one of early Islam's most effective military leaders. He led the campaign that captured Damascus in AD 634, just two years after Muhammad's death, and the army that defeated Roman forces at the Battle of Yarmouk in 636. That victory, rated by some experts as one of the most consequential battles in all of history, permanently altered the balance of power in the Middle East and led to the fall of Jerusalem in AD 637.

Al-Walid's words are echoed by violent jihadis today, fourteen centuries later. Yet "virtually no one in the West understands that they are quoting the verbatim words—and placing themselves within the footsteps—of their jihadi forbears."[154]

As we noted earlier, even the term "the West" has its roots in the bloody history of Islam.

> The West is actually the westernmost remnant of what was a much more extensive civilizational block that Islam permanently severed.... It further implies that all those "eastern" lands conquered by Islam were never part of "Western civilization," when in fact they were the original inheritors of its Greco-Roman and Christian heritage.[155]

In the fourth century, Constantine the Great moved the capital of the Roman Empire to Byzantium, later called Constantinople and now Istanbul, because it was closer to most of the wealth and civilization of the Roman world. Even though Rome and the western half of the empire collapsed in the fifth century, the Eastern Roman Empire—which never called itself "Byzantine" or "Eastern," just Roman—lasted another thousand years. For most of that time, it was the most powerful economic and military force in Europe, an odd and unfamiliar fact to most of us educated in "the West."

If Constantinople had fallen before 1453, the history of Europe would be very different indeed. In 1683, more than one hundred sixty years after Spain established a colony in the Americas, and more than sixty years after the Pilgrims landed at Plymouth Rock, the army of the Ottoman Empire assaulted the walls of Vienna, Austria. The Ottoman forces were led by Kara Mustafa Pasha, an Albanian Muslim who served as Grand Vizier to Sultan Mehmed IV. Mustafa was described as "fanatically anti-Christian." After capturing a Polish town in 1674, he had the citizens flayed alive and sent their stuffed hides to Mehmed.[156]

Only the last-minute arrival of a relief army led by heroic Polish king, Jan III Sobieski, prevented the Ottomans from taking the city and controlling key trade routes between the Austrian capital and the Mediterranean and

Black seas. This was critical, because Vienna was essentially the gateway to Europe. "From it, Italy (and Rome) to the south and the disunited German kingdoms to the north could easily be invaded."[157] If not for Sobieski, Saint Peter's Basilica in Rome might have been turned into a mosque decades before the American colonies declared independence.

But even after the Ottoman defeat at Vienna, Muslim pirates made life on and around the Mediterranean dangerous. Robert C. Davis, a professor at the Ohio State University, estimated in his 2003 book *Christian Slaves, Muslim Masters* that more than one million Europeans may have been enslaved by Muslim pirates between 1530 and 1780.[158]

We've forgotten that America's first war as an independent nation began even before George Washington was elected its first president. Fighting against the Muslim pirates of North Africa dragged on for more than thirty years, prompting Congress to create the United States Navy in 1794, a war that finally ended in 1815. One of the battles inspired the famous line in the Marines' Hymn, "to the shores of Tripoli."

Western academics often rationalize these encounters by citing the Crusades, as though the Vatican is solely responsible for violence done in the name of Allah. President Barack Obama famously scolded Americans at the National Prayer Breakfast in 2015, drawing a moral equivalence between the Islamic State and the Crusades of nine hundred years ago:

> "Humanity has been grappling with these questions throughout human history," he told the group, speaking of the tension between the compassionate and murderous acts religion can inspire. "And lest we get on our high horse and think this is unique to some other place, remember that during the Crusades and the Inquisition, people committed terrible deeds in the name of Christ. In our home country, slavery and Jim Crow all too often was [sic] justified in the name of Christ."[159]

The former president's view is shared by many academics, who have an undeniable blind spot when it comes to the Crusades. When the history of post-Roman Europe is reviewed, the terms "Arabic," "Turk," "Tatar," "Moorish," and "Ottoman" are used easily enough, but "Muslim" and "Islamic" rarely appear—as though the shared religion of the armies that nearly conquered all of Christendom is coincidental to their actions.

The truth is the Crusades were a response to centuries of Muslim war against the West. Yes, atrocities were committed by the Crusaders, and no, "they did it first" does not justify those atrocities. The difference is that only one of the two religions involved in those wars taught that bloodshed for profit was a sacrament, and it's not the one that fought under the banner of the cross.

As Saudi journalist Abdelrahman al-Rashid wrote in 2004: "It is a certain fact that not all Muslims are terrorists, but it is equally certain, and exceptionally painful, that almost all terrorists are Muslims."[160]

The rider on the red horse, the war-god by whatever name he/she/it chooses to use, is the same spirit behind the bloodlust of Islam. Its work is not exclusive to Islam, but this spirit inspires humans to engage in unimaginable acts of violence, forcing us to join him/her/it in a long, bloody war against the Creator.

At this point, you might wonder what role Islam plays in the end times. That's a good question; it's not clear from prophecies in the Bible that Islam has an obvious role. There are more than a billion and a half Muslims on the earth as of this writing, so any timeline of the Apocalypse that doesn't take Islam into account is incomplete.

We'll refer you again to Derek's book *Bad Moon Rising* for details of our proposal on the prophetic timeline, but to summarize, there is no clearly defined role for what is rapidly becoming the world's largest religion, because things end badly for Islam in the last days. In a nutshell, we believe Islam will be sacrificed by the principalities and powers behind it to dupe Israel—and Christians, if we are still present on earth—into accepting the Antichrist as Messiah in the flesh.

Consider a war triggered by rising tensions in the Middle East. Perhaps a terror event on Israeli soil triggers a muscular response from the Israel Defense Force, which in turn provokes a military response from its

Muslim neighbors. This could be the start of the prophesied war analyzed in detail by Bill Salus, author of *Psalm 83: The Missing Prophecy Revealed*.

The first eight verses of Psalm 83 seem to foretell a war between Israel and the neighboring Muslim states. Below is a chart of the participants and their modern-day names.

TRIBAL NAME	MODERN NATION
Edom	Jordan
Ishmaelites	Saudi Arabia
Moab	Jordan, Palestinians of West Bank
Hagrites (after Hagar, Abraham's servant)	Egypt
Gebal (city in ancient Phoenicia)	Hezbollah (Lebanon)
Ammon	Jordan
Amalek	Bedouins, Arabs in Sinai
Philistia	Hamas, Palestinians of Gaza
Tyre	Hezbollah
Asshur (Assyria)	Syria and northern Iraq

If we pair this information with Daniel 11, we get what appears to be an overwhelming victory for Israel under the leadership of a messiah-like figure:

At the time of the end, the king of the south shall attack him, but the king of the north shall rush upon him like a whirlwind, with chariots and horsemen, and with many ships. And he shall come into countries and shall overflow and pass through. He shall come into the glorious land. And tens of thousands shall fall, but these shall be delivered out of his hand: Edom and Moab and the main part of the Ammonites. He shall stretch out his hand against the countries, and the land of Egypt shall not escape. He shall become ruler of the treasures of gold and of silver, and all the precious things of Egypt, and the Libyans and the Cushites shall follow in his train. But news from the east and the north shall alarm him, and he shall go out with great fury to destroy and devote many to destruction. And he shall pitch his palatial tents between the sea and the glorious holy mountain. Yet he shall come to his end, with none to help him. (Daniel 11:40–45)

Here's a summary of how we think the rider on the red horse factors into this end-times conflict:

- Muslim nations launch a surprise attack against Israel (Psalm 83:1–8; Daniel 11:40).
- A dynamic military and/or political figure leads Israel to an overwhelming victory (Daniel 11:40–43).
- This leader "comes into the glorious land" as a victor (Daniel 11:41).
- "News from the east and the north" provokes the next phase of Antichrist's war, and possibly strikes against Muslim nations farther away such as Turkey, Iran, or even Pakistan (Daniel 11:44).
- Jordan is spared (Daniel 11:41), but Israel's territory may be expanded (Obadiah 1:9).
- This leader will "come to his end," just like the Beast from the sea in the book of Revelation: One of its seven heads "seemed to have a mortal wound, but its mortal wound was healed, and the whole earth marveled as they followed the beast."[161]
- Not only would this miraculous victory over Israel's enemies cause Jews to welcome this leader—the Antichrist—as their Messiah, but the rest of the world, amazed by a seemingly miraculous recovery, will accept him as the savior they've been waiting for, too. The world's 1.6 billion Muslims, stunned by the crushing defeat of its armies, especially if the king of the south is from Arabia and Mecca is destroyed in the conflict, no longer offer resistance to the apparent savior of Israel as a global leader.

This is speculative, we know, as is much of end-times prophecy, but the destruction of Islam as a ploy seems the most plausible scenario we can imagine to lure the Jews into welcoming and worshiping the Antichrist. Why would the spirits that created the false religion of Muhammad sacrifice its followers? Chemosh/Ares/Mars/Athtar, the rider on the red horse, is the god of mindless, bloody violence. Look at the death toll racked up by war over the ages. *He hates us*, even those who do his bidding.

Sadly for those who follow the teachings of Muhammad, they are nothing more in the eyes of the war-god than useful idiots. The greatest service they can render to this god in the end-times is to die and draw God's chosen people into welcoming the False Christ as their Messiah.

RIDER THREE: FAMINE

When he opened the third seal, I heard the third living creature say, "Come!" And I looked, and behold, a black horse! And its rider had a pair of scales in his hand. And I heard what seemed to be a voice in the midst of the four living creatures, saying, "A quart of wheat for a denarius, and three quarts of barley for a denarius, and do not harm the oil and wine!"

—REVELATION 6:5–6

It's understood by most prophecy scholars that the rider on the black horse brings famine with him when he rides. But it's more than that. This rider also brings economic inequality, slavery, and a financial yoke that subjects the world to the control of a newly formed, global government.

As with any Scripture, we need to dig into the original language in which it was written, as well as the culture of the time, to get a better sense of its meaning. English doesn't always capture the nuances of Hebrew, Aramaic, and Greek, and we don't always understand their *idioms*, those figures of speech that were commonly used two or three thousand years ago on the other side of the planet.

The Greek word translated "scales" is ζυγός (*zygos*). In this context, a set of scales makes perfect sense. The rider on the black horse causes economic hardship; when food is scarce, prices go up and everything is more expensive. A denarius in the first century AD was equal to one day's wages for a laborer. The amount of wheat and barley described is just enough to keep one person alive.

Now, think about that: As of this writing, in the United States, activists are fighting for a $15 hourly wage. Using that rate, because it's a nice, round number, that's $120 for an eight-hour workday. After deducting about 30 percent for various taxes,[162] a laborer working for $15 an hour takes home roughly $84 for a day's work.

Now, imagine paying $84 for just enough wheat or barley to keep you alive for a day. Just you—nothing left over for your spouse or children. Then you have to do it again tomorrow, and the next day, and the next. Forget about weekends off unless you plan to fast every Saturday and Sunday.

And such a wage leaves nothing for housing, utilities, transportation, or medical expenses.

Harsh, grinding poverty. Desperation. That's what we're talking about here.

It's hard to imagine such scarcity for those of us blessed to live in the Western world. Here in the United States, the bread lines of the Great Depression might be the most recent example of widespread hunger, although we don't know what the months ahead may bring. As we write this, nearly forty-one million Americans have filed for unemployment compensation over the previous ten weeks,[163] far and away the most in US history.[164] But as a society, we still find the resources to cushion the impact for many who are out of work through no fault of their own.

However, spirit-crushing hunger is all too common in the third world. As of this writing, as many as thirteen million people in Yemen face food shortages because of the ongoing civil war there.[165] In fact, at least three of the riders have circled through the land of Yemen recently: War, Famine, Death. Last year, over one million died there as a result.

Less than a century ago, another man-made famine, caused by Joseph Stalin's policy of forced collectivization, led to six or seven million deaths in Ukraine.[166]

Yet one of Stalin's lieutenants in Ukraine stated in 1933 that the famine was a great success. It showed the peasants "who is the master here. It cost millions of lives, but the collective farm system is here to stay."[167]

We don't claim to see into the spirit realm, but it's safe to say that lieutenant's twisted point of view was inspired by supernatural evil.

As horrific as it was, the *Holodomor* Campaign (meaning "to kill by starvation") in Ukraine was surpassed by a number of famines in history that claimed even more victims: The Great Chinese Famine of 1959–61 (between fifteen and forty-three million),[168] drought in northern China between 1928 and 1930 (between three and ten million),[169] Persia 1917–19 (as many as ten million),[170] and these are just the ones within the last century or so. A quick check shows ten more famines that killed at least a million people each happened in the nineteenth century, including the Great Irish Famine of 1845–49 and several in China that may have killed more than one hundred million in total between 1810 and 1873.[171]

There is no doubt that things will be grim for those on the earth during the seven-year period called the Great Tribulation, but the sheer number of deaths from famine and war during recorded human history should be enough to convince anyone that the riders on the black and red horses have been roaming the earth for a very long time.

The sense of Revelation 6:6 seems pretty plain: When the rider on the black horse comes along, people struggle to survive and they often fail. But we need to go back for a closer look at that Greek word *zygos*. It's only used in six verses in the New Testament, so it's easy to check its use in other contexts.

It turns out that *zygos* is translated "scales" in only one of those six verses. In every other case the English word is "yoke," the wooden crosspiece used to harness oxen to a cart or a plow. For example:

Take my **yoke** upon you, and learn from me, for I am gentle and lowly in heart, and you will find rest for your souls. For my **yoke** is easy, and my burden is light. (Matthew 11:29–30; emphasis added)

Now, therefore, why are you putting God to the test by placing a **yoke** on the neck of the disciples that neither our fathers nor we have been able to bear? (Acts 15:10; emphasis added)

For freedom Christ has set us free; stand firm therefore, and do not submit again to a **yoke** of slavery. (Galatians 5:1; emphasis added)

What John conveyed in Revelation 6:6 is *both* senses of the Greek word *zygos*: A pair of scales, which would have been balanced on a wooden crosspiece similar to a yoke, and, at the same time, an instrument of bondage. The rider on the black horse brings not just famine, but economic slavery as well.

As Paul noted: "For the love of money is a root of all kinds of evils."[172] God is obviously aware of this, and this is why He directed Moses to include certain rules of economic justice in the Law.

At the end of every seven years you shall grant a release. And this is the manner of the release: every creditor shall release what he has lent to his neighbor. He shall not exact it of his neighbor, his brother, because the Lord's release has been proclaimed. Of a foreigner you may exact it, but whatever of yours is with your brother your hand shall release.

If among you, one of your brothers should become poor, in any of your towns within your land that the Lord your God is giving you, you shall not harden your heart or shut your hand against your poor brother, but you shall open your hand to him and lend him sufficient for his need, whatever it may be. Take care lest there be an unworthy thought in your heart and you say, "The seventh year, the year of release is near," and your eye look grudgingly on your poor brother, and you give him nothing, and he cry to the Lord against you, and you be guilty of sin. You shall give to him freely, and your heart shall not be grudging when you give to him, because for this the Lord your God will bless you in all your work and in all that you undertake. For there will never cease to be poor in the land. Therefore I command you, "You shall open wide your hand to your brother, to the needy and to the poor, in your land."

If your brother, a Hebrew man or a Hebrew woman, is sold to you, he shall serve you six years, and in the seventh year you shall let him go free from you. And when you let him go free from you, you shall not let him go empty-handed. You shall furnish him liberally out of your flock, out of your threshing floor, and out of your winepress. As the Lord your God has blessed you, you shall give to him. (Deuteronomy 15:1–3, 7–14)

Did you catch that? God directed the Hebrews to *cancel all debts every seven years.* In our modern age of ten-year auto loans and thirty-year mortgages, this is inconceivable!

And that is precisely the point: Bankers, with the help of powerful friends in government, have rigged the game to fix a *zygos* onto our necks. Too many of us, lured in by the love of having the coolest and newest things, have willingly become economic slaves; yoked to banks by easy credit for clothes, cars, our homes, even our educations—remaining in debt and financial servitude, *for our entire adult lives.*

Let's look at some examples. For instance, many of us were brought up believing that the key to financial success is a college degree. In generations past, that was probably true, but is no longer the case. The student debt burden in the United States is currently $1.54 trillion.[173] For borrowers with federal student loans, which is about 92 percent of student loans, the average debt is more than $35,000.[174] The average monthly payment on college loans in 2016 was nearly $400,[175] and one study found that, on average, it will take college graduates in America today more than twenty-one years to repay their debt.[176]

A survey found that recent American college grads naively believe they'll have their school debt paid off in about six years.[177] Imagine the shock when they realize they'll be in their forties before they make that last payment. Imagine the further shock when they discover that student loans, unlike nearly every other kind of debt, normally cannot be discharged through bankruptcy in the United States.[178]

Student debt is now the largest form of consumer debt in the US, other than mortgages, having surpassed auto loans and credit cards.[179] Nearly 11 percent of student loans are, as of this writing, at least ninety days delinquent.[180] That's a bad sign, because that statistic was compiled *before* the tsunami of unemployment filings caused by the COVID-19 economic crash. Sadly, unless Congress changes the law, student debt will remain non-dischargeable in bankruptcy. (Technically, it can happen, but it's rare. Filers have to jump through a lot of legal hoops.) Student borrowers who are granted a forbearance during the COVID crisis will add additional interest charges to the principal, extending the time it will take for those loans to be paid off.

As it is, a typical $35,000 loan borrowed at 4.66 percent interest and paid off over ten years will cost $43,853. Paid off over twenty years (the norm), that's $53,871. Now, while there are other considerations—like the rate of inflation, which lowers the real cost of borrowing—you can still see why banks are happy to make loans available and "cheap" to college students. By extending payments out over ten or twenty years, new graduates entering the workforce represent a constant income stream to banks.

You can see why lobbyists who represent banking interests managed to convince the US Congress to make it harder to discharge those loans back in 1984.[181]

Credit card debt is also bad, but for different reasons. Because cards are relatively easy to get, charge outrageously high interest rates, and look for opportunities to hit consumers with extra fees, revolving debt is a trap—a devastating financial treadmill that lures in the unwary with slick advertising emphasizing the convenience of swiping plastic to pay for everything from entertainment to groceries.

For those running on this exhausting treadmill, credit cards can be a nightmare. True, the cards can be useful (try traveling without one, especially if you need to rent a car), but if the balances are carried over from month to month, that "ease of transaction'" is very soon offset by the crippling cost of interest charges and late fees added to the purchase.

The average American credit card balance as of this writing is $6,194. To pay off that balance by making the minimum monthly payment of 2 percent of the principal, and using the average interest rate of 14.87 percent, it would take more than six years—and add about $3,521 in interest charges.[182]

Credit cards can be a useful tool, but without the discipline or ability to pay them off as quickly as possible, they become a *zygos*—a heavy yoke, trapping consumers in a never-ending cycle of trying to stay one payment ahead of the credit cycle. Tragically, it's often when people are most desperate that they reach for the plastic, hoping that their temporary situation can be sorted out when things get better.

But for some, better days never come. Often, the highest average credit card debt in the US rests on the backs of those who have the least—households with a net value of zero or less.[183]

By making credit easily available and stretching payments for cars, clothes, college, and housing out to ten, twenty, and thirty years, and then turning those debts into complicated financial instruments that can be traded like stocks, we have become oxen—our necks locked in yokes of debt as we tread out grain for our financial overlords.

This, as much as famine, is the work of the rider on the black horse.

How did we get here? Isn't America the land of opportunity, where a good idea and hard work leads to prosperity and happiness? To a degree, yes; but remember, *the love of money leads to all kinds of evil*, and the rider on the black horse has been spreading his influence for a very long time.

After the American Civil War, the rapid rise of industry in the United States was accompanied by the growth of investment banks to facilitate the rising demand for capital. Unlike commercial banks, investment bankers weren't allowed to accept deposits or issue notes. Instead, they served as intermediaries, bringing together investors with those who needed capital. By 1890, a few powerful firms, led by J. P. Morgan & Co., dominated US investment banking. In 1913, a House committee found that the officers from J. P. Morgan sat as directors on the boards of 112 corporations, with a market capitalization of $22.5 billion—at a time when the total capitalization of the New York Stock Exchange was about $26.5 billion.[184]

Lax regulation in the United States allowed banks to operate commercial and investment divisions with no internal firewall, until the Glass-Steagall Act at the height of the Great Depression. This meant that, until 1933, deposits from the commercial side of a bank provided a ready in-house supply of capital for the investment side. Glass-Steagall was passed after the collapse of a large portion of the commercial banking system. The act required banks to separate according to the type of business they pursued. For example, J. P. Morgan & Co. continued as a commercial bank, while Morgan Stanley was formed as an investment bank.

Glass-Steagall was partly repealed by the Gramm-Leach-Bliley Act of 1999, which passed Congress with bipartisan support. The GLBA became law shortly after Citicorp's merger with Travelers Group. The new corporation, Citigroup, offered commercial banking, insurance products, and securities. Going forward, the GLBA allowed other similar mergers, as well as removing a provision in Glass-Steagall that banned the "simultaneous service by any officer, director, or employee of a securities firm as an officer, director, or employee of any member bank."[185] Thus, the cross-pollination of retail banking, investment banking, and securities trading was restored.

In 2000, J. P. Morgan & Co. merged with Chase Manhattan Bank to enter retail banking as Chase Bank, and in 2016, Goldman Sachs, another of the world's largest investment banks, expanded into consumer banking by launching Marcus, an online bank named for Marcus Goldman, who founded the company in 1869.

You might be wondering: A bank with no physical locations? Why not? With direct deposit, debit cards, and ATMs everywhere, money in the twenty-first century is mostly bits and bytes. All banks really need are sophisticated computers and software to record credits and debits in their virtual ledgers.

Of course, this means that whoever controls the virtual ledgers controls the financial well-being of those who trust the banks to keep an accurate count of their bits and bytes.

The cause of the Great Depression is debated by economists to this day. Derek's opinion, which is not the majority view, is that rapid expansion of credit through speculative investing in the 1920s created a wealth bubble that burst when the unsustainable credit cycle inevitably collapsed—which happened again during the subprime mortgage collapse in late 2007.

How is this bubble inflated? The full answer is too convoluted for this chapter, but in three words: fractional reserve banking. In a nutshell, it's a system in which banks are required to keep only a fraction of bank deposits on hand in the form of actual cash. In theory, this expands the economy by freeing up more money for lending.

In theory.

However, the trend in the US over the last century has been away from wealth creation and toward wealth manipulation. Commercial and investment banks, rather than bringing together investors and entrepreneurs, focus on trading exotic financial instruments such as collateralized debt obligations (CDOs), credit default swaps, tri-party repos, and others.

A short definition: CDOs, which were at the heart of the 2007 subprime mortgage meltdown, are securities backed by a variety of income-generating assets, such as corporate bonds, government bonds issued by less developed countries, or, of course, mortgage loans—which encouraged lenders during the real estate boom of the 1990s and early 2000s to approve as many as possible.

In one morbid example, German investors accused Deutsche Bank of fraud in 2009 for selling more than $750 million worth of shares in funds, based on American life insurance policies! Apparently, the Germans who'd sunk their money into these investments were upset because Americans weren't dying fast enough for them to turn a profit.[186]

As the old song goes, money makes the world go 'round, and speculation is the name of the tune. The value of the global market for financial derivatives is estimated at more than $558 trillion,[187] a staggering sum, and the five biggest Wall Street banks hold more than 90 percent of all derivatives contracts.[188] To give you an idea of just how much money that is, the annual gross domestic product (GDP) of the United States is about $20.5 trillion. Global GDP in 2018 was estimated at $86 trillion.[189]

Let that sink in. The biggest banks in America hold contracts on speculative investments worth about *seven times more than the combined annual economic output of the entire planet!*

After the bubble burst in 2007, Wall Street and Washington, DC, worked together to protect the big banks from the consequences of their actions. They're doing the same in the COVID-19 crisis of 2020. Since hitting a low of 18,591.93 on March 23, 2020, the Dow Jones Industrial Average has rebounded by about 50 percent as of this writing, five months later. Over the same span, more than fifty-five million Americans filed first-time claims for unemployment compensation. That makes no sense whatsoever, until one realizes that the Federal Reserve Bank of the United States, created a hundred years ago as the lender of last resort to prevent financial institutions from collapsing during bank runs, is now essentially investing directly in the stock market.[190]

Meanwhile, those newly unemployed Americans with college loans will wait and watch as their loan balances grow until they can afford to start paying them down again. This is precisely the type of debt slavery that God intended to prevent with the *shmita* (also spelled "Shemitah" and "Shemittah") every seventh year. And this is what the rider on the black horse has been working for two thousand years to circumvent. His goal is to establish the financial infrastructure for a world ruler by making people dependent on government for their economic survival.

In a very real way, this is a return to Babel. To explain what we mean, let's turn back the clock about five thousand years.

As we noted earlier in the book, Nimrod is usually identified as the builder of the Tower of Babel. Our best guess is that he lived sometime between 3800 and 3100 BC,[191] during the Uruk Expansion.

But the point here is not what happened at the Tower of Babel. We're interested in how Nimrod administered his kingdom. And to analyze that, we return to the crudely made, mass-produced Urukian pottery we mentioned previously: the beveled-rim bowl.

During its heyday, Uruk dominated Mesopotamia along the Tigris and Euphrates rivers from the Persian Gulf to southeastern Turkey. The dominant civilization in Mesopotamia just before the Uruk period, the Ubaid culture (c. 6500–3800 BC) became more stratified as people moved from rural settlements to cities. The Ubaid civilization produced high-quality pottery, identified by black geometric designs on buff or green-colored ceramic. Then, around 3800 BC, the emerging Uruk culture developed the world's first mass-produced product, a primitive type of pottery called the beveled-rim bowl.

These bowls are very rough compared to the pottery from the Ubaid culture, a step backward in technique and quality. Beveled-rim bowls are described as "the simplest and least attractive of all Near Eastern pots… among the crudest vessels in the history of Mesopotamia pottery."[192] This is odd because other aspects of the Uruk culture, including large temples, complex administrative systems, and sophisticated works of art, clearly show that these were not simple, uneducated people.

And yet, the most common artifacts from the Uruk period are these coarsely made bowls. Archaeologists have dug up a *lot* of them. About three-quarters of all ceramics found at Uruk sites are beveled-rim bowls. One of the defining characteristics of a dig site from the Uruk period is the presence of lots and lots of beveled-rim bowls!

Scholars agree that these simple, undecorated bowls were made on molds rather than wheels, probably in cone-shaped depressions in the ground. Most important for this topic, however, is evidence that these bowls were probably used to dole out barley and oil for workers' daily rations.[193]

The bowls were too porous for liquids like water or beer. They were cheap and easy to make—so cheap, in fact, that they were apparently disposable. At some sites, large numbers of used, unbroken bowls have been found in big piles. These bowls were essentially the Sumerian equivalent of fast-food containers. The Sumerian picture sign for "bread," NINDA, looks just like a beveled-rim bowl, and the sign for "to eat" is a human head with a beveled-rim bowl at its mouth.[194]

This is what brings us back to the third rider of Revelation 6: Rationed food means that there's a central authority doling out daily bread to the people. It's not a coincidence that these crude bowls appeared alongside Uruk's emergence as the world's first empire. After Noah's Flood, which we believe marked the end of the Ubaid civilization, the growing population in Mesopotamia gravitated to cities where evidence suggests they exchanged their freedom for guaranteed government rations.

It appears that Nimrod and his successors, including the legendary Gilgamesh, controlled their subjects by moving them off the land and into cities, keeping a tight rein on the production and distribution of food and resources.

Things haven't changed all that much over the last five thousand years.

A similar situation developed in the last years of the Roman republic. Populist politicians realized they could win the support of the people by expanding the *Cura Annonae* ("care for the grain supply"). Regular distribution of grain at below-market prices began for the poorer citizens of Rome in 123 BC. It was expanded and made free by 58 BC, and may have supplied grain to as much as 20 percent of Rome by the first century AD. The emperor Tiberius, recognizing the problems a starving population could create, said in AD 22 that neglecting the Cura Annonae would lead to "the utter ruin of the state."[195]

The poet Juvenal, writing about seventy-five years later, saw how easily and cheaply ambitious rulers had lured Roman citizens into trading away the republic:

> Nowadays, with no vote to sell, their motto is "couldn't care less." Time was their plebiscite elected generals, heads of state, commanders of legions; but now they've pulled in their horns, there's only two things that concern them: bread and circuses.[196]

What may have begun as a temporary solution to a food shortage became a means to ensure a compliant and docile population. That was Juvenal's point—the people of Rome had abdicated their responsibilities as citizens of a republic, content to place their necks in the government's yoke in exchange for an allotment of free bread and tickets to the Colosseum.

What happened in Uruk and Rome is happening today in the United States. Universal basic income (UBI), a guaranteed monthly stipend from the government, is a modern take on the Urukian and Roman grain doles, and it's getting a trial run during the COVID-19 crisis. Millions of Americans, anyone who'd filed an income tax return the previous year, received a $1,200 handout from the US Treasury as part of the Coronavirus Aid, Relief, and Economic Security (CARES) Act. The bill passed Congress with overwhelming bipartisan support and was signed by President Donald Trump on March 27, 2020.

But that wasn't enough for some. So-called progressives in Congress, unaware that their policies are neither progressive or new, introduced a bill in April, 2020 that would send two thousand dollars a month to "every American age 16 or older earning less than $130,000 annually."[197] Senate Democrats unveiled a similar plan shortly thereafter, offering to make the payments retroactive to March, 2020, and continuing until three months after the Department of Health and Human Services declares an end to the public health emergency.[198] Of course, this assumes there *will be* an end to the emergency.

Please understand that we are sympathetic to the financial hardship caused by shutting down the global economy. We've been there. Our home went to foreclosure during the subprime mortgage crisis in 2007, and for a time we literally got by on free bread. It wasn't the most nutritious diet, but it kept us from going hungry. However, this "economic relief" from the government sets a disturbing precedent. The $1,200 disbursements weren't means-tested. Americans got checks whether we needed them or not.

Politicians presumed the money would be spent to keep the economy from locking up as businesses shut down. Call us skeptical, but it appears that the main beneficiaries of the $2.2 trillion relief plan were bankers, whose livelihoods depend on collecting monthly payments for credit cards, auto loans, mortgages, and student debt, and the complicated collateralized debt obligations created by packaging those debts into securities.

We wouldn't be surprised to see some form of UBI in the United States within our lifetimes. Although Sen. Bernie Sanders of Vermont wasn't able to ride a growing socialist sentiment among younger voters into the White House, the fact that fully half of Democrat voters hold a favorable impression of socialism[199] is a startling change from Cold-War America. And that poll reflected voters' attitudes *before* COVID-19 shut down the economy and threw fifty-five million Americans out of work.

While the current crisis may not be the event that brings the Antichrist to power, when it does happen, it's going to look a lot like this. The world will be in crisis, and people will gratefully place their necks in the yoke of a government led by a dynamic leader who promises a way out of what appears to be a hopeless situation. We can only speculate on what that crisis will be, but we believe it's probably the devastation created by the opening of the sixth seal in Revelation 6:12, which we believe coincides with the Rapture of the Church.

Recall our chapter on the seventy-weeks prophecy that the angel Gabriel told Daniel were "decreed about your people and your holy city."[200] The sixty-ninth week ended when "an anointed one," Jesus, was "cut off" in or about AD 32. The "weeks," seven-year periods of time, were "about your people" (Daniel's people, the Jews). Therefore, the final "week," the seven-year period commonly called the Great Tribulation, doesn't begin until the Church is removed from the earth.[201]

Until we get there, the rider on the black horse continues to ride, preparing the world for the ultimate yoke—one that not only requires contact tracing so that authorities know where everyone has been and with whom, but one that will literally compel citizens to choose between worshiping this venerated world leader and going without food, clothing, and shelter.

This leads us to an obvious question. John identified the rider on the pale horse as Thanatos (Death), and we've made our case for the entities riding on the white and red horses—Apollo and Mars. Who, then, is the rider on the black horse?

In the time of Abraham, around the eighteenth century BC, a deity known as Nabû emerged in Babylon as the god of wisdom, writing, prophecy, and scribes.[202] That role had previously been assigned to a Sumerian goddess called Nisaba or Nidaba, but it appears that active female deities, other than Inanna (later called Ishtar and Astarte), were deemphasized after Babylon became the dominant power in southern Mesopotamia around 1750 BC.

Nabû's symbol was a wedge-shaped cuneiform mark, representing a stylus at rest on a clay tablet, the tools of the scribe.[203] He was believed to be the son of Marduk, who began as the city-god of Babylon and eventually replaced Enlil at the top of the pantheon. Marduk, in turn, was the son of Enki (also called Ea), the profoundly influential Sumerian god of fresh water, knowledge (as in the foundational concepts of human civilization), and creation. Some of these traits were eventually ascribed to Nabû, including Enki's association with the planet Mercury.[204]

By the time of David and Solomon, around 1000 BC, Nabû's profile had risen in the pantheon. He was considered the vizier of Marduk, the "one who fixes destinies."[205] As kings in the ancient Near East learned to rely on bureaucracy to administer their territories, the importance of

Nabû grew. Bureaucrats require records and communication, leading to the emergence of a scribal class, and thus the god of scribes grew in importance to become the right-hand deity of the chief god, Marduk.

When Assyria surpassed Babylon as the dominant regional power in the late tenth century BC, around the time of Solomon's grandson Abijah, Marduk was replaced at the head of the pantheon by Ashur (essentially the Assyrian version of Enlil), but Nabû remained in his role as vizier to the high god. When Babylon reasserted itself in the late seventh century BC, Marduk was restored at the top of the pantheon, the Assyrian gods faded into obscurity, and Nabû became Marduk's co-regent.[206] In fact, Nabû was considered so important to the ruling class that he continued to receive worship long after Babylon ceased to be an independent kingdom.

Nabû's status in the Neo-Babylonian Empire is highlighted by his popularity as the theophoric element (the "god-name") of the names of the best-known Chaldean kings: Nabopolassar ("Nabû protect my son"),[207] Nebuchadnezzar ("Nabû defend my firstborn son"),[208] and Nabonidus ("Nabû is to be revered").[209] The Bible also mentions Nebuzaradan ("Nabû has given seed"),[210] the captain of Nebuchadnezzar's guard,[211] and Nebu-sar-sekim[212] ("Nabû has established his rule"),[213] the Rab-saris (chief eunuch),[214] whose existence has been confirmed outside the Bible by a small clay tablet confirming a donation of gold by Nebu-sar-sekim to the temple of Nabû at the city of Borsippa.

Nabû played a key role during the annual *akitu* festival celebrated after the barley harvest in the month of Nisan (March), around the spring equinox. The *akitu* festival featured a dramatization of the Babylonian creation story in which Marduk defeated the chaos-monster Tiamat. Near the end of the festivities, on the eleventh of Nisan, Marduk and Nabû decreed the fate of the land for the coming year and Nabû recorded it on his tablet. This is similar to the book kept by God to record the names of those who please Him,[215] the "book of life" examined in the end times,[216] and, of course, the seven-sealed scroll of Revelation 5 and 6 that released the Four Horsemen of the Apocalypse to roam the earth.

And here we come to the connection between Nabû and the *zygos*, the economic yoke we described in the early part of this section. Not only was Nabû the god of wisdom and writing; as the patron of scribes, he was also the god who kept track of debits and credits. A small temple in Babylon, built during the reign of Nebuchadnezzar near the main ziggurat for Marduk, was dedicated to Nabû-ša-hare—"Nabû of Accounts."[217]

Scribes came from the elite class of Mesopotamian society.[218] Their ability to read and write set them apart from most of the people, who were illiterate. Their function was to write documents for others, an invaluable skill not just for preserving the king's decrees, but for documenting the mundane aspects of any advanced civilization—tax rolls, astronomical observations, property deeds, wills, and even contracts for laundry service.[219]

In other words, Nabû wasn't just the god of scribes; he was the god of contracts, law, and ledgers—a spirit who undoubtedly feels right at home in the modern world. Who rules the world today if not lawyers, accountants, and bankers?

As we noted above, the veneration of Nabû extended long past the end of Babylon, surviving into the Christian era. Through contact between the ancient Near East and the western Mediterranean, Nabû was introduced to the West as Hermes in Greece and Mercury in Rome. As with Nabû, whose name basically means "the announcer,"[220] Hermes/Mercury was considered by the Greco-Roman world to be the herald of the gods. The Greeks believed Hermes was also a god of trade and merchants (and thieves).[221] The Romans did, too, but they were more specific, as Mercury's name was based on the Latin root *merx*, from which we get the modern English words "merchant," "merchandise," and "commerce."[222]

So, Mercury/Hermes/Nabû is a god of scribes (meaning records, ledgers, and accounts), merchants, and trade who was closely associated with the Neo-Babylonian kingdom of Nebuchadnezzar, which represents the end-times religion of the Antichrist, Mystery Babylon. The economic slavery and poverty represented by the *zygos*, the scales and yoke, carried by the rider on the black horse of Revelation 6, is apparently intended to compel the world to accept the Antichrist's solution to a world in turmoil. This is the same deal offered by Nimrod and the emperors of Rome to their subjects: a government dole in exchange for their liberty.

Significantly for our study, Hermes and Mercury—along with their Etruscan equivalent Turms and the Egyptian god of scribes and wisdom, Thoth—were believed to serve as a psychopomp, a spirit guide who conducted the dead to the netherworld.[223] While that wasn't a role ascribed to Nabû, it does seem relevant to John's description of the rider on the black horse, an entity who uses financial serfdom to deprive the world of life, liberty, and happiness.

Here's one last piece of the puzzle. It may be coincidence, or it could be the spirit realm having a laugh at our expense: In April 2009, following the global economic meltdown touched off by the subprime mortgage crisis, MasterCard introduced a new fee on all transactions with its credit card. That fee is currently set at just under two cents per transaction.[224] That doesn't sound like much, but if you're a merchant with an active business—say, a coffee shop that sells several hundred cups of coffee a day, paid for with credit or debit cards—it adds up quickly. The fee is non-negotiable and paid directly to MasterCard. (VISA, Discover, and American Express have their own variants of this fee.)

We can only assume that whoever came up with the name of this fee for MasterCard has an odd sense of humor or was perhaps guided from beyond in their choice. The acronym is ominously relevant to this chapter; dealing, as it does, with the financial shackles used by the banks of the world, and their allies in government, to turn free people into debt slaves.

You see, for more than a decade, businesses have been billed a small amount by MasterCard for every credit or debit card transaction. This charge was formerly called the "Acquirer Access Fee." But in April of 2009, it was renamed the "Network Access and Brand Usage" fee—the NABU.

How prophetically appropriate.

16

RIDERS FOUR AND FIVE: DEATH AND HADES

Peste: 1. pest [noun] a troublesome person or thing. 2. **pestilence** [noun] (literary, old-fashioned) any type of deadly epidemic disease, especially bubonic plague.

—CAMBRIDGE ENGLISH DICTIONARY (EMPHASIS ADDED)

I will bring a sword against you, that shall execute vengeance for the covenant. And if you gather into your cities, I will send pestilence among you, and you will be delivered into the hand of the enemy.

—LEVITICUS 26:25

Into the eternal darkness, into fire and into ice.

—DANTE ALIGHIERI, *THE DIVINE COMEDY*

In 2003, Sharon wrote a novel called *The Armageddon Strain* about a manmade disease that provides an excuse for governments to enslave all the world beneath the yoke of a New World Order. Though the book was written nearly two decades ago, the plot now plays out before our very eyes—only, we know it as a disease called COVID-19.

According to a March 13, 2020, article posted to the *South China Morning Post*, the first known SARS-CoV-2 patient entered a Hubei hospital on November 17, 2019. This fifty-five-year-old male presented with flu-like illness and atypical pneumonia of unknown etiology, but it's doubtful he was Patient Zero in what would become a pandemic. Because the hallmark symptom of the illness in these early stages was pneumonia, no one recognized the cause as anything novel. By December 15, twenty-seven cases would later be traced to the outbreak, and by end of December, the case count would rise to 266. January 1 would see a sharp rise, with that day's case count at 381.

Looking back, epidemiologists have followed contact tracing, travel patterns, and hospital records to determine the earliest patterns of the novel disease that would come to be called COVID-19. It is one of those shocks to the world system that resonates like a punch in the proverbial gut, and it came as a complete surprise, which is why experts refer to this type of event as a "black swan." (Most swans are white, and though black swans can occur, they usually don't.)

Did China or another human group manufacture SARS-CoV-2 as a bioweapon—as in the plot of *The Armageddon Strain*? Perhaps, but as of this moment, there is no definite proof of it. However, there is evidence that the disease may have been part of a research project into possible mutations of the original SARS virus. At some point during the fall of 2019, one of these mutated forms escaped from a Wuhan lab and infected Patient Zero. This cannot yet be proven, but as of this writing, it a likely scenario.

No matter how SARS-CoV-2 emerged into the world of men, this much is fact: Rider number four has taken control of every aspect of modern society and government. After six months, most travel remains at a standstill, affecting every industry with which it's associated: airlines, car rentals, hotels, restaurants, retail, tourism, and entertainment. Public gatherings have been curtailed, canceled, or limited; and most states require we wear a mask when shopping or walking through a park. In short, our freedom of movement is strictly controlled.

Government leaders put on their perfectly practiced smiles for the camera as they explain why our freedoms have vanished—making it sound as though governors and legislators are our protectors. But behind closed doors, every man and woman wrings his or her hands in anguish, fearing the possibility of dissent—or worse, voter disappointment. As we write these lines, it's the height of summer, a time when most scientists expected us to be long past the outbreak. But are we?

Not by a longshot.

Lockdowns have come and gone, only to come back around again. Schools that released their students early with plans to reopen in August now question the rationality of such a plan. Headlines shouting about rising numbers of children testing positive for the virus dominate the media. In fact, there is talk of canceling the school year in its entirety.

Control, control, and more control. It's as though the third rider is singing an off-key duet with the fourth: *Unhappy trails to you! Until we meet again—in hell.*

All the world is caught in a mind-numbing scenario, best played out in fiction—but it is all too real.

Business meetings and conferences are now conducted via Zoom, Skype, and Meet. Easter, Mother's Day, Father's Day, Independence Day, and even Memorial Day Weekend were primarily celebrated at home. Churches cannot meet unless they defy governors, and parishioners must watch online as pastors deliver messages to empty pews. Sports are played to empty stands, but you can buy the right to have your face pasted to a cardboard cut-out. It's the Summer of the Second Wave, and everyone is ordered to stay home to stop the spread—again. Protesters, however, are given a pass, it seems. Yes, they wear masks, but they do so to protect their identities; not to protect others.

We're promised that, one day, travel will resume, schools will reopen to full classrooms, and filled sports stadiums and sizzling hot dogs will make a comeback. Sandy beaches will once more host happy families wearing sunny smiles and golden tans. Planes will fly and cruise ships will set sail.

But underneath all of it, we will wonder. We will fear. We will worry. Will it come back? And if it does, will it be worse?

And what about the vaccine? Will I be forced to take it? Will my children be permitted to enter school without it? Can I board a plane?

Even if SARS-CoV-2 vanished tomorrow like a thinning shadow, humanity can never be truly safe from Thanatos and his hellish ride. If not this pandemic, another will arise—and then another, followed by another—until God Almighty shouts the final command, "Come!" to Thanatos and the last pandemic of the world as we know it commences. Death will be given permission to ride to such an extent that his passage will end the lives of 25 percent of the world's population.

One out of four will die.

Compare that to the estimated case fatality rate for COVID-19: 0.5–1 percent. In other words, we ain't seen nothin' yet!

God has been warning mankind for millennia to turn from our evil ways, to stop worshiping false gods who promise a golden age but deliver only ruin and the grave. In fact, that's their ultimate aim: to see every human writhing and wailing in outer darkness. God has given us years and years of His bountiful grace, but our time is nearly up. The final seven years of Daniel's seventy-weeks prophecy are nearly here. And then, all hell will break loose.

Four seals. Four riders. Four spirits with one thing on their minds: Destroy humanity to prevent Christ's return. Sword, conquest, warfare, economic disaster, slavery, pestilence, and death. Four riders and a whole lotta trouble. They've hated us since the Garden. Remember what we covered earlier?

> I will put enmity between you and the woman,
> and between your offspring and her offspring;
> he shall bruise your head, and you shall bruise his heel.
> (Genesis 3:15)

As we studied previously, Satan (the *nachash* tempter in the garden) is able to perpetuate his evil lineage through a type of "seed." It's likely that this is a prophecy of the Mount Hermon event, when numerous (Enoch says two hundred) Watcher-class *bene ha'elohim* ("sons of God") descended on the mount with plans to engender offspring through copulation with human females (consensual or otherwise). The resultant breed of "mighty men" are remembered in Greek history as the demigod heroes of the Golden Age, but these same hybrid beings had far older names, beginning with the pre-Flood era (an age whose language is now lost).

As we covered in the chapter on "Rider One: Conquest," Nergal, Enlil's son, is the oldest known version of the god Apollo (AKA Resheph). Both Nergal and Apollo are liminal figures. Both serve as gatekeepers and/ or rulers of the underworld. Both ride horses. Both are healers who also use a bow to fire deadly arrows that kindle plagues and pestilence. And both may well be represented in the first rider in the book of Revelation. There's no need to unpack it again here, so suffice it to say that the Garden tempter did indeed have "children" who continue to enforce his laws and enact his will upon the children of Adam.

There is deep hatred between the two camps: God's and Satan's. When Christ rose from the tomb and ascended to His Father in heaven, He immediately began to unseal a legal document that gave Him full authority and ownership of the earth. Adam had relinquished the earth (which should have fallen under his dominion) to the deceiver, but Christ bought it back, through His blood.

John has recorded Christ's arrival in the book of Revelation: As the Lord breaks the first few seals, we see the reaction within the fallen realm. First, their leader, a false Christ, leads the charge of the same unholy triumvirate so often seen in the Old Testament: Sword, Famine, and Death. Conquest is none other than Apollo, who wears a victor's crown and impersonates the true Victor right down to the white horse.

Behind Apollo rides the Red Horse Spirit, followed by the Black (Famine), and finally Death joins the team, with Hades coming along for this hellish ride. The recent COVID-19 outbreak has certainly caused a surge in Bible purchases. Many who never even opened a Bible now eagerly thumb through the pages of Revelation looking for answers.

The Pale Rider's reputation reaches beyond our Sunday pews.

In January of 2018, Sharon authored an article for *SkyWatchTV Magazine*, whose first lines now seem eerily oracular, though they were based solely on scientific observation, logic, and her strong belief in God's prophetic Word:

> Something is brewing out there. Mutating. Recombining. Running through species after species to perfect its nature; becoming more transmissible, more pathogenic. And it will be deadlier than anything yet seen upon the earth. Zika. Avian influenza. Marburg. Ebola. Smallpox. Will it be one of these or an unknown chimera virus; one that will take us by surprise; one that is secretly readying itself to jump from animals to humans; a *"therion"* creature that accompanies the Pale Rider Thanatos?

Now, in case you've never studied Revelation, if you have never dug deeply into the Greek behind our English translations, let us explain two points: *Thanatos* is the name of the rider on the fourth horse, and *therion* (meaning "little beasts") is one of his weapons.

Pandemics are nothing new. Viruses are often, but not always, the culprit. Sometimes, bacteria can cause widespread destruction and loss of life.

As we've learned in recent months, viruses cause unspeakable diseases in humans. Avian influenza, smallpox, HIV, mumps, measles—all are caused by tiny machines known as viruses. Though not actually alive, these microscopic entities can inflict major harm to vulnerable populations.

Usually, the outer envelope of the virus contains a protein that allows it to merge with a membrane receptor protein in the target cell (plant, animal, or human). Once the viral protein and the host receptor protein conjoin (rather like docking to a space craft), the virus is permitted entry into the cell, where it forces the native cellular system to construct new viral particles.

You might say the virus converts our own DNA and associated proteins (histones, ribosomes, mRNA, tRNA, etc.) to become a molecular copy-machine. The result of this invasion is disease. Our immune systems react to the invader, causing fever, local or systemic swelling, vascular damage, and even organ failure and death. As our bodies try to expel the pathogen through sneezing, bleeding, urination, and defecation, the virus uses these reactions to infect new victims, creating a vicious cycle of stolen life— leading to death or debilitation of the host organism.

Some of the worst viruses known to mankind are also the tiniest. Collectively named as family *filoviridae*, Ebola and Marburg weaken the immune and vascular systems and induce massive blood loss in order to spread themselves to others. As humans continue to interact with remote caves and forests, we risk encountering new species that play host to silent killers.

But the risk is nothing new. For millennia, mankind has suffered plagues and pestilence. Thanatos, the rider known as Death, has been mounted and riding across the earth for a very long time.

In the Bible, sword, famine, and pestilence often ride together as a trio. The word "pestilence" occurs forty-seven times in the KJV, while "plague" makes ninety-eight appearances. In the Old Testament, these are translations of the Hebrew word *nega*, referring to a spot or scab on the skin. Twenty-six times, however, the OT writers chose to use the word *maggephah*, implying plague is a divine judgment. Inherent within *maggephah*'s meaning is the picture of slaughter or a sudden, fatal blow, rather like being butchered.

Secularists would bristle if we used only the Old Testament as proof of ancient plagues. For these scholars, we will use the great writers of antiquity. Among these is Thucydides., who kept notes on a plague that commenced in 430 BC:

> As a rule, however, there was no ostensible cause; but people in good health were all of a sudden attacked by violent heats in the head, and **redness and inflammation in the eyes**, the inward parts, such as the throat or tongue, **becoming bloody** and emitting an unnatural and fetid breath. These symptoms

were followed **by sneezing and hoarseness, after which the pain soon reached the chest, and produced a hard cough.** When it fixed in the stomach, it upset it; and **discharges of bile of every kind named by physicians ensued,** accompanied by very great distress. In most cases also an **ineffectual retching** followed, producing **violent spasms,** which in some cases ceased soon after, in others much later. Externally the body was not very hot to the touch, nor pale in its appearance, but **reddish, livid, and breaking out into small pustules and ulcers.** But internally it burned so that the **patient could not bear to have on him clothing or linen even of the very lightest description; or indeed to be otherwise than stark naked.** What they would have liked best would have been to throw themselves into cold water; as indeed was done by some of the neglected sick, who plunged into the rain-tanks in their agonies of **unquenchable thirst;** though it made no difference whether they drank little or much. Besides this, the miserable feeling of not being able to rest or sleep never ceased to torment them.

(Translation by R. Crawley, in M. I. Finley's *The Viking Portable Greek Historians,* pp. 274–75;[225] emphasis added)

We've highlighted several of the symptoms, including red eyes, bloody cough, diarrhea, pain to the touch, ripping off clothing due to being "hot" internally, and bloody pustules on the skin. All these are hallmarks of hemorrhagic fever viruses (HFV), which include Ebola and Marburg. It's not uncommon for Ebola patients to strip off their clothing—almost as though a type of madness seizes them. They can become violent and try to escape their hospital beds, as if the virus were driving them to escape, to go outdoors and spread the contagion to others.

First-century-BC writer Titus Lucretius Carus composed a poem about the Great Athens Plague, which includes symptoms that are all too familiar to those suffering during an HFV epidemic:

If any then
Had 'scaped the doom of that destruction, yet
Him there awaited in the after days
A wasting and a death from ulcers vile
And **black discharges** of the belly, or else
Through the clogged nostrils would there ooze along
Much **fouled blood**, oft with an **aching head**.[226]
(Emphasis added)

Ebola is but one of a larger family of HFVs that include filoviruses, arenaviruses, bunyaviruses, and flaviviruses. All arenaviruses were discovered and named in the twentieth century, most within the last few decades. These include LCMV, Junin, Machupo, Lassa, Guanarito, Sabia, Chapare, and Lujo.

Usually, the natural hosts for arenaviruses are rodents of some kind that are near or inside victims' homes and urinate/defecate onto beds and furniture and in corners. This allows the virus to become airborne whenever someone sweeps. Such an airborne virus can then enter human nostrils and gain access to the lungs. Also, these microscopic particles can land in food or water, which then spreads the virus to the gastrointestinal system—completing the cycle by excretion and further infection.

Bunyaviridae (bunyaviruses) include Hanta, Dugbe, Bunyamwera, Rift Valley, and Crimean-Congo. Bunyaviruses are transmitted by arachnids, primarily ticks.

However, Hanta is a rodent-borne disease, most memorable for the epidemic that broke out in the American southwest in the 1990s. *Sin Nombre* (Spanish for "nameless") was what the Mexican-Americans called the unknown killer that struck in the Four Corners region where Colorado, New Mexico, Arizona, and Utah meet. According to the Centers for Disease Control, the fatality rate during the *Sin Nombre* outbreak of Hanta was almost 67 percent. The deer mouse was determined to be the natural host, and urine/feces the means of infection. Spring cleaning had created airborne virus particles that infected nasal passages and lungs as women and children swept their homes.

Though most have never heard of it, the Hantavirus received its name in the middle of the twentieth century, during its initial known outbreak in South Korea near the Hantan River. (It is often customary to name an HFV for the nearest river or town.) The South Korean event ran from 1950–1953 and initiated the modern medical battle against HFV. More than three thousand troops, both American and South Korean, developed the disease. The mortality rate was calculated at 10 percent. This is considered low for HFV, which can run as high as *90 percent*. Remember, the mortality rate for COVID-19 is estimated at 1 percent or less.

What caused that original Hanta outbreak? What "little beast" helped carry the microscopic *therion*? Karl M. Johnson, an American virologist, partnered with South Korean virus hunter Ho-Wang Lee to ferret out the culprit: the striped-field mouse.

Flavivirus family members (*genera*) are well-known to most who follow epidemiological news. These include West Nile virus, Dengue, tick-borne encephalitis, and yellow fever. Flavus is the Latin term for "yellow," hence the family name. Victims are often jaundiced as a result of liver impairment, giving their skin a yellow cast.

In 1793, yellow fever—sometimes called the "American Plague"—killed more than 9 percent of Philadelphia's population. *Over 9 percent.* The vectors? Arthropods and arachnids, mosquitoes, and ticks are the primary culprits.

The final family of HFVs is the serpent. Why do we refer to this particular virus in such a manner? Because it looks like a serpent. The morphology (or "shape") of most other virus families is round (like a small sphere or even a Koosh ball), but family Filoviridae are shaped like ropes, shepherd crooks, worms, or *snakes* due to their unusual appearance. These have a linear portion that ends either in a curved, hook-like appendage or a circle (sometimes called the "Cheerio").

In Sharon's 2014 book, *Ebola and the Fourth Horseman of the*

Apocalypse, she documented the various phases of that terrible outbreak and the public reaction to it. In 2013, Ebola virus disease (EVD) was virtually unknown to the citizens of West Africa. Previously, the virus had struck only in Sudan, Uganda, and Zaire, where the other riders, Famine and War, had already left their marks.

Remember, Christ arrived in heaven and began to open the seals.

> And when he had opened the fourth seal, I heard the voice of the fourth beast say, Come and see. And I looked, and behold a pale horse: and his name that sat on him was Death, and Hell followed with him. And power was given unto them over the fourth part of the earth, to kill with sword, and with hunger, and with death, and with the beasts of the earth. (Revelation 6:7–8, KJV)

And in chapter 1, we learn that all that John wrote would soon come to pass:

> The revelation of Jesus Christ, which God gave him to show to his servants the things that **must soon take place**. He made it known by sending his angel to his servant John, who bore witness to the word of God and to the testimony of Jesus Christ, even to all that he saw. (Revelation 1:1–2; emphasis added)

The Greek word translated "soon" is *tachos*. It refers to something which is speedy or quick. It's used in the parable of woman who petitions the judge day and night for justice. Our Lord then uses this to make a promise:

> And will not God give justice to his elect, who cry to him day and night? Will he delay long over them? I tell you, he will **give justice to them speedily**. Nevertheless, when the Son of Man comes, will he find faith on earth?" (Luke 18:7–8; emphasis added)

The elect who are crying day and night in this parable may be the souls shown beneath the throne in the opening of the fifth seal:

When he opened the fifth seal, I saw under the altar the souls of those who had been slain for the word of God and for the witness they had borne. They cried out with a loud voice, "O Sovereign Lord, holy and true, how long before you will judge and avenge our blood on those who dwell on the earth?" (Revelation 6:9–10)

Since the first moment when man tasted death, those who place their faith in the Creator have pleaded for mercy and justice. Our enemy roams the earth as a ravenous lion, hunting us down and looking for easy prey, but our Lord sees it all—and He will take vengeance. That is the ultimate end of the long war between God and the fallen realm—the day when Christ judges the giants (demon spirits of the Nephilim), the small-*g* gods, and the dragons, along with all those who follow them.

We've studied the first rider at length. Conquest, most likely Apollo, who carries a bow. But did you know this word carries a double meaning?

The Greek word translated as "bow" is *toxon*, a very curious word that literally means "bow," but is derived from verb *tikto*, which means "to travail, to bring forth, to give birth." This picture of childbirth echoes a warning given by Jesus to His followers and to all of us: that TEOTWAWKI ("the End of the World as We Know It") will commence after much travail.

When His disciples asked what would be the signs for the coming of "the end of the age," Christ replied:

For many shall come in my name, saying, I am Christ; and shall deceive many. And ye shall hear of wars and rumors of wars: see that ye be not troubled: for all these things must come to pass, but the end is not yet. For nation shall rise against nation, and king-dom against kingdom: and there shall be famines, and pestilences, and earthquakes, in diverse places. All these are the beginning of **sorrows.** (Matthew 24:5–8, KJV; emphasis added)

Christ tells the disciples that imposters would arise and try to fool the people; wars would break out; and there would be famines and pestilences, but all these would be just the beginning of the sorrows. The word "sorrows" is *odin* (no, not the Norse god) in the original Greek, referring to "intolerable anguish" or "the pain of childbirth."

Christ is telling us that the Tribulation period, that final week of Daniel's prophecy, will be preceded by birth pangs.

If you're a woman who's given birth or if you have witnessed childbirth, then you know the intense pain that precedes and accompanies this awe-inspiring miracle. You may also know that birth pangs can be felt weeks before a child is due to be born. Most often, these early pangs are called "Braxton Hicks"[227] contractions (Dr. John Braxton Hicks lived in nineteenth-century London and makes an appearance in *The Redwing Saga*). These contractions feel like the real thing, but they are prodromal, a reminder that a child is on the way.

Prophetically speaking, they are harbingers of something about to be born—a new age, when the enemy—that old serpent—will set up a false kingdom and attempt to unseat Christ. Remember that, in Matthew 24, the disciples asked Jesus to tell them when the "end of the age" would occur. The time is now. Humanity is closing in on the final moments of the current age. Satan will try to set up *his* kingdom, but Christ's return will stop this seven-year lie in its unholy tracks.

One hundred years ago, the world was in the grip of a deadly wave of influenza. When the pandemic at last ended, the final tally of dead equaled anywhere from 2–5 percent of the global population. We know it today as H1N1, dubbed by the mainstream media of the day as the Spanish Flu.

The commonly quoted root of the pandemic lists the initial occurrence at Camp Funston, a US Army training camp in Fort Riley, Kansas.

However, recent research indicates that the pandemic started much earlier, as many as five to ten years earlier, in fact, as a localized epidemic in the Far East, probably China.[228]

When discussing influenza outbreaks, we need to wrap our heads around several terms. A "deme" refers to a local area or population. A village might be a "deme," or a cave filled with bats might be a deme. An "endemic" disease is one that lives and thrives within a "deme" without killing more individuals than replacement numbers can resupply. Such endemic diseases can even become symbiotic, meaning they serve a mutually advantageous purpose to the host species.

Wild animal populations often serve as hosts for endemic diseases. Bats, for instance, carry diseases like Marburg and Ebola alive. The animals might sicken; a few may even die. But overall, they learn to coexist with the pathogen. Occasionally, endemic viruses jump from their host to a different, vulnerable population, one never before exposed to it—and therefore lacking immunity. For instance, a pathogen could infect a human who wanders into a cave and touches bat guano (excrement). If the human becomes ill, he or she can infect friends and family, leading to a potential epidemic or even pandemic.

The 1918 Spanish Flu pandemic most likely originated in China as a local epidemic. The virus had probably been living within a local host population for decades or even centuries. When Chinese laborers were shipped to Canada and England, as well as to parts of Europe to serve as construction workers, because most young men were serving as soldiers in World War I, some of those aboard the ships were listed as ill or became ill during the voyage. These ships stopped at ports along the way for supplies, and the sailors enjoyed a little shore leave. Perhaps the "cargo"—the Chinese laborers—also had a chance to get off the ship for a few hours. Either way, it's believed that influenza literally *jumped ship* at these cities, infecting local populations with no immunity.

After arriving in their host countries, the Chinese men infected Canadians, Brits, Europeans, and any Americans who traveled to these locales.

Bottom line: The Spanish Flu was actually the Asian Flu.

Interestingly enough, another Asian flu infected all the world in the late nineteenth century. In May 1889, this virus emerged simultaneously in parts of India and the Crimea. It appeared in Russia and Turkey in August of that year, and by late December had reached nearly every country on the planet. How did it circle the globe so quickly? Travel. Ships had become much faster, crossing the Atlantic in just eight days, and railroads crisscrossed most of the world, moving carloads of humans for pennies a trip.

Called either the Russian or Asiatic Flu, the illness broke out in three waves:

The first caused many to fall ill. Paris reported *half its population* had taken to their beds, as did those in Constantinople and St. Petersburg. But most who contracted the disease recovered in a few days, and the symptoms were relatively light.

Wave number two hit a few years later, and those who'd suffered in round one became ill again; only this time, their symptoms proved much more severe, often leading to pneumonia and death. Paris newspapers wrote of bakeries shutting down and butcher shops falling silent, and the only people who worked at all were the funeral directors, who conducted as many as five hundred funerals a day!

Round three hit a few years after round two, and as before, the virus re-infected its previous victims. And once again, its virulence had increased during the lull. Numerous nobles and notables died during this wave, including Helena Blavatsky and Prince Albert Victor, the Queen's grandson.

So, what happened in the 1880s and '90s that might have prepared the Pale Rider for a worldwide spree twenty years later? Most likely, the virus, which lived in a local population of Asia, had mutated and begun to infect people more easily and efficiently. As with today's avian influenzas, which are endemic in domestic and wild birds, the Asiatic flu may have lived in local ducks, swans, or seagulls. Even today, Asian farmers often keep both birds and pigs in the same location, and pigs catch avian influenza very easily. Pigs can then spread the mutated avian flu to humans.

Birds to pigs to humans is a typical pathway for zoonotic influenza to take. "Zoonotic" means the virus jumps from animal hosts to humans. Pigs make efficient "mixing vessels" for viruses. Inside such an intermediate host, viruses can share genes, leading to genetic shift—a sudden alteration of the virus's DNA or RNA.

The wave-one virus in the nineteenth century most likely mutated on its own (a slower process called "genetic drift"), but it may have encountered other viruses inside local animals. Researchers don't really know what particular influenza virus caused the nineteenth-century pandemic, but it's thought to be a strain of H3. The *H* and *N* of virus names stand for "hemagglutinin" and "neuraminidase," respectively. The *H* protein allows the virus to enter a cell, and the *N* helps it get out so it can infect other cells.

Remember, a virus hijacks the human cell's molecular machinery and forces it to create copies of itself. These viral copies require a working neuraminidase to exit the cell, and they emerge wrapped in our own cell-membrane "coats." This makes it difficult for our immune systems to identify these viruses as invaders. Sneaky, huh?

BODY: "Hey, you're wearing one of our uniforms. You must be a good guy. Carry on with whatever it is you're doing."

VIRUS: "Yep, that's right. I'm one o' the good guys. Now, where did you say the lungs are again?"

Though the COVID-19 pandemic has removed it from the headlines, there's an H3 influenza strain making its way around the world. H3N2 is causing a spike in pneumonia cases in younger individuals, much like the nineteenth century pandemic did in waves two and three, and despite our health care advances, there is no treatment that currently works against it.

When the Pale Rider gallops across the globe, he brings with him many types of pestilence, but influenza certainly captures the imagination, with its historic death toll numbers—over a million in the nineteenth century, and as high as 5 percent of the world population during World War I.

We know that the type of influenza virus that devastated whole cities in the early twentieth century was H1N1, the first identified and numbered influenza virus, but we can only guess at what caused the three nineteenth century waves. Currently, there are no samples of the nineteenth-century virus available, for most of the bodies lay in hastily buried, unmarked graves. Also, influenza wasn't always listed as the cause of death in the doctor's notes. Sometimes, they say "laryngitis," "pneumonia," or even "headache." It seems that whatever symptom screamed the loudest was recorded as the cause.

Pandemics have caused the deaths of large swaths of populations for millennia, but Scripture makes it clear that, as we near the return of Christ, these will increase in number and severity. As devastating as it's been, COVID-19 is but a Braxton Hicks event.

Somewhere out there lurks an endemic virus, waiting for the perfect storm of mixing vessel, availability, access to vulnerable populations through travel, and brewing time.

Invisibility is a superpower. Ask any biological entity. For millennia, these microscopic creatures have managed to avoid detection and even recognition as a factor in disease. They've stealthily invaded human tissues and caused myriad maladies, reducing populations and sometimes wiping out whole cities. "Germ theory" is relatively new, commencing only in the mid-nineteenth century, but prior to Lister, Koch, and Pasteur, armies of *therion* marched unhindered through mankind's history.

Rider Four's name is *Thanatos*, who is one of a pair of psychopomp twins who escort the dead to the underworld. Thanatos takes the condemned unjust to hell, whilst Hypnos carries away the "just" or "justified," those who "fall asleep."

Hades (Hell) rides along with Thanatos, so it's no coincidence that the Pale Rider carries a *rhomphaia*—a curved blade, which looks very similar to the blade carried by Kronos, who used his to castrate his father, Ouranos.

You see, Hades and Kronos are both linked with the underworld—in fact, they're often named as rulers there.

Here's a clue embedded within the original Greek that escaped us for years. It's the actual meaning of the word translated "follow" (as in "Hades followed with him"). We've always pictured Hades as the big guy acting as the final, deadly aspect of this one-two punch. However, the Greek word, *akoloutheo,* implies a follower in the sense of a disciple or personal attendant. In other words, Hades is pictured as *subservient to Thanatos.*

This is the reverse of how most mythologies depict their relationship. According to most legends, Thanatos and his brother Hypnos serve Hades, not the other way around; yet verse 8 leads us to conclude that Hades is a bit of a "fan-boy," or even a squire, to Thanatos!

Come on. Since when is Hades, son of the Titan king, Kronos, anyone's servant? Is there more here than meets the eye? Possibly. After all, Thanatos is given pride of place in the list of four. He is the only rider who is *named,* and he is the last to arrive. The others are nothing but his warm-up acts.

So, who is Thanatos, anyway? According to Greek mythology, Thanatos was born of Nyx ("Night") by her brother Erebus.

And Erebus is the son of the primordial dragon, Chaos.

Get that? Thanatos is the grandson of *Chaos.* Nice family, huh?

Erebus's union with his sister Nyx produced Aether, Hymera, Hesperides, Hypnos, Moirai, Geras, Styx, Charon, and the twins Thanatos and Hypnos.

Here's the kicker: "Erebus" is another name for "Tartarus."

Did you get that?

The primordial dragon *Chaos* fathered *Tartarus,* who fathered *Death.*

Bottom line: The Pale Rider is way more than Clint Eastwood on an oddly colored horse. He is a very powerful rebel who is rising up out of Tartarus with Hell riding along as his disciple. When Death makes his final ride, the devastation to humanity will end the lives of one-quarter of all mankind.

We mentioned the *rhomphaia* carried by Thanatos (one very similar to that carried by Kronos), but Thanatos uses other weapons to end the lives of humans.

Here's the quote:

Power was given to them over the fourth part of the earth to kill with **the sword** and **with hunger** and **with death** and **with beasts**. (Revelation 6:8, KJV; emphasis added)

The Sword

Killing with a blade implies military actions or even terrorism. Recent headlines indicate a sharp rise in the number of blade-related crimes throughout the world, especially in England. Gangs of balaclava-wearing thieves on mopeds now use "zombie knives" to slash their victims' arms or wrists in order to steal purses, messenger bags, phones, or watches. These zombie knives can be purchased online and are advertised as the only weapon that will get you through the "Zombie Apocalypse." They also don't require a permit, background check, or even ammunition.

Guns don't kill people. Sin kills people.

But is this "sword" in Thanatos's hand merely a sign of chaotic crime sprees in the last days before Christ's return? It's one possibility, but we suspect it's much more. Greeks believed Thanatos used the *rhomphaia* to harvest souls. Depictions of Death often show a skeletal figure wearing a hooded, black robe. Usually, Death carries a curved blade; sometimes shown with a long staff like the scythe, other times carrying a shorter-handled, curved blade, as in a sickle—both denote the idea of harvesting.

HUNGER

This is the second manner of death employed by Thanatos and his hellish, fan-boy follower. During times of military actions, thousands, if not millions, of people lose their homes, their breadwinners, or both. This can lead to empty bellies. However, the Greek here is *limos*, and it means much more than missing a meal or two.

And, wait for it...

Limos is the name of the goddess of starvation.

Yep, Limos is another spirit entity, not merely a tactic. Limos is the daughter of Eris, the female aspect of chaos or discord. Homer saw Eris as the equivalent to Enyo, a war-goddess. Eris is also a daughter of Nyx, making Limos Thanatos's niece. Nepotism in the spirit realm. Hmm...

Limos is anything but beautiful. Ovid describes Limos thusly:

Her hair was coarse, her face sallow, her eyes sunken; her lips crusted and white; her throat scaly with scurf. Her parchment skin revealed the bowels within; beneath her hollow loins jutted her withered hips; her sagging breasts seemed hardly fastened to her ribs; her stomach only a void; her joints wasted and huge, her knees like balls, her ankles grossly swollen.[229]

Virgil tells us that Limos stands at the entrance to the underworld, beside the River of Lamentation, her ugly jaws open wide to swallow the dead as they arrive. No surprise then that Limos would accompany Thanatos on his ride.

She's been working with Uncle Thanatos all along.

DEATH

The third weapon is "death" (*thanatos*). This seems like a redundancy. Death killing with death? There must be a reason, so let's dig deeper.

The root word of *thanatos* is *thnesko*, which refers to spiritual death. While it's impossible to know precisely what John and the Holy Spirit want us to deduce from this passage, it could mean several things:

1) A loss of mortal life (physical death)
2) A loss of spiritual life (eternal death)
3) Or perhaps even a *living death*

What if the idea of a zombie apocalypse has merit? OK, we've passed into speculation land here, but bear with us for a minute. Numerous prophecies in the Bible refer to hordes of zombie-like soldiers that swarm into a city like a cloud of locusts (Joel 2, for example, but also see Isaiah 29 and Revelation 9). When the riders of Revelation start to radically alter the world, the current order will yield to Chaos; out of this, a New World Order will emerge.

We see glimpses of this shift now, such as the previously mentioned zombie knife gangs in London. Chaos, father of Erebus, who fathered Thanatos, seeks to reign once again on earth. The chaos-dragon has been clamoring to regain control of humanity and the earth since the moment the Spirit hovered over the face of the waters (Hebrew *tehowm*, meaning "chaos" or "Apsu," that is, the primordial chaos-dragon, Leviathan, in Genesis 1:2).

Bottom line: Chaos is using his kids to pave the way for his return. Like a netherworld general—who's hiding in plain sight—Leviathan sends out his troops to corrupt human souls, play upon our sinful natures, and mold us into images of himself. Thanatos and his spirit companions form the final stage of this massive strategy.

After all, invisibility is a superpower.

BEASTS

Therion is the final weapon in Thanatos' arsenal. The general translation of *therion* is "beasts of the earth." While true, there's much more to it.

First of all, it may refer to actual "beasts" or wild animals. As chaos arises across the earth (in the wake of the Four Riders' travels), city services and infrastructure will break down, and zoos will likely empty. Starving animals will flee their enclosures (especially if cages are locked electronically), but also, research animals in the world's thousands of laboratories could escape. Picture what might have happened in Reston, Virginia, if the Ebola-ridden monkeys housed at the animal facility there had escaped back in 1989, and then multiply that by a factor of ten thousand or more.

A second meaning to *therion* might refer to the virus riding in the bloodstreams of those escaped monkeys, or to an emerging disease not yet discovered. "Little beasts" is the proper translation of the Greek term, for *therion* is a diminutive of *thera*. Thera can mean "wild animals" (as in game animals, such as boars), or it can be used metaphorically, as in "preparing the destruction of men."

"Little beasts" may also refer to microscopic "beasts," which until the nineteenth century evaded detection with their invisibility superpowers. We think we know all about them today, but most are still poorly understood, and some are mutating into more pathogenic forms. Yet others still hide within host organisms, awaiting their chance to infect a wary hunter or tourist.

Therion is also the Greek name for a constellation, and this gets us into *Redwing Saga* territory again. *The Redwing Saga* is about spiritual warfare, focusing on the battle between the good guys (the inner circle) and the bad guys (Redwing, and later Blackstone, and finally the White Council). Redwing experiments with human and angelic partnerships, hybridizing humans with wolf "germ plasm" (we'd call it DNA).

How does Therion take us there? You see, the constellation Therion is also called Lupus.

Yep. The Wolf. The Greeks called this southern-sky constellation after their word for "little beast." Lupus dwells in the stars with the Centaur, Hydra, and Scorpion constellations. It's thought that the constellation Therion might be based on a Babylonian figure called "The Mad Dog," a hybrid with the head and torso of a man, and the legs and tail of a lion. The Mad Dog is often linked to another Babylonian figure called the "Bison-man," an intercessor for Marduk.

Derek wrote about bison-man imagery in *Last Clash of the Titans*, revealing how the theriomorphic species of spiritual villain is connected with—yep, you guessed it—the Titans:

> The Akkadians believed that the primordial chaos-dragon Tiamat was served by a host of demonic creatures, one of which was the *kusarikku,* or "bison-man."[230] This chimera was human above

and bovine below, a sort of bullish centaur but with horns on the human head. The *kusarikku* was defeated by the god Ninurta, but it was also associated with—surprise!—**the Titans, by way of the ancient Amorite Ditanu tribe.**

A similar creature called the *kusarikku*, or **bison-man**, was also a common figure in Mesopotamian religious art as far back as the Sumerian Early Dynastic period (2900–2350 BC). The bison-man was a type of demon, possibly originally associated with the sun-god Shamash. Later, in the Babylonian creation myth, **the *kusarikku* appears in the army of the chaos serpent Tiamat in her battle against Marduk.**[231] (Emphasis added)

Derek provides a strong case that Kronos and Molech may be the same entity. Both are bovid, or bull-like, in appearance (the name "Kronos" actually means "horned one").

And there's a real twist in this description of the disease-spreading rider upon the fourth horse. If he's wielding weapons that relate to a host of entities (Limos, Therion, and even Thnesko, as "Death"), then are these really weapons or something else?

Might they be his partners?

Aspects of his personality?

Followers on hell's version of a social media site?

It's difficult to reach a rock-solid conclusion, but the fact that these words indicate *both weapons and entities* is a major clue. Another is the notion of "plague" in the primary weapon, *therion*. Why?

Simple.

Rephaim.

First Titans and now the Rephaim? Derek has spent years researching the connection between the Titans and the biblical Rephaim.

References to the Valley of Rephaim/Titans also occur in 2 Samuel 23:13 and 1 Chronicles 11:15. Another mention of the Titans occurs in the apocryphal (for Protestants) book of Judith:

The Assyrian came down from the mountains of the north;
he came with myriads of his warriors;
their numbers blocked up the wadis,
and their cavalry covered the hills.
He boasted that he would burn up my territory,
and kill my young men with the sword,
and dash my infants to the ground,
and seize my children as booty,
and take my virgins as spoil.
But the Lord Almighty has foiled them
by the hand of a woman.
For their mighty one did not fall by the hands of the young
men,
nor did the sons of the Titans strike him down,
nor did tall giants set upon him;
but Judith daughter of Merari
with the beauty of her countenance undid him.
　　(Judith 16:3–6, NRSV; emphasis added)

Since the oldest text of Judith available to us today is from the Septuagint, we don't really know the book's original language.[232] It may have been composed in Greek, since the earliest Hebrew copy is from the Middle Ages.

The point? By the time the Greeks controlled the lands of the Bible, after the conquests of Alexander the Great in the fourth century BC, the religious scholars and scribes of the Jews had no problem directly linking the Titans to the Rephaim and identifying them specifically as giants—the Nephilim, sons of the rebel gods who'd rejected the authority of the Creator.

Okay, then, we can connect Thanatos to Kronos and perhaps even Molech through the idea of theriomorphic (bovid or bull-like) imagery. It's tenuous but bear with us.

Rephaim has numerous connotations, all based on how we interpret the root word, *rpu*.

First of all, they're sometimes called "healers." The root of the word rendered "healer" is *rp'*, the same one behind the name "Rephaim." We see this idea of healing in the attributes of ancient gods (read that as "spiritual rebels") like Asclepius and Apollo, who is also a god of plague, carrying a two-edged sort of weapon in his hand—bringing plague or health, depending on how he feels about you that day, or whether you are willing to appease him.

There's another aspect to the name Rephaim that undergirds the notion of this scenario being way more than Death on a green horse. Again, using Derek's excellent research, let us quote from a section of chapter 4 of *Last Clash of the Titans*, "The Great Ones":

> Searching for hints about the Rephaim in texts outside the Bible gets more difficult as you go farther back in history. While most scholars lean toward a definition of the Semitic root *rp'* as "healers," another meaning has been proposed:
>
> In the light of the repeated occurrence of *rp'um* in military and heroic contexts and the inadequacy of alternative hypotheses, the significance of Ugaritic *r-p-'* might best be understood in the light of Akkadian *raba'um* "to be large, great," and its derivative *rabium* (< *rabûm*) "leader, chief." **Thus, the *rp'um* would be "the Great Ones" or "the Mighty Ones."**[233] (emphasis added)

Mighty Ones? Great Ones? Sounds familiar, doesn't it? How about "Men of Renown"?

Boom. Nephilim. Rephaim. Titans.

Our conclusion?

Death and his entourage are Titans, possibly accompanied by members of the Rephaim, who, as we noted earlier, are the demons who've plagued the world for thousands of years. Maybe all of the Horsemen are Titans, or perhaps the first three are just the opening acts to a final grouping.

Does this sound far-fetched, this connection between the Bible's prophecies of the end of the age and the Greek mythology we were taught in school?

It wasn't strange at all to the early church.

As we showed you in an earlier chapter, the second-century theologian Irenaeus, a student of Polycarp, who in turn was a disciple of the apostle John, concluded that the most likely name of "he who is to come"—the Antichrist—is "Titan." Bear in mind that Irenaeus wrote *Against Heresies* around AD 180,[234] about ninety years after John wrote Revelation.

Remember, John's disciple Polycarp was Irenaeus' mentor. While there is no evidence one way or the other, it's possible that Irenaeus' thoughts about the Antichrist might have come from John himself.

The bottom line is this: These entities have been riding across our world, acting as spies and warriors, bringing wars and plagues with them during times of great stress. However, these have been but Braxton Hicks contractions—prodromal events presaging the final ride.

Soon, these Titans will bring back their own brand of chaos and havoc to our space/time continuum.

Oh, and there's one more tactic Death is convincing his human acolytes to use: transhumanism.

The primary goal of tranhumanists is to eradicate death from our world—at least, death as it relates to humans. They seek to upgrade themselves, using technology and medicine. But they fail to realize that, in so doing, they are worshiping at the cloven feet of Thanatos and his buddies.

But here's the kicker. From Revelation 9, we see this:

And the fifth angel blew his trumpet, and I saw a star fallen from heaven to earth, and he was given the key to the shaft of the bottomless pit. He opened the shaft of the bottomless pit, and from the shaft rose smoke like the smoke of a great furnace, and the sun and the air were darkened with the smoke from the shaft. Then from the smoke came locusts on the earth, and they were given power like the power of scorpions of the earth. They were told not to harm the grass of the earth or any green plant or any tree, but only those people who do not have the seal of God on their foreheads. They were allowed to torment them for five months, but not to kill them, and their torment was like the torment of a scorpion when it stings someone. **And in those days people will seek death and will not find it. They will long to die, but death will flee from them.**

In appearance the locusts were like horses prepared for battle: on their heads were what looked like crowns of gold; their faces were like human faces, heir hair like women's hair, and their teeth like lions' teeth; they had breastplates like breastplates of iron, and the noise of their wings was like the noise of many chariots with horses rushing into battle. They have tails and stings like scorpions, and their power to hurt people for five months is in their tails. **They have as king over them the angel of the bottomless pit. His name in Hebrew is Abaddon, and in Greek he is called Apollyon.** (Revelation 9:1–11; emphasis added)

Note the appearance of these locusts. It is theriomorphic (beastlike), just like Kronos the Titan, the horned king of the old gods now locked away in the abyss. These Titans—these giants, gods, and dragons—are coming back, and in one final act of rebellion, one of their theriomorphic leaders will inflict a plague upon mankind and slay a fourth part of the earth.

But then, in a Crazy Ivan course correction, he will turn about 180 degrees and remove the option for death. Men will seek death, and it will flee from them.

The transhumanist desire for eternal life will suddenly flip into a desire to die, but a release from hell on earth will be denied to them—to all those who deny the saving blood of Jesus Christ, who join the Titan agenda.

As you read this, a division of Thanatos's *therion* soldiers surround you.

It's called COVID-19, but this "little beast" has lots of friends who've yet to be deployed. They linger upon your surfaces, sit beside your children, and ride upon the molecules of the air like hellish ghosts with tiny teeth.

We are at war, but most of us have no idea that we stand upon a battlefield. If you consider the ultimate origin of all these *therion* beasts, then you'll understand the nature of our enemy. It is spiritual at its rotten core. Thanatos is an entity. Hades is an entity. And *therion* are supernaturally organized battalions who follow Death.

CONCLUSION

"Oh, make no mistake, we are in the end times," the preacher said. "But the exact day and hour? Jesus said even He didn't know… No, Agent Unes, anyone who says he's figured out the precise date is probably selling something."

—Pastor Ed Harper to FBI Special Agent Joe Unes, Chapter 15 of *The God Conspiracy* by Derek P. Gilbert

He who testifies to these things says, "Surely I am coming soon." Amen. Come, Lord Jesus!

—Revelation 22:20

The Lord is telling us that the final days are here. Chaos in our streets, locust swarms across Africa and Asia, earthquakes in odd places, strange weather phenomena, green comets, volcanoes, and a fire outside the nuclear plant called "Wormwood."

How do we respond? Consider all this as joy, dear friends, for as James 1:3 tells us:

…the testing of our faith produces steadfastness. And let steadfastness have its full effect, that you may be perfect and complete, lacking in nothing.

We're living in a spiritual pressure cooker right now, a refiner's furnace—or perhaps a threshing floor, where the chaff is separated and burned. The Holy Spirit within us withstands all such pressures and leaves us purer, stronger, more on fire for Him.

Yes, the Titans are coming. The giants, the gods, and the dragons—Satan and his seven-headed commander-in-chief, the Beast—want to kill us, but remember that Jesus created all of them.

And He won the war on the cross. Our job today isn't to worry, grumble, or hide our lights under bushels. No! We're to lift up Christ—crucified, risen, and coming again! The warning bells are sounding, and our response should be to run towards the battle, wearing the armor God has given us.

In John 12:31–32 Jesus declares His victory:

Now is the judgment of this world; **now will the ruler of this world be cast out.** And I, when I am lifted up from the earth, will draw all people to myself. (Emphasis added)

Satan is about to be cast out as "ruler of this world." Christ shed His blood to win the spiritual war that has raged since Genesis. He is the fulfillment of the promise God made to Adam and Eve in the Garden. Christ, the seed of woman, will soon, once and for all time, crush the heads of Leviathan.

That's the good news, and right now, those hiding in fear of a virus are primed to hear it. Let's preach it while we still have the freedom to do so!

NOTES

1. Tom Embury-Dennis. "Anak Krakatau Eruption, Indonesian Volcano Which Triggered Deadly Tsunami in 2019 Erupts Again," *The Independent*, April 10, 2020. https://www.independent.co.uk/news/world/asia/anak-krakatau-volcano-eruption-news-indonesia-ash-tsunami-island-a9460491.html, retrieved 8/12/20.
2. Charles P. Pierce. "An Extremely Normal Weekend of Pestilence, Locusts, a Fire in Chernobyl, and a Volcano," *Esquire*, April 13, 2020 . https://www.esquire.com/news-politics/politics/a32127561/volcano-chernobyl-fire-locusts-weekend/, retrieved 8/12/20.
3. 1 Chronicles 5:4.
4. Hesiod. *The Homeric Hymns and Homerica with an English Translation by Hugh G. Evelyn-White. Theogony* (Cambridge, MA: Harvard University Press; London, William Heinemann Ltd., 1914).
5. J. W. Van Henten. "Typhon," in K. van der Toorn, B. Becking, & P. W. van der Horst (Eds.), *Dictionary of Deities and Demons in the Bible* 2nd extensively rev. ed. (Leiden; Boston; Köln; Grand Rapids, MI; Cambridge: Brill; Eerdmans, 1999), p. 879.
6. Hesiod. op. cit.
7. Apollodorus. *Library and Epitome (English)*. J. G. Frazer, Ed. (Medford, MA: Perseus Digital Library), p. 47.
8. Irenaeus. *Against Heresies*, Book V, Chapter 30.
9. Luke 22:3.

10. 2 Corinthians 11:4.

11. Numbers 21:4–9.

12. Genesis 3:24.

13. J. A. Black, G. Cunningham, E. Fluckiger-Hawker, E. Robson, and G. Zólyomi. "The Sumerian King List: Translation," *The Electronic Text Corpus of Sumerian Literature* (http://etcsl.orinst.ox.ac.uk/section2/tr211.htm), retrieved 12/24/16.

14. C. S. Coon. "The Eridu Crania: A Preliminary Report," *Sumer* 5, 1949, p. 103.

15. Kirsi O. Lorentz. "Ubaid Headshaping: Negotiations of Identity Through Physical Appearance?" in *Beyond the Ubaid: Transformation and Integration in the Late Prehistoric Societies of the Middle East,* Robert A. Carter and Graham Philip eds. (Chicago: University of Chicago Oriental Institute, 2010), pp. 141–142.

16. Rose Solecki, Peter M. M. G. Akkermans, Anagnostis Agelarakis, Christopher Meiklejohn, and Philip E. L. Smith. "Artificial Cranial Deformation in the Proto-neolithic and Neolithic Near East and Its Possible Origin: Evidence from Four Sites," *Paléorient,* 1992, vol. 18, no. 2, pp. 83–97.

17. Gil Stein. "Economy, Ritual, and Power in Ubaid Mesopotamia," in *Chiefdoms and Early States in the Near East: The Organizational Dynamics of Complexity,* Gil Stein and Mitchell Rothman eds. (Madison, WI: Prehistory Press, 1994), pp. 35–46.

18. Stephanie Dalley. "Babylon as a Name for Other Cities Including Nineveh," *Proceedings of the 51st Rencontre Assyriologique Internationale,* eds. R.D. Biggs et al (Chicago: Oriental Institute of the University of Chicago, 2008), pp. 25–33.

19. Fu'ād Safar, Seton Lloyd, Muḥammad 'Alī Muṣṭafá, Mu'assasah al-'Āmmah lil-Āthār wa-al-Turāth. *Eridu* (Baghdad: Republic of Iraq, Ministry of Culture and Information, State Organization of Antiquities and Heritage, 1981), p. 46.

20. Ibid.

21. J. A. Black, G. Cunningham, E. Fluckiger-Hawker, E. Robson, and G. Zólyomi. "Enmerkar and the Lord of Aratta," *The Electronic Text Corpus of Sumerian Literature* (http://etcsl.orinst.ox.ac.uk/cgi-bin/etcsl.cgi?text=t.1.8.2.3#), retrieved 12/17/16.

22. J. A. Black, G. Cunningham, E. Fluckiger-Hawker, E. Robson, and G. Zólyomi. "A *cir-namcub* to Inana (Inana I)," *The Electronic Text*

Corpus of Sumerian Literature (http://etcsl.orinst.ox.ac.uk/cgi-bin/etcsl.
cgi?text=t.4.07.9&charenc=j#), retrieved 12/17/16.

23. A. W. Sjoberg. "In-nin Sa-gur-ra: A Hymn to the Goddess Inanna," *Zeitschrift
fur Assyriologie* 65, no. 2 (1976), p. 225.

24. "Enmerkar and the Lord of Aratta," op. cit.

25. Ibid.

26. Samuel N. Kramer. "The Babel of Tongues: A Sumerian Version," *Journal of
the American Oriental Society* 88 (1968), pp. 108–11.

27. William Harms. "Evidence of Battle at Hamoukar Points to Early Urban
Development," *University of Chicago Chronicle* 26:8 (2007). http://chronicle.
uchicago.edu/070118/hamoukar.shtml, retrieved 8/10/20.

28. Safar, et al, op. cit.

29. Edward Lipiński. "El's Abode: Mythological Traditions Related to Mount
Hermon and to the Mountains of Armenia," *Orientalia Lovaniensa Periodica*
2 (1971), p. 19.

30. Dr. Michael S. Heiser. "The Nephilim," *SitchinisWrong.com* (http://www.
sitchiniswrong.com/nephilim/nephilim.htm), retrieved 12/16/16.

31. Dr. Michael S. Heiser. "Deuteronomy 32:8 and the Sons of God," *Bibliotheca
Sacra* 158 (January–March 2001), p. 54.

32. Amar Annus. "On the Origin of Watchers: A Comparative Study of the
Antediluvian Wisdom in Mesopotamian and Jewish Traditions," *Journal for
the Study of the Pseudepigrapha* 19.4 (2010), pp. 277–320.

33. "Gilgamesh Tomb Believed Found," *BBC News*, April 29, 2003. http://news.
bbc.co.uk/2/hi/science/nature/2982891.stm, retrieved 7/29/20.

34. David Livingston. "Who Was Nimrod?" *Ancient Days*, http://davelivingston.
com/nimrod.htm, retrieved 7/29/20.

35. Translation of the Mount Hermon stela by George Nickelsburg.

36. British Museum entry for the Mount Hermon stele can be found online
in the museum's catalogue: https://www.britishmuseum.org/collection/
object/G_1903-0422-1 (accessed May 18, 2020).

37. Sir Robert Anderson. *The Coming Prince, Or, the Seventy Weeks of Daniel: With
an Answer to the Higher Criticism* (London: James Nisbett and Company,
1915).

38. It sounds bizarre, but it's true. Our home is too far from trees for the
mysterious visitor to be a raccoon or a big cat, and besides, the footsteps are
bipedal and much too heavy. The sound is that of a man walking across the
roof.

39. Derek P. Gilbert. *Bad Moon Rising* (Crane, MO: Defender, 2019), pp. 77–80.

40. Adam Clarke. *The Holy Bible: Containing the Old and New Testaments with a Commentary and Critical Notes to a Better Understanding of the Sacred Writings, Vol. IV* (New York: Abraham Paul, 1825) p. 336.

41. Adam Clarke. *Bible Commentary on Book of Daniel* (1831). https://www. studylight.org/commentaries/acc/daniel-11.html, accessed August 1, 2020.

42. See *The Great Inception* for Derek's reasons for believing that Eridu was the city built by Cain.

43. "The Sumerian King List: Translation," op. cit.

44. "Enmerkar and the Lord of Aratta: Translation," op. cit.

45. Safar, et al, op. cit., p. 46.

46. John 14:30 and 16:11.

47. Matthew 24:24.

48. Jaap Doedens. *The Sons of God in Genesis 6:1–4* (Leiden: Brill, 2019), pp. 250–252.

49. Jeremy Hultin. "Jude's Citation of 1 Enoch," in *Jewish and Christian Scriptures: The Function of "Canonical" and "Non-Canonical" Religious Texts*, James H. Charlesworth and Lee M. McDonald, eds. (Edinburgh: T & T Clark, 2010), p. 114.

50. See, for example, the commentary by A. W. Fausset on Revelation 6: https:// www.blueletterbible.org/Comm/jfb/Rev/Rev_006.cfm?a=1173001, retrieved 5/4/20.

51. "Toxic." *Dictionary.com*. https://www.dictionary.com/browse/toxic, retrieved 5/4/20.

52. Revelation 19:15.

53. Strong's G4735. https://www.blueletterbible.org/lang/lexicon/lexicon. cfm?t=kjv&strongs=g4735, retrieved 5/4/20.

54. Revelation 19:12.

55. Matthew 27:29, Mark 15:17, John 19:2, 5.

56. Revelation 12:3.

57. Revelation 13:1.

58. Deuteronomy 8:15, Numbers 21:6, 8.

59. Ezekiel 1:20.

60. Giovanni Pettinato. *The Archives of Ebla: An Empire Inscribed in Clay* (Garden City, NY: Doubleday & Company, Inc., 1981), p. 247.

61. Baal became king of the pantheon by defeating the sea-god, Yam, in single combat. By parting the sea at a place called Baal-Zephon (Exodus 14:2),

named for the mountain in Turkey where Baal's palace was located, God demonstrated His power over Baal's domain.

62. "Erra (god)." *Ancient Mesopotamia Gods and Goddesses*, http://oracc.museum. upenn.edu/amgg/listofdeities/erra/, retrieved 5/5/20.

63. Peter Machinist. "Rest and Violence in the Epic of Erra," *Journal of the American Oriental Society* 103.1 (1983), p. 221.

64. Paolo Xella. "Resheph," in K. van der Toorn, B. Becking, & P. W. van der Horst (Eds.), *Dictionary of Deities and Demons in the Bible* (2nd extensively rev. ed.). (Leiden; Boston; Köln; Grand Rapids, MI; Cambridge: Brill; Eerdmans, 1999), p. 702.

65. Ramesses erected a commemorative stela dedicated to Baal and Ramesses' father, Seti I.

66. Xella, op. cit., p. 701.

67. Maciej M. Münnich. *The God Resheph in the ancient Near East* (Tübingen: Mohr Siebeck, 2013), p. 102.

68. Douglas N. Petrovich. "Amenhotep II and the Historicity of the Exodus Pharaoh," http://exegesisinternational.org/pdf/ExodusPharaohArticle.pdf, retrieved 9/15/20.

69. Pettinato, op. cit., p. 248.

70. Joshua 8:30–35.

71. Deuteronomy 11:29.

72. Assaf Kamar. "A Rare Visit to the Supposed Altar of Prophet Joshua." *Ynet News*, August 9, 2016 (https://www.ynetnews.com/articles/0,7340,L-4838962,00.html), retrieved 5/5/20.

73. Xella, op. cit., p. 702.

74. It is not a coincidence that the creators of the current HBO science-fiction drama series *Westworld* named the company that created the godlike synthetic "hosts" Delos.

75. Wilfred G. Lambert. *Babylonian Oracle Questions* (Winona Lake, IN: Eisenbrauns, 2007), p. 1.

76. Mark Cartwright. "Delphi," *Ancient History Encyclopedia*, https://www. ancient.eu/delphi/, retrieved 5/16/20.

77. Diodorus Siculus. *Library of History*, Book XVI, 26:1–4.

78. H5172, *Strong's Hebrew Lexicon*. https://www.blueletterbible.org/lang/lexicon/lexicon.cfm?strongs=H5172&t=KJV, retrieved 5/17/20.

79. R. Van den Broek. "Apollo," in K. van der Toorn, B. Becking, & P. W. van der Horst (Eds.), *Dictionary of Deities and Demons in the Bible*, 2nd extensively

rev. ed. (Leiden; Boston; Köln; Grand Rapids, MI; Cambridge: Brill; Eerdmans, 1999), p. 76.

80. Eusebius. *Life of Constantine* 2.50. Translated by Ernest Cushing Richardson. From *Nicene and Post-Nicene Fathers*, Second Series, Vol. 1. Edited by Philip Schaff and Henry Wace (Buffalo, NY: Christian Literature Publishing Co., 1890). http://www.newadvent.org/fathers/2502.htm, retrieved 5/17/20.

81. Elizabeth Depalma Digeser. "An Oracle of Apollo at Daphne and the Great Persecution," *Classical Philology*, Vol. 99, No. 1 (January 2004), p. 73.

82. Lactantius. *On the Deaths of the Persecutors* 11.7. https://people.ucalgary. ca/~vandersp/Courses/texts/lactant/lactpers.html#XI, retrieved 5/17/20.

83. Paul Pavao. "Diocletian and the Great Persecution," Christian History for Everyman. Greatest Stories Ever Told. 2014. https://www.christian-history. org/diocletian.html, retrieved 5/17/20.

84. Michael Gaddis. *There Is No Crime for Those Who Have Christ: Religious Violence in the Christian Roman Empire* (Berkeley, Los Angeles, and London: University of California Press, 2005), p. 29.

85. Ramsay MacMullen and Eugene Lane. *Paganism and Christianity, 100–425 C.E.: A Sourcebook* (United States: Fortress Press, 1992), p. 287.

86. Eusebius. *Church History* Book VIII, 16.4 (https://www.newadvent.org/ fathers/250108.htm, retrieved 5/17/20); and Lactantius, *Of the Manner in Which the Persecutors Died* 16 (https://www.newadvent.org/fathers/0705.htm, retrieved 5/17/20).

87. Josephus. *Antiquities of the Jews*, Book XVII 6.5 (https://www.ccel.org/j/ josephus/works/ant-17.htm, retrieved 5/17/20).

88. Acts 12:23.

89. *Divine Institutes* 1.7.1.

90. R. Van den Broek, op. cit.

91. Pausanias, *Description of Greece* 10.7.8. https://www.theoi.com/Text/ Pausanias10A.html, retrieved 5/18/20.

92. Jon D. Mikalson. *Ancient Greek Religion* (Chichester: Wiley-Blackwell, 2011), p. 103.

93. Ibid.

94. Titus Livius (Livy). *The History of Rome*, Book 4.25.3.

95. Philip V. Hill. "The Temples and Statues of Apollo in Rome." *The Numismatic Chronicle and Journal of the Royal Numismatic Society*, Seventh Series, Vol. 2 (1962), p. 126.

96. Michael C. Astour. *Hellenosemitica: An Ethnic and Cultural Study in West Semitic Impact on Mycenaean Greece* (Leiden: Brill, 1965), p. 247.

97. Homer. *Iliad* 1:250. Translated by Murray, A T. Loeb Classical Library Volumes 1 (Cambridge, MA, Harvard University Press; London, William Heinemann Ltd., 1924). https://www.theoi.com/Text/HomerIliad1.html, retrieved 5/18/20.

98. Amar Annus. "Are There Greek Rephaim? On the Etymology of Greek *Meropes* and *Titanes*," *Ugarit-Forschungen* 31 (1999), pp. 14–15.

99. Strong's Concordance H7495. https://www.blueletterbible.org/lang/lexicon/lexicon.cfm?strongs=H7495, retrieved 8/12/20.

100. Isaiah 14:9.

101. Isaiah 26:13–14. The "lords" in v. 13 are the "shades" (Rephaim) of v. 14.

102. For an in-depth exploration of the evidence behind this paragraph, please see our previous book *Veneration*.

103. F. Graf. "Heros," in K. van der Toorn, B. Becking, & P. W. van der Horst (Eds.), *Dictionary of Deities and Demons in the Bible* 2nd extensively rev. ed. (Leiden; Boston; Köln; Grand Rapids, MI; Cambridge: Brill; Eerdmans, 1999), p. 414.

104. David K. Osborn. "The Asclepeions: Sanctuaries of Healing," GreekMedicine.net, www.greekmedicine.net/mythology/asclepions.html, retrieved 5/18/20.

105. See Daniel 4. Nebuchadnezzar, the Chaldean king of Babylon, was punished for his excessive pride "by the decree of the Watchers."

106. Isaac Roberts and Patrick Brewer. "Apollo: Foreigner in Rome," *MQ Ancient History: City of Rome Blog* (https://ancient-history-blog.mq.edu.au/cityOfRome/ApolloBlog), retrieved 5/12/20.

107. Hill, op. cit., p. 130.

108. Miriam T. Griffin. *Nero: The End of a Dynasty* (London: Routledge, 2000), pp. 41–42.

109. Edward Champlin. "Nero, Apollo, and the Poets," *Phoenix*, Vol. 57, No. 3/4 (Autumn–Winter, 2003), p. 282.

110. Jennifer Zilm, ed. "Sibylline Oracles." Edition 1.0. In *The Online Critical Pseudepigrapha*. Edited by Ian W. Scott. (Atlanta: SBL Publishing, 2010), http://www.purl.org/net/ocp/SibOr, retrieved 5/20/20.

111. Augustine of Hippo. *City of God* XX.19.3. https://www.newadvent.org/fathers/120120.htm, retrieved 5/20/20.

112. 1 Corinthians 2:6–8.

113. "Number of Military and DoD Appropriated Fund (APF) Civilian Personnel Permanently Assigned by Duty Location and Service/Component (as of March 31, 2020)." Defense Manpower Data Center. May 8, 2020.

https://www.dmdc.osd.mil/appj/dwp/rest/download?fileName=DMDC_
Website_Location_Report_2003.xlsx&groupName=milRegionCountry,
retrieved 8/12/20.

114. Stephanie Savell and 5W Infographics. "This Map Shows Where in the
World the U.S. Military Is Combatting Terrorism," *Smithsonian Magazine*,
January 2019. https://www.smithsonianmag.com/history/map-shows-
places-world-where-us-military-operates-180970997/, retrieved 8/12/20.

115. Revelation 9:1.

116. Manfred Hutter. "Abaddon," in K. van der Toorn, B. Becking, & P. W.
van der Horst (Eds.), *Dictionary of Deities and Demons in the Bible* (2nd
extensively rev. ed.). (Leiden; Boston; Köln; Grand Rapids, MI; Cambridge:
Brill; Eerdmans, 1999), p. 1.

117. See the Rephaim Texts from Ugarit, KTU 1.20–1.22.

118. See Raymond Ibrahim's excellent book, *Sword and Scimitar: Fourteen
Centuries of War Between Islam and the West.*

119. 1 Kings 11:7; 2 Kings 23:13.

120. Pettinato, op. cit., p. 257.

121. Ibid., 292.

122. Jeremiah 46:2; 2 Chronicles 35:20; Isaiah 10:9.

123. Genesis 19:37.

124. "The Stela of Mesha." Livius.org (http://www.livius.org/sources/content/
anet/320-the-stela-of-mesha/), retrieved 12/27/18.

125. Diodorus Siculus. *The Library of History*, Book XX, Chapter 14, *Lacus
Curtius* (http://penelope.uchicago.edu/Thayer/E/Roman/Texts/Diodorus_
Siculus/20A*.html), retrieved 12/27/18.

126. Anthony J. Spalinger. "A Canaanite Ritual Found in Egyptian Reliefs,"
Journal of the Society for the Study of Egyptian Antiquities 8 (1978), p. 50.

127. David Flusser. *Judaism of the Second Temple Period: Sages and Literature*
(Grand Rapids, Mich.; Cambridge; Jerusalem: William B. Eerdmans
Publishing Company: Hebrew University Magnes Press, 2009), p. 41.

128. 1 Enoch 69:6.

129. Book of Jubilees 10:8, 17:15–16.

130. "Jewish Concepts: Angels and Angelology," *Jewish Virtual Library* (https://
www.jewishvirtuallibrary.org/angels-and-angelology-2), retrieved 12/28/18.

131. C. Houtman. "Queen of Heaven," in K. van der Toorn, B. Becking, & P.
W. van der Horst (Eds.), *Dictionary of Deities and Demons in the Bible* (2nd
extensively rev. ed.) (Leiden; Boston; Köln; Grand Rapids, MI; Cambridge:
Brill; Eerdmans, 1999), p. 678.

132. Ibid.

133. Robert G. Hoyland. *Arabia and the Arabs: From the Bronze Age to the Coming of Islam* (London; New York, Routledge), p. 140.

134. Collin Cornell. "What Happened to Kemosh?" *Zeitschrift für die alttestamentliche Wissenschaft* 128(2) (2016), p. 10.

135. Ibid., p. 12.

136. See Genesis 4:17–24. Lamech was of the line of Cain. As Derek argues in *The Great Inception*, the oldest Sumerian city, Eridu, home of Enki's temple *E-abzu* ("House of the Abyss") was probably built by Cain and named for Lamech's great-grandfather, Irad. The link between the line of Cain and the god of the abyss may help explain Lamech's murderous response to being insulted.

137. University of Chicago. "Earliest Evidence for Large Scale Organized Warfare in The Mesopotamian World," *ScienceDaily*, 16 December 2005. <www.sciencedaily.com/releases/2005/12/051216092426.htm>, retrieved 5/23/20.

138. "List of Wars by Death Toll." *Infogalactic*, https://en.wikipedia.org/wiki/List_of_wars_by_death_toll, retrieved 5/22/20.

139. "World War II Casualties." *Infogalactic*, https://infogalactic.com/info/World_War_II_casualties, retrieved 5/22/20.

140. "The Future of World Religions: Population Growth Projections, 2010–2050." Pew Research Center, April 2, 2015 (https://wayback.archive-it.org/all/20150429153811/http://www.pewforum.org/files/2015/03/PF_15.04.02_ProjectionsFullReport.pdf, retrieved 5/22/20), p. 70.

141. In Matthew 12:22–26, Jesus links Satan to Beelzebul ("Baal the prince"), and in Revelation 2:13, He calls Pergamum the city "where Satan dwells," probably a reference to Pergamum's famed altar of Zeus, who was the Greek equivalent of Baal.

142. Actually, "henotheism" is a more accurate term. It's the belief in multiple gods, but only one supreme, transcendent God.

143. E. A. Knauf. "Qos," in K. van der Toorn, B. Becking, & P. W. van der Horst (Eds.), *Dictionary of deities and demons in the Bible* (2nd extensively rev. ed.) (Leiden; Boston; Köln; Grand Rapids, MI; Cambridge: Brill; Eerdmans, 1999), p. 676.

144. Karen Armstrong. *Islam: A Short History* (New York: Random House. 2002), pp. 18–19.

145. Raymond Ibrahim. *Sword and Scimitar: Fourteen Centuries of War Between Islam and the West* (New York: Da Capo Press, 2018), p. 2.

146. Ibid.

147. Ibid., p. 6.

148. The conquest of Canaan was neither. For an excellent treatment of the concept of *kherem*, or "under the ban," see chapter 25 of Dr. Michael Heiser's book *The Unseen Realm.*

149. Matthew 10:14; Mark 6:11; Luke 9:5, 10:11.

150. Dinesh D'Souza (quoting President George W. Bush). *The Enemy at Home: The Cultural Left and Its Responsibility for 9/11* (New York: Doubleday, 2007), p. 13.

151. Leon de Winter. "Europe's Muslims Hate the West," *Politico*, March 29, 2016 (https://www.politico.eu/article/brussels-attacks-terrorism-europe-muslims-brussels-attacks-airport-metro/), retrieved 1/19/19.

152. Ibrahim, op. cit., p. 13.

153. John Hinderaker, "The American Blood Is Best, and We Will Taste It Soon," Powerline (https://www.powerlineblog.com/archives/2015/11/the-american-blood-is-best-and-we-will-taste-it-soon.php), retrieved 1/19/19.

154. Ibrahim, op. cit., p. 296.

155. Ibid., p. 9.

156. Ibid., p. 267.

157. Ibid.

158. Rory Carroll. "New Book Reopens Old Arguments about Slave Raids on Europe," *The Guardian*, March 11, 2004 (https://www.theguardian.com/uk/2004/mar/11/highereducation.books), retrieved 1/19/19.

159. Juliet Eilperin. "Critics Pounce after Obama Talks Crusades, Slavery at Prayer Breakfast," *Washington Post*, February 5, 2015 (https://www.washingtonpost.com/politics/obamas-speech-at-prayer-breakfast-called-offensive-to-christians/2015/02/05/6a15a240-ad50-11e4-ad71-7b9eba0f87d6_story.html), retrieved 1/19/19.

160. Magdi Abdelhadi. "Arab Journalist Attacks Radical Islam," *BBC News*, September 7, 2004 (http://news.bbc.co.uk/2/hi/middle_east/3632462.stm), retrieved 1/23/19.

161. Revelation 13:3.

162. Beverly Bird. "How Much Does the Average American Pay in Taxes," *the balance,* August 28, 2019. https://www.thebalance.com/what-the-average-american-pays-in-taxes-4768594, retrieved 5/24/20.

163. Rebecca Rainey. "2.1 Million New Unemployment Claims Filed Last Week, as Workers Still Struggle to Get Benefits," *Politico*, May 28, 2020. https://apple.news/ACV5mSHdURKuQgptNQZl5dg, retrieved 5/29/20.

164. Jeff Cox. "Jobless Claims Total 2.4 Million, Still Elevated Levels but a Declining Pace from Previous Weeks," CNBC, May 21, 2020. https://www.cnbc.com/2020/05/21/us-weekly-jobless-claims.html, retrieved 5/24/20.

165. Susan Shand. "Yemen's Famine: Not Enough Food, and Plenty of Blame," *Voice of America*, August 12, 2019. https://learningenglish.voanews.com/a/yemen-s-famine-not-enough-food---and-plenty-of-blame-to-go-around/5035977.html, retrieved 5/24/20.

166. "Ukrainian Famine." *Library of Congress*, August 31, 2016. https://www.loc.gov/exhibits/archives/ukra.html, retrieved 5/24/20.

167. Ibid.

168. Peng Xizhe. "Demographic Consequences of the Great Leap Forward in China's Provinces," *Population and Development Review* 13, no. 4 (1987), pp. 639–70.

169. Lilian Li. *Fighting Famine in North China: State, Market and Environmental Decline, 1690s–1990s* (Stanford University Press, 2007), p. 284.

170. Mohammad Gholi Majd. *The Great Famine and Genocide in Persia, 1917–1919* (Lanham, MD: University Press of America, 2003).

171. "List of Famines," *InfoGalactic*. https://infogalactic.com/info/List_of_famines, retrieved 5/24/20.

172. 1 Timothy 6:10.

173. Travis Hornsby. "Student Loan Debt Statistics in 2020: A Look at The Numbers," *Student Loan Planner*, May 5, 2020. https://www.studentloanplanner.com/student-loan-debt-statistics-average-student-loan-debt/, retrieved 5/24/20.

174. Ibid.

175. Natalie Issa. "U.S. Average Student Loan Debt Statistics in 2019," *Credit.com*, June 19, 2019. https://www.credit.com/personal-finance/average-student-loan-debt/, retrieved 5/24/20.

176. Abigail Hess. "College Grads Expect to Pay Off Student Debt in 6 Years—This Is How Long It Will Actually Take," *make it*, May 23, 2019. https://www.cnbc.com/2019/05/23/cengage-how-long-it-takes-college-grads-to-pay-off-student-debt.html, retrieved 5/24.20.

177. Ibid.

178. It is possible, but rare. The filer has to prove financial hardship and meet certain other conditions.

179. Federal Reserve Bank of New York, *Quarterly Report on Household Debt and Credit*, 2020:Q1 (May 2020).

180. Ibid.

181. Rebecca Safier. "Discharging Student Loans in Bankruptcy: A Brief History," *Student Loan Hero*, September 1, 2019. https://studentloanhero. com/featured/discharging-student-loans-bankruptcy/, retrieved 5/24/20.

182. John S. Kiernan. "How Much is the Average Monthly Credit Card bill?" *Wallet Hub*, April 23, 2020. https://wallethub.com/answers/cc/average-monthly-credit-card-bill-2140706350/, retrieved 5/29/20.

183. Joe Resendiz. "Average Credit Card Debt in America: May 2020," *ValuePenguin*, May 27, 2020. https://www.valuepenguin.com/average-credit-card-debt, retrieved 5/29/20.

184. Robert F. Bruner, Sean D. Carr. *The Panic of 1907: Lessons Learned from the Market's Perfect Storm* (Hoboken: John Wiley & Sons, 2007), p. 149.

185. Julia Kagan. "The Gramm-Leach-Bliley Act of 1999 (GLBA)," *Investopedia*, May 11, 2020. https://www.investopedia.com/terms/g/glba.asp, retrieved 5/29/20.

186. Anne Seith. "Short Selling American Lives: Deutsche Bank Life Insurance Fund in Hot Water," *Spiegel Online International*, November 20, 2009, http://www.spiegel.de/international/business/short-selling-american-lives-deutsche-bank-life-insurance-fund-in-hot-water-a-662447.html.

187. "Semiannual OTC Derivatives Statistics." Bank for International Settlements, updated May 7, 2020, http://www.bis.org/statistics/derstats. htm, retrieved 5/24/20.

188. Ben Protess. "Big Banks Get Break in Rules to Limit Risks," *New York Times*, May 15, 2013, http://dealbook.nytimes.com/2013/05/15/compromise-seen-on-derivatives-rule/?_r=0.

189. "GDP (Current US$)." The World Bank Data, https://data.worldbank.org/indicator/NY.GDP.MKTP.CD, retrieved 5/24/20.

190. The Federal Reserve Bank of the United States is actually purchasing Exchange-Traded Funds, or ETFs, as of this writing. Since ETFs are investment funds traded on stock exchanges that own stocks, commodities, and bonds, it's only one step removed from the Fed investing directly in specific stocks. Any way you look at it, this distorts the valuation of securities by creating demand where it doesn't normally exist.

191. Kjetil Sundsdal. "The Uruk Expansion: Culture Contact, Ideology, and Middlemen," *Norwegian Archaeological Review* 44:2, pp. 164–185.

192. A. R. Millard. "The Bevelled-Rim Bowls: Their Purpose and Significance," *Iraq*, Vol. 50 (1988), pp. 49–50.

193. Ibid.

194. Ibid.

195. G. E. Rickman. "The Grain Trade Under the Roman Empire," *Memoirs of the American Academy in Rome* 36 (1980), p. 263.

196. Juvenal. *Satires* 10.77–81, in J. P. Toner, *Leisure and Ancient Rome* (Cambridge: Polity Press, 1995), p. 69.

197. Christina Marcos. "House Democrats Propose $2,000 Monthly Payments to Americans," *The Hill*, April 15, 2020. https://thehill.com/homenews/house/492950-house-democrats-propose-2000-monthly-payments-to-americans, retrieved 5/25/20.

198. Megan Henney, "Proposal to Give $2,000 Per Month to Americans Gains Traction in Senate," *Fox Business*, May 8, 2020. https://www.foxbusiness.com/money/sanders-markey-harris-proposal-2000-payments-coronavirus, retrieved 5/25/20.

199. Domenico Montanaro. "Poll: Sanders Rises, But Socialism Isn't Popular with Most Americans," NPR.org, February 19, 2020. https://www.npr.org/2020/02/19/807047941/poll-sanders-rises-but-socialism-isnt-popular-with-most-americans, retrieved 5/25/20.

200. Daniel 9:24–27.

201. We recommend the excellent book *Earthquake Resurrection* by David W. Lowe for an in-depth study on the connection between the resurrection of the dead in Christ and the massive earthquake described in Revelation 6:12.

202. Joshua J. Mark. "Nabû," *Ancient History Encyclopedia*. 10 Jan 2017. https://www.ancient.eu/Nabû/, retrieved 5/28/20.

203. Johanna Tudeau. "Nabû (god)," *Ancient Mesopotamian Gods and Goddesses*, Oracc and the UK Higher Education Academy (2013). http://oracc.museum.upenn.edu/amgg/listofdeities/Nabû/, retrieved 5/29/20.

204. James R. Lewis. *The Astrology Book: The Encyclopedia of Heavenly Influences* (Detroit: Visible Ink Press, 2003), p. 442.

205. Joachim Schaper. "The Death of the Prophet: The Transition from the Spoken to the Written Word of God in the Book of Ezekiel," in Michael H. Floyd and Robert D. Haak, eds., *Prophets, Prophecy, and Prophetic Texts in Second Temple Judaism* (London: Bloomsbury Academic, 2006), p. 72.

206. Francesco Pomponio. *Nabû: Il culto e la figura di in dio del Pantheon babilonese ed asiro* (Roma: Istituto di Studi del Vicino Oriente, Università di Roma, 1978), p. 100.

207. "Nabopolassar." *BiblicalTraining.com*, https://www.biblicaltraining.org/library/nabopolassar, retrieved 5/29/20.

208. Edward E. Hindson and Daniel R. Mitchell. *Zondervan King James Version Commentary: Old Testament* (Grand Rapids, MI: Zondervan, 2010), p. 557.

209. "Nabonidus." *BiblicalTraining.org*, https://www.biblicaltraining.org/library/nabonidus, retrieved 5/29/20.

210. International Standard Bible Encyclopedia, "Nebuzaradan." *BibleHub.com*, https://biblehub.com/topical/n/nebuzaradan.htm, retrieved 5/29/20.

211. 2 Kings 25:8–20; Jeremiah 39:9–13, 40:1, 41:10, 43:6 52:12–30.

212. Jeremiah 39:3.

213. Warren Reinsch. "Nebo-Sarsechim Tablet Confirms a Biblical Babylonian General," *Watch Jerusalem*, January 2, 2019. https://watchjerusalem.co.il/514-nebo-sarsechim-tablet-confirms-a-biblical-babylonian-general, retrieved 5/29/20.

214. Ibid.

215. Exodus 32:32–33; Psalm 69:28, 139:16.

216. Revelation 3:5; 20:12, 15; 21:27.

217. Eleanor Robson. "The Production and Dissemination of Scholarly Knowledge," in K. Radner and E. Robson (eds.), *The Oxford Handbook of Cuneiform Culture* (Oxford: Oxford University Press, 2011), p. 560.

218. Laurie E. Pearce. "The Scribes and Scholars of Ancient Mesopotamia," *Civilizations of the ancient Near East* IV (1995), p. 2265.

219. Caroline Waerzeggers. "Neo-Babylonian Laundry," *Revue d'assyriologie et d'archéologie orientale* 100 (2006), pp. 83–6.

220. Mark, op. cit.

221. L. H. Martin. "Hermes," in K. van der Toorn, B. Becking, & P. W. van der Horst (Eds.), *Dictionary of Deities and Demons in the Bible* (Leiden; Boston; Köln; Grand Rapids, MI; Cambridge: Brill; Eerdmans, 1999), p. 405.

222. Donald L. Wasson. "Mercury (Deity)," *Ancient History Encyclopedia*. Last modified November 6, 2018. https://www.ancient.eu/Mercury_(Deity)/, retrieved 5/29/20.

223. Martin, op. cit., p. 409.

224. Ben Dwyer. "NABU Fee—Network Access Brand Usage," *CardFellow*, April 6, 2020. https://www.cardfellow.com/blog/nabu-fee-network-access-brand-usage/, retrieved 5/29/20.

225. Excerpt from "The Viking Portable Greek Historians" found at Wikipedia, link: http://en.wikipedia.org/wiki/Plague_of_Athens, retrieved 10/2/14.

226. http://www.poemhunter.com/poem/book-vi-part-04-the-plague-athens/, retrieved 10/2/14.

227. Braxton Hicks contractions are named for the John Braxton Hicks, the English doctor who first discovered them. For more on this phenomenon

of pregnancy, see "What Are Braxton Hicks Contractions?" at the online site Baby Center via http://www.babycenter.com/0_braxton-hicks-contractions_156.bc, retrieved 10/2/14.

228. Dan Vergano. "1918 Flu Pandemic That Killed 50 Million Originated in China," *National Geographic*, Jan. 2014. https://www.nationalgeographic.com/news/2014/1/140123-spanish-flu-1918-china-origins-pandemic-science-health/, retrieved 9/15/20.

229. Ovid, *Metamorphoses*. A. D. Melville, translator (Oxford: Oxford University Press, 1998), pp. 195–197.

230. Amar Annus. "The God Ninurta in the Mythology and Royal Ideology of Ancient Mesopotamia," *State Archives of Assyria Studies*, Volume XIV (Helsinki: The Neo Assyrian Text Corpus Project, 2002), pp. 111–112.

231. Amar Annus. "The Antediluvian Origin of Evil in the Mesopotamian and Jewish Traditions," in Dietrich M./Loretz O., eds., *Ideas of Man in the Conceptions of the Religions* (Münster: Ugarit-Verlag, 2012), p. 25.

232. Barbara Schmitz. "Holofernes's Canopy in the Septuagint," in *The Sword of Judith: Judith Studies Across the Disciplines* (Cambridge: Open Book Publishers, 2010). http://books.openedition.org/obp/990, retrieved 9/15/20.

233. Brian B. Schmidt. "Israel's Beneficent Dead: The Origin and Character of Israelite Ancestor Cults and Necromancy," doctoral thesis (University of Oxford, 1991), pp. 158–159.

234. Gustaf Wingren. "Saint Irenaeus," *Encyclopedia Britannica*. https://www.britannica.com/biography/Saint-Irenaeus, retrieved 8/12/20.